MEMORY, HISTORY,
and OPPOSITION

THE PUBLICATION OF THE ADVANCED SEMINAR SERIES
IS MADE POSSIBLE BY GENEROUS SUPPORT FROM
THE BROWN FOUNDATION, INC., HOUSTON, TEXAS

School of American Research
Advanced Seminar Series
Douglas W. Schwartz, General Editor

MEMORY, HISTORY, AND OPPOSITION
Contributors

Robert M. Hayden
Department of Anthropology
University of Pittsburgh

Caroline Humphrey
Department of Anthropology
Cambridge University

Stephen F. Jones
Program for Russian and Slavic Studies
Mount Holyoke College

Ellen R. Judd
Department of Anthropology
University of Manitoba

Andrew Lass
Department of Sociology and Anthropology
Mount Holyoke College

Paul G. Pickowicz
Department of History
University of California–San Diego

Vera Schwarcz
East Asian Studies Program
Wesleyan University

Rubie S. Watson
Peabody Museum and Department of Anthropology
Harvard University

MEMORY, HISTORY, AND OPPOSITION

UNDER STATE SOCIALISM

EDITED BY

RUBIE S. WATSON

SCHOOL OF AMERICAN RESEARCH PRESS ▮
SANTA FE ▮ NEW MEXICO

SCHOOL OF AMERICAN RESEARCH PRESS
Post Office Box 2188
Santa Fe, New Mexico 87504-2188

Director of Publications: Joan K. O'Donnell
Editor: Jane Kepp
Designer: Deborah Flynn Post
Indexer: Douglas J. Easton
Typographer: Tseng Information Systems, Inc.

Library of Congress Cataloging-in-Publication Data:

Memory, history, and opposition under state socialism / edited by
   Rubie S. Watson.
      p.   cm.—(School of American Research advanced seminar series)
Includes bibliographical references and index.
   ISBN 0-933452-86-1 (cloth)—ISBN 0-933452-87-X (paper)
   1. Communist countries—Historiography.   I. Watson, Rubie S.
(Rubie Sharon), 1945– . II. Series.
D847. M46   1994   93-46594
909'.09717—dc20   CIP

Catalog Card Number 93-46594.
International Standard Book Numbers 978-0-933452-87-9 (paper).
First edition. Third paperback printing 2019.

Cover: "Lenin statue comes down." Bucharest, Romania, March 5, 1990.
Photo by Radu Sigheti. Reuters/Bettman.

Contents

Preface and Acknowledgments

MANY PEOPLE AND INSTITUTIONS have contributed generously to the project from which this book grew. It began as a panel at the 1991 annual meetings of the Association for Asian Studies in New Orleans. Three of the chapters included here (those by Paul Pickowicz, Vera Schwarcz, and me) were first presented at those meetings. Although Arthur and Joan Kleinman contributed a paper to the panel, pressures of other work made it impossible for them to participate in the School of American Research advanced seminar upon which this book is based. Their continuing interest in and support of the project, however, has been extremely generous and helpful.

This volume grew out of an advanced seminar sponsored by the School of American Research in Santa Fe, New Mexico, and held on October 19–25, 1991. On behalf of my fellow contributors I take this opportunity to express our gratitude to the School's staff for taking such good care of us during our stay in Santa Fe. We are especially grateful to Douglas W. Schwartz, president of the School of American Research, Jane Kepp, at that time the School's director of publications, and Joan K. O'Donnell, the present director of publications, who contributed both their time and their wisdom to the seminar and the volume.

In Santa Fe, the papers of four Soviet and Eastern European specialists (Robert Hayden, Caroline Humphrey, Stephen Jones, and Andrew Lass) and a paper by Ellen Judd, a China anthropologist, were added to the by now revised and enlarged panel papers. We were indeed fortunate to have Gail Kligman and Richard Madsen as our seminar discussants. Their interest, enthusiasm, and good counsel added greatly to our seminar deliberations. As volume editor, I am especially indebted to Gail and Dick for the time they took in advising me on revisions for my introduction. They gave generously of their time to the entire project, and we are all most grateful.

During much of the time that this project was taking shape, I was a member of the anthropology department at the University of Pittsburgh, and I wish to acknowledge the support of the Asian Studies Program and the Endowment for Chinese Studies there for help in preparing both the seminar papers and the final manuscript. As colleague and chair of the department of anthropology, Jerry Sabloff encouraged me throughout the project, and I am grateful for his support.

Many people have read, discussed, and commented on parts or the whole of this volume. Leonard Plotnicov kept me well supplied with newspaper clippings that helped me stay abreast of events in Eastern Europe and what was then the

Soviet Union. I owe special debts to Robert Hayden, who was always "just down the hall" and therefore easy prey for impromptu discussions of memory and history; Hue-tam Ho Tai, who was the discussant for the Association of Asian Studies panel when the ideas presented here were taking form; Michael Herzfeld, who helped me think about representing the past outside of as well as within the context of socialism; and James Watson, who, as always, read, listened, and offered his sound advice. Finally, I wish to acknowledge the assistance of Eric Miller and Yan Yunxiang, who helped with the documentary research for my chapters, and Terri Teleen, who constructed the joint bibliography for the volume.

Memory, History, and Opposition under State Socialism
An Introduction

RUBIE S. WATSON

THIS BOOK IS ABOUT REPRESENTING the past in societies where history writing has been the prerogative of a single-party state and its agents. From the very beginning, Communist party leaders grounded their claims to legitimacy in their special understanding of the principles of scientific socialism. According to the Soviet historian Geoffrey Hosking, a mastery of the objective laws of social evolution justified the right of the party faithful to direct society (1989:115; see also Clark 1981). Under state socialism, Marxism-Leninism was not one ideology or political economy among many, but rather was the inevitable and glorious outcome of a discernible historical process.

If one of the primary justifications of communist rule is its inevitability, then the production of history takes on tremendous significance—political, ideological, and moral. Under state socialism the past was read from the present, but because the present changed (leaders, plans, and lines of thinking came and went), the past also had to change. Hosking reports a Soviet anecdote from the imaginary "Armenian radio" that beautifully captures the problem: "Armenian radio is asked 'Is it possible to foretell the future?' Answer: 'Yes, that is no problem: we know exactly what the future will be like. Our problem is with the past: that keeps changing'" (1989:115). As Stephen Jones notes in chapter 8, in Soviet historiography the primary standard by which events or figures were incorporated into official histories was their usefulness in establishing the legitimacy of the current power holders.

In China, too, policies and leaders were justified by their inevitability. During the early stages of Chinese communist organizational development, for example,

Mao Zedong created the terms of political discourse—created correct thought—
by transforming his reading of the past into the only possible reading. He thereby
justified his own leadership and that of his party by writing himself into history—
by making himself, his followers, and his "line" the inevitable result of historical
forces (see Saich 1994; see also chapter 4, this volume). In such an environment,
incorrect understandings are judged to be not only wrongheaded but also trea-
sonous; they are by definition antiparty and therefore antistate. The production
of history in China, Mongolia, the Soviet Union, and Eastern Europe was deemed
too important to be left to those who had no appreciation for the "true march of
events."

Given the logic of Communist party thinking, it is not surprising to find that
enforced historical orthodoxies, guided by what Gail Kligman calls "monologic
historical explanation" (1990:395), gained considerable adherence in the societies
discussed here. If that were the whole story, however, there would be no reason for
this book. In the chapters that follow, contributors demonstrate that official histories, while plentiful, never precluded the active construction and transmission of
unofficial pasts. Indeed, even as the creators of "correct" history jealously guarded
their right to produce historical texts, alternative remembrances and alternative
histories survived and on occasion even prospered in Eastern Europe (e.g., Verdery 1991a:215–55), in the Soviet Union (e.g., Heer 1971), and in China (e.g.,
Barme and Jaiven 1992; Goldman, Cheek, and Hamrin 1987; Wagner 1990). Con-
testation both within communities of historians and among ordinary people over
how the past was to be represented was never fully eradicated.

In this volume we seek to contribute to what Peter Burke has labeled "a social
history of remembering" (1989:100) by considering the mechanisms that make
unsanctioned remembrance possible under state socialism. The contributors have
moved into and beyond the usual domain of written, narrative history to examine
how representations of the past are contested in situations where one historical
interpretation was meant to be accepted by all. In the following chapters, personal and shared memories, commemorations, theater and drama, and secret and
oppositional histories are the venues within which alternative remembrances are
located and analyzed.

Although unauthorized representations of the past are the subject matter of
this book—they are the windows through which we seek to understand socialist
systems—it is important that we do not credit the socialist state and its agents
with too much power or its citizens with too much boldness. State socialism was
never as omnipotent as the cold war warriors of the 1950s claimed it to be, nor
was it the paper tiger that some present-day celebrants of its demise proclaim. It
is also important not to lose sight of the fact that state socialist regimes had the
capacity to be both brutally coercive and vulnerable at the same time.

As the contributors to this volume can testify, it is difficult to find a vocabulary that captures the elaborate and subtle forms of repression and subversion—
of compliance and resistance—that are so characteristic of state socialisms. For

many years totalitarian models dominated our understanding (see, e.g., Arendt 1951; Conquest 1968; Kornhauser 1959; Wittfogel 1957). Those who developed these models stressed the repressive nature of state power and argued that compliance was coerced by means of terror and intimidation. In the last two decades, totalitarian theories have been severely criticized as being too blunt an instrument to produce the kinds of nuanced analyses that are needed. They offer, it is argued, little insight into what scholars like Rudolf Bahro (1978) have called "actually existing socialism."

With some notable exceptions, centralized dictatorial control under state socialism has not been as effective as totalitarian models would lead us to expect.[1] In recent years attention has focused on the failures and weaknesses of state socialism, including the growth of personalistic networks and clientelism, inefficiencies in production and distribution, and an enveloping cynicism that seems to have characterized party elite and masses alike. These analyses come from American and European scholars as well as from Eastern European sociologists, economists, philosophers, and dissenting intellectuals.[2] Katherine Verdery makes the important point that "indigenist" theorizing about Eastern European socialism by Eastern Europeans has proved to be both sophisticated and provocative (1991a:74).

Over the years, studies of clientelism, of the second, or underground, economy, and of what have been called "everyday forms of resistance" have increased in number and sophistication.[3] Of course, as I pointed out earlier, state socialism was not as fragile as some now think. It did not collapse because peasants resisted collectivization or because industrial workers bargained, dissembled, or engaged in silent protests—yet neither were these activities irrelevant or epiphenomenal. As Michel Foucault has argued (see, e.g., 1978, 1982), there is much to be gained by linking the study of power to the analysis of resistance. The history of state socialism can be written in various ways depending on whether one takes a structuralist or a more processual view of the events; however, the construction and utilization of power and the forms of resistance that countered that power must be central to all these analyses.

Many students of state socialism feel uneasy not only with views that embrace totalitarian models but also with views that privilege resistance.[4] In chapter 2 of this volume, Caroline Humphrey warns against reading opposition and dissent into the ambiguous situations one finds in societies where mistrust is pervasive and public demonstrations of compliance are expected of everyone. Ideas about resistance, Humphrey argues, have been developed primarily in the context of colonial and class encounters and not in the context of the centralizing party states described in this volume.

Understanding state socialism in its many forms, including both its strengths and its weaknesses, requires, as Sally Falk Moore has argued for the social sciences generally, a scholarship that gives weight not only to people's struggles to construct order but also to those actions that undo order (1987:735). In many respects the demise of state socialism seriously challenges theorists concerned with practice, process, and agency.[5] In Eastern Europe, the former Soviet Union, and even in China (although not so forthrightly), we confront, on the one hand, the dramatic, orchestrated construction of state socialism, and on the other, its equally dramatic, seemingly unorchestrated, "happeninglike" transformation. The dynamic tension between structure and action, society and countersociety, determinacy and indeterminacy is strikingly evident as we put state socialism under the microscope.

Over the years, millions of ordinary Soviet, Eastern European, and Chinese people have found it advantageous, sometimes necessary, to bypass "the system" in order to feed, clothe, and shelter themselves. Even bureaucrats, apparatchiks, and factory managers resorted to backdoor trade-offs to get their jobs done. In this world—where a friend of a friend might offer a better chance of getting what was needed than reliance on the channels of central distribution—scholars are presented with a rare opportunity to study the ways in which many small, incremental acts can alter structures and institutions that once seemed entrenched and inviolate.

For our part, we contributors to this volume examine how small acts of sometimes private, sometimes public, unsanctioned remembrance kept alive memories and histories that produced and were produced by this shadow world. Our examination of memory and secret histories takes on an added significance when we consider that many of these unapproved rememberings are now the stuff of which new histories and new states are being created.

In this book we have restricted our discussion to state socialist societies for a variety of reasons. There are, of course, important differences among the societies discussed here, and no one model or description fits them all. But for our purposes it is important to note that prior to 1989 these societies shared certain features. They were dominated by a single-party state that claimed the exclusive right to exercise political power, to organize the production and distribution of goods and services, and to authorize the production of cultural texts, including historical ones. These rights, as I argued earlier, were based upon claims to a uniquely scientific understanding of the historical process as revealed in the writings of Marx and Lenin. The would-be historian's loyalty, or at least compliance, was secured—as it also was in the European democracies, for example—through education, enculturation, socialization, and the calculation of personal self-interest. But unlike the situation in those democracies, official censorship prevailed, and compliance also was obtained by direct and officially sanctioned threats to withdraw goods and services controlled by the party and/or its apparatchiks. In state socialist societies, "history" implied official history, and contending representations of the past were forced underground. The price for noncompliance was high.

In my view, there is much to be gained by focusing on socialist states. An enhanced ability to scrutinize the process of cultural production—including the production of oppositional forms—in situations where a single party dominated political power is certainly one such gain. This kind of scrutiny has the potential to enlarge our understanding of both state socialism and opposition. Beyond this, however, a focus on state socialism makes it possible to contextualize many of the compelling issues of the postsocialist era. It is difficult to imagine how we can begin to appreciate the transitions from socialism that are now taking place if we do not first understand what preceded those transitions.

DISAPPEARING WORLDS

Since the conferences that led to this book began, the societies of Eastern Europe and the Soviet Union have been radically transformed, and the twists and turns of their transformation have produced some formidable challenges to all of us who have worked on this volume. In some cases contributors have had to revise several times to cope with dramatic changes, renamed countries, and redefined borders. Since the autumn of 1989, it has been necessary to discuss state socialism in Eastern Europe in the past tense: the Soviet Union has become the former Soviet Union, while Yugoslavia seems to have disappeared altogether in a frenzy of "ethnic cleansing."

Besides these national appearances and disappearances, there has also been an amazing transformation of one-time commissars, seemingly overnight, into politicians in the best tradition of American ward politics. And perhaps most important for many of the societies discussed here, the rhetoric of fraternal socialism has given way to the strident language of nationalism. There is no doubt that our burden of analysis has been expanded by these changes. Because of recent events we have added a second set of research questions. In addition to our concern with contending representations of the past under state socialism, contributors also consider the ways in which unsanctioned memories and histories have become the raw material from which new societies and nations are being created. These questions of transition are taken up most explicitly in the chapters dealing with Czechoslovakia, Georgia, and Yugoslavia.

We are also confronted with China—an apparent socialist survivor. At the end of 1989, Eastern Europe and China seemed to be moving in opposite directions. As Chinese leaders boasted that they were saving socialism, the Eastern Europeans proclaimed they were destroying it (in its statist form, that is). For China we can, at this writing, still speak of state socialism in the present tense, but it is a pale version of Mao's robustly centralizing, "politics-in-command" socialism of the 1950s and 1960s.

In the aftermath of the Beijing Massacre (June 4, 1989), contacts with Western countries continue, as do many of the economic reforms instituted in the 1980s. China, however, has not embraced the concept of glasnost. Contrary to developments in Eastern Europe and the Soviet Union, Deng Xiaoping continues to argue that political and economic reforms can be separated. There are many who doubt the ability of Deng and his followers to maintain this separation—to produce reform with Chinese characteristics. In this volume, no one suggests that China is the country that stood still; changes are occurring and further changes are inevitable, but, in my view, China does represent a failure to create and sustain a national framework for political reform. As I argue in chapter 4, China appears to have neither a message nor a messenger that can mediate among the warring elites who seek to "speak for," but do not seem able to "speak with," the masses. State social-ism in Asia is not dead, although it is being transformed, and for this reason alone China makes an interesting contrast to the postsocialist countries described here.

The dramatic events in Beijing, Berlin, Prague, Bucharest, and eventually Mos-cow and Leningrad (now renamed St. Petersburg) remind one in the most dramatic terms that constructing the new is deeply embedded in reconstructing the old. There is, of course, nothing particularly novel in the idea that new environments produce "new pasts." As Bernard Lewis points out: "The invention of history is no new invention" (1975:13). Until recently, however, discussions of reinventing the past have focused primarily on history making outside the Soviet and Chinese orbits.[6] In this book we consider how new pasts are created in societies where, as Vera Schwarcz argues in chapter 3, "the technology of amnesia" has produced an enforced forgetfulness. In one way or another each of the contributors to this vol-ume seeks to assess the effectiveness of that technology.[7]

Given the changes taking place in Eastern Europe, the former Soviet Union, and China, many important issues now turn on how the past is represented. New national charters are being constructed out of long-suppressed histories and shared memories. Judging from the mounting evidence for the survival of alterna-tive versions of the past, it is clear that the party's gatekeepers were not as success-ful in mandating what could be remembered as we had assumed. How, we ask, do people encounter and counter historical orthodoxies? How do they remember events that "did not occur" or were described in terms unfamiliar to those who had experienced them?

As the effects of glasnost and later the "velvet revolutions" of 1989 widened and deepened, people in Eastern Europe and the Soviet Union could be seen en-gaging in a feast of remembrance. Their counterparts in China also remembered, but with different consequences. In all these societies, however, alternative repre-sentations of the past were publicly recalled, recharged, and even relived in ways that would have been impossible a decade earlier. There was a sense that ordinary people were recovering pasts that, because they contradicted official history, had remained hidden and protected. Some of these "recoveries" took place before our eyes as newly minted official histories lent their support to emerging nation states (for examples, see the chapters by Hayden, Jones, and Lass).

For the countries discussed in this book, the 1980s were a time when "for-gotten" people and "forgotten" deeds could be commemorated. Sidney Monas has written of the great potency of the "return of the repressed" in societies that have been dominated by strict censorship (1989). In a recent paper, Susan Gal (1991) provides a fascinating account of the composer Bartok's reburial on Hungarian soil in 1988. Similar memorial rites have taken place with increasing urgency, including (again in Hungary) the reburial of the executed leader Imre Nagy, memorial services for well-known victims of China's Cultural Revolution, and public commemorations for Polish officers slaughtered during the Second World War. These memorials testify to the recognition of the forgotten dead and to the "nonevents" that occasioned those deaths. In chapter 9, Robert Hayden describes how, in 1990–91, the victims of communist and fascist massacres in Yugoslavia received elaborate funerals after having lain for decades in unmarked graves.

Although these rememberings were often encouraged and orchestrated by emergent power holders, remembrance was by no means confined to the choreographed event. There were also fragmented and sometimes highly ritualized, personal acts of memory and homage: the flowers placed on an empty pedestal that was to have supported a monument commemorating the American liberation of Pilsen; the photos and personal documents of Stalin's "disappeared" posted on a Moscow street; the creation of an unauthorized cemetery in a Soviet gulag; candles lit at the mass graves of "secret" Yugoslav massacres; and silent vigils commemorating violent confrontations with police in Czechoslovakia, Poland, and Romania.[8] Before 1989—during the early days of glasnost—people sometimes used their own bodies to proclaim the unofficial past. The unsanctioned mourning of Zhou Enlai in January 1976 is an example of such a proclamation (chapter 4, this volume). Often these acts of remembrance were both simple and silent; they were, as Humphrey argues in chapter 2, "inherently ambiguous," managing to appear individual and collective, silent and noisy at the same time. As Andrew Lass points out in chapter 5, many of these symbolic acts took place in public places like Wenceslas Square in Prague, where for decades secret histories of opposition had been quietly but effectively nurtured.

Transmitting the Past

In asking how people remember what is meant to be forgotten, matters of transmission—the mechanics of shared memory and hidden histories—take center stage. We are only beginning to understand these processes, and it is here that the authors of this book make, I believe, a special contribution. In societies where unofficial histories are seditious and the photographer's air brush is an effective tool of historical annihilation, the production and survival of unsanctioned memories must be problematical.

Much has been written about shared, collective, or social memory and about the relationship between memory and history.[9] In chapter 5, Lass provides an excellent discussion of various scholarly treatments of the latter. In this volume, the term *history* is most often used to describe representations of the past that appear in written, narrative form—although it is important to note that for definitional purposes no one would wish to imply that the term should be so rigidly confined. In chapter 7, Paul Pickowicz analyzes a remarkable oppositional history written by a Chinese villager. Of course, a history may become oppositional whether the author intends such a reading or not; the ongoing battle over how to remember China's May Fourth Movement (1919), for example, has transformed official accounts into oppositional ones and back again as political regimes have come and gone (see Schwarcz 1991c; Wasserstrom 1990).

Memory may be a reservoir of history, but it is not the same as history. As Stephen Owen argues: "It is easy to forget that we do not read memory itself but its transformation through writing" (1986:114). People maintain personal memories—memories of events and situations that they themselves experienced. These personal memories may remain private, they may be passed on in conversation or storytelling, they may be lost, or they may be written down in the form of diaries, memoirs, and autobiographies. There are also collective or shared memories that are not dependent on a single individual's direct experience of the past. That is, we may "remember" an event—have a shared understanding that is represented as a "memory"—that we ourselves did not experience. Many Americans "remember" the American Civil War and many Jews "remember" the Nazi Holocaust, but not because they personally experienced those events or because they have read master narratives written by professional historians detailing the great battles or the sufferings in the camps. Rather, they "remember" because they share with others sets of images that have been passed down to them through the media of memory—through paintings, architecture, monuments, ritual, storytelling, poetry, music, photos, and film.

These rememberings are not constructed in an overtly logical, intellectualized manner—they rarely provide a clearly organized story or narrative. Rather, they are fragmented, much like a Dalí painting or a collage. Often these rememberings are visual, producing powerful and compelling images that speak to the passions as well as to the intellect. Such memories re-present the past and give people the sense that they are reexperiencing an event that may have occurred long before their birth. Museums and monuments often give a physicality to memory, as do the rituals that commemorate the dead and their deeds. The visual arts, poetry, memoirs, and novels contribute to memory construction in part because they make us *feel* as well as *think* the past.

Although definitional exercises may not be very satisfying, in my view shared memory and history should not be collapsed, nor should those who are concerned with the past eschew the realm of memory altogether, leaving it, as so often has been the case, to the cognitive psychologists and philosophers. I do not wish to invoke the dichotomies between Lévi-Strauss's hot and cold societies, nor do I wish to deny that there are many kinds of history (for discussion, see Rappaport 1990). However, for those of us who are concerned with unorthodox transmissions of unapproved pasts, memory is a word that is too precious to abandon.

The construction of memory and the construction of history do not take place in isolation from each other. As Lass points out (indeed, as all the contributors

show), personal memory, shared memory, and narrative (written) history inter-
act in highly complicated ways, shaping each other as versions of the past are
constructed and reconstructed (see also Burke 1989). The important point is that
shared memory and history tend not only to represent but also to transmit the
past in characteristically different ways. A number of the contributors to this book
suggest that in situations where alternative understandings of the past are tantamount to treason, shared memory expressed in oral and visual forms provides a
particularly adaptive medium for expressing disagreement, dissent, opposition,
and resistance.

In *The Politics of Memory*, Joanne Rappaport describes the appeal of the novelist's vision of the past. A writer like Gabriel García Márquez creates a powerful
image of the past as he seeks to tell his stories "before the historians have time to
arrive" (cited in Rappaport 1990:16). Shared memories produce powerful images
by taking up themes, telling stories, and making it possible to reexperience events
in ways that are significantly different from the history of the professional historian. In creating shared memories we construct visions of the past rather than
chronologies. Time itself may be collapsed or made inconsequential as these memory visions are evoked, shared, transmitted, and continuously altered—while remaining ostensibly the same.

ENCAPSULATION, SOCIALISM, AND THE PAST

For purposes of understanding how the past was used and abused under state
socialism, it is important to differentiate those societies upon which Marxism-
Leninism was imposed from those where it developed in situ. China, discussed
in chapters 3, 4, 6, and 7, is an example of the latter. But for the Czechoslovaks,
Georgians, and Mongolians described in chapters 2, 5, and 8, state socialism was
perceived as an alien intrusion. It is not that people failed to adjust to the new
order—there were certainly Czechoslovakian, Georgian, and Mongolian communists—but rather that Moscow, not Prague, Tbilisi, or Ulan Bator, stood as the
guarantor and the ultimate enforcer of that order. Because of Yugoslavia's history
and internal divisions, its situation is more complicated. Increasingly, the Croatians, Slovenians, and Bosnians have equated socialism with Serbian hegemony;
the Serbs, not surprisingly, have taken a different view (see chapter 9).

In Soviet-dominated Eastern Europe and Georgia, representations of a cultural past were by no means free of party manipulation, yet these representations
continued to play a significant role in constructing national and personal identities. E. M. Simmonds-Duke (1987) and Katherine Verdery (1991a:99) argue that
a discourse on the nation was so powerfully instituted in Romanian culture and
political life that it subverted the discourse of Marxism itself. For Romanians and
others, the universalism of communism never managed to drown out the "local-
ism" of the nation. During the 1960s, policy shifts in the Soviet Union seemed

to encourage, even promote, national distinctiveness (although, of course, local party officials defined what was to be "distinctive"). According to Jones (in chapter 8), this proved to be particularly important in Soviet republics like Georgia, where it was possible to sustain, sometimes surreptitiously, memories of a pre-Soviet past. In Mongolia, as Humphrey points out, Soviet dominators appear to have been especially rigorous in their control over the production of history and culture, but there too, the past, in the form of a hidden religious history transmitted through a rich oral tradition, continued to exist in a world of us versus them.

In some important respects the capacity to externalize communism—to give it a foreign origin, to associate it with an outside Soviet dominator—encouraged the retention and elaboration of national histories. Although this externalization was never completely successful—the dominated always had their own locally produced dominators—Georgians, Mongolians, and Czechoslovakians could maintain an attitude toward their national past that was significantly different, I believe, from the attitude we find in China.

In China, where socialism under Mao was accepted as a homemade affair and where there was considerable popular support for a Maoist version of socialism that promoted economic equality and industrial growth, the past has remained a forbidding, and often forbidden, territory. While the past in the form of a traditional culture was never fully rejected in China, there is no doubt that rituals, religious beliefs, and physical manifestations of cultural practices (i.e., texts, temples, ancestral halls, domestic altars, tombs, genealogies) were forthrightly and consistently attacked. In contrast to Georgia, Czechoslovakia, and Mongolia, in China the past became a highly problematical resource for the construction of identity. Myron Cohen describes what has happened in China as "cultural warfare" and argues that it has resulted in a nationalism that is "amazingly devoid of elaborated cultural content" (1991:128). Although China's cultural turmoil is, to a considerable degree, a consequence of Maoist iconoclasm, Cohen points out that the long-standing and deeply held antitraditionalism of Chinese intellectuals should not be underestimated.

REMEMBERING UNOFFICIAL PASTS: "SILENT DISAGREEMENT" AND OPPOSITION

Under state socialism, the space for resistance, opposition, alternative views, and disagreement has been extremely small. As John Keane puts it in his preface to *The Power of the Powerless*, "in Soviet-type regimes . . . no citizen is innocent before the state," and "public opposition of any kind is always regarded by the State authorities as seditious" (1985:8). In the present book, contributors probe the limits of state socialism in its capacities to colonize and dominate the private and public spaces of ordinary people. "The public sphere," Kligman writes, "belonged to the party-state, which appropriated unto itself the rights to space, privilege, discourse, and communication" (1990:398). In many of the societies described in the following chapters, the public sphere was indeed expansive as it encroached on the private realm, sometimes shrinking it to alarmingly small dimensions.

Under state socialism, party apparatchiks strived to control the bodies and minds not only of dissidents and counterrevolutionaries but also of ordinary workers and peasants. What could be written and what could be said was of central and abiding concern to the state. Because, as Verdery points out, the socialist order is a self-consciously constructed one, having been produced more through discourse than practice (1991b:430), control over the discursive realm is fundamental (on this point, see also Burawoy and Lukacs 1992). Under such circumstances, opposition must be camouflaged; Keane refers to the "silent disagreement" that is common in such societies (1985:8).

In chapter 2 of this volume, Humphrey develops the idea of the "evocative transcript" in order to capture the subtlety of what might be labeled a form of "non-oppositional opposition." Although Humphrey acknowledges her debt to the work of James Scott (1990), she argues that Scott's concept of the hidden transcript is not fully applicable to "encapsulated societies subject to Soviet-type domination." As Humphrey defines the term, an evocative transcript is not specific to a class or circle of people but is a common resource available to everyone in Mongolian society. In this respect, she argues, it is different from Scott's hidden transcripts, which are produced by enduring groups within their own social space. Evocative transcripts are inherently ambiguous and come to the fore when the restricted codes of classes and ethnic groups are replaced by new kinds of discourse. According to Humphrey, these transcripts are intended to elicit or evoke a reaction beyond their surface meaning. Humphrey describes these new discursive forms as "highly ideological, stilted, and mostly written official discourse, and 'all the rest,' which may be oral and informal but nevertheless must maintain a semblance of conformity in public." Humphrey shows how jokes, written texts, and various actions may be "deliberately designed to evoke a dual reaction." For example, a visit to a spring may commemorate a goddess-spirit, it may recall a dead empress, or people may simply say they are "taking a cure."

In Schwarcz's chapter on Chinese intellectuals, we are allowed a glimpse into the process by which private, unapproved memories are hesitantly and painfully shared. Schwarcz describes how, in May 1989, in the midst of the official commemorations of the seventieth anniversary of the May Fourth Movement, the "survivor-rememberer" Chen Hengzhen struggled to find a place "at the margin" where he could join personal memory to public history. According to the official version of Chinese history, communism is the only true outcome of May Fourth and of China's struggles to attain a prosperous and independent nation-state (see Schwarcz 1991c; Wasserstrom 1990). In a series of unofficial conferences at the fringes of public commemoration, however, forgotten figures of May Fourth could be talked about without the burden of correct criticism.

At one of these unofficial conferences, Schwarcz met Chen, the 60-year-old son of a victim of China's antirightist campaign, who was seeking "to rehabilitate his mother's reputation in the annals of the Chinese revolution." The mother, a French literature specialist who had helped found the Paris cell of the Chinese Communist party in 1921, had been labeled a rightist (and therefore a nonperson) in 1957. At the conference, Schwarcz recounts, the son was engaged in a rectification of history as he attempted to find a place for an acceptable memory of his mother in a newly emerging public, but not quite official, account of May Fourth. Outside the conference format, however, during a lunch break, Chen's talk changed as he spoke to Schwarcz of more personal, less palatable remembrances—memories of his mother's betrayal, of violent political campaigns, and of his own suffering. "She tried to protect herself and ended by blackening twenty years of my life," Chen said of his mother. In 1958, "when she could no longer defend herself, she went mad" and ended her life by committing suicide. "She trusted the authorities with everything," he exclaimed, "as if the party were a benevolent, faultless father. She sacrificed her son for this father." Schwarcz's description of a son who strives to contribute to a new representation of modern Chinese history, yet struggles with private memories that have no history, no framework, to which they can be attached and thereby given meaning, captures the conflicting, eruptive nature of memory in a China that is still deeply at odds with its past.

In a recent essay, Lisa Rofel, who, like Schwarcz, discusses a victim of the Cultural Revolution, writes of the way in which memories of violence are lived in silence but may suddenly erupt only "to disappear again, seemingly without a ripple" (1991:1). In the 1980s, Rofel argues, memories of the Cultural Revolution were officially acceptable if they replicated a version of the master narrative that placed blame on the Gang of Four and characterized the violence as senseless. For many, however, it has not been easy to connect their own memories to this accepted understanding of events. Bad memories of the Cultural Revolution, according to Rofel, are sayable if they "draw a clear border between then and now." But there are those who refuse to weave together their fragmented memories "into a tale of progress and redemption" (1991:10). Neither the Cultural Revolution victim Rofel describes nor the son Schwarcz discusses (both of whom, it is worth noting, were betrayed by a family member), has resolved his or her personal memories, and so their "cultural revolutions" remain unfinished business. In this, they are certainly not alone.

Whereas Schwarcz describes a failed attempt to transform personal memory, Lass is concerned with the process of transformation itself. He examines the making of histories in postsocialist Czechoslovakia and asks how "individuals' events [become] society's history." Like Hayden and Jones, he examines how the "new histories" of the 1990s are being created. Lass is concerned with the complicated interplay between recollection, memory, and narrative history—the process by which private recollection structures and is structured by historically marked events. How, he asks, does "my past" become "our past?" Transformations of recollection into memory and memory into history, he argues, are thought by some to involve the construction of distance through a process of rethinking rather than reliving—of remembering rather than recollecting. Lass maintains, however, that there is a "lived" aspect to the new histories of Czechoslovakia as the events of 1989 are turned into an artistic drama about the past. The closer we get to the "new histories," Lass concludes, the more history comes alive again as it is reproduced as art, as spectacle, as final absolution.

In chapter 4 I am concerned, like Schwarcz and Lass, with the transmission of an unofficial past, and I consider the expressive forms that are available for creating shared meaning out of personal mourning in Chinese society. In examining how the anonymous victims who died during the violent political upheavals of Maoist China are remembered, I discuss the elaborate, state-orchestrated memorials of the 1980s. Of special importance are the eruptions of unsanctioned remembrance that, on at least two occasions (in 1976 and 1989), overwhelmed official acts of memorialization. In China, mourning is highly charged with moral significance and continues, as in the past, to provide a dramatic medium for expressing injustice. I am concerned with what happens when personal memory is so much at odds with official history that the former would be branded subversive if it were shared. What is the cost for the individual and for society when there is no meaningful framework for publicly exploring traumatic memories of political violence?

In chapter 6, Ellen Judd discusses a form of opera that in China has long been associated with the transmission of the past. The explosive potential of folk drama is highlighted as Judd describes the meticulous control a group of Chinese officials exercised over a 1989 (post–Beijing Massacre) performance of *The Story of Mulian*. Although many traditional operas were revived in China during the 1980s, this particular opera, in part because of its timing and the presence of foreign guests, was too invested with political significance to be "just an opera." One is reminded of the "civilizing" and controlling attempts of China's imperial literati as Judd describes a popular opera from which the populace has been excluded. The "erasure of the popular audience" (only official guests were allowed to attend) considerably augmented, Judd argues, the complex mix of official and unofficial politics that the authorities hoped to dampen or avoid.

In Judd's view, the danger of Mulian opera lies not in its portrayal of "hungry ghosts" or the promotion of "superstitious beliefs," but rather in the way in which the central tenets of Chinese political culture are presented. Conflict and ambiguity, play, and magical transformation make this drama hugely complex and in some fundamental sense uncontrollable. Paraphrasing Walter Benjamin (1969), Judd argues that it is memory's ability to flash up at a point of historical danger that frightens China's ruling elite.

TOTALITARIAN MODELS, MEMORY, AND OPPOSITION

No state is completely successful in domesticating the old to construct the new; in practice, there are always varying degrees of success. Official historians, try as they might, are unable to turn their fellow citizens into blank pages upon which the new can be inscribed. This observation should not, however, make us lose sight of the fact that under state socialism party elements jealously guarded the cultural realm—including the domain of memory and forgetting. Censors, state-supported writers' organizations, state-employed thought workers, and, ultimately, the security police oversaw this realm. Beyond these external sanctioning agents lay self-censorship. As Miklos Haraszti so eloquently points out in *The Velvet Prison* (1987), compliance is not always or even primarily coerced from above. In a discussion of intellectuals living under "totalitarian socialism," Haraszti writes: "Censorship is no longer a matter of simple state intervention. A new aesthetic culture has emerged in which censors and artists alike are entangled in a mutual embrace" (1987:5).[10] Andrew Walder describes the more prosaic embrace that characterized Chinese factory workers, managers, and party officials in the 1970s, when, as he argues, political loyalty was "rewarded systematically with career opportunities, special distributions, and other favors that officials in communist societies are uniquely able to dispense" (1986:6).

Scholars working with totalitarian models argue that the public destroys the private under statist regimes. Control, they contend, is effectively exerted as the state engulfs its citizens (see, e.g., Arendt 1951; Kornhauser 1959; Wittfogel 1957). Given that one's livelihood and access to such basic resources as employment, housing, food, health care, education, and travel are controlled by organs of the party state, active protest is something that only a few consider. Yet even under harsh regimes, certain domains of personal and community life remain uncolonized. Jones shows in chapter 8 that although texts of "correct histories" were lavishly produced in Soviet Georgia, one could also find unofficial histories, often in the form of oral literature. In China, the state maintained a vigilant population-reduction program during the 1980s, but had little concern for nonreproductive domestic matters, including family violence. In effect, the Chinese state claimed control over women's bodies as instruments of reproduction but took little interest when those same bodies were subjected to physical aggression (see Gilmartin 1990; cf. Kligman 1990:424).

It is clear that under state socialism resistance, passive or otherwise, did and does exist, and not only among intellectuals of Solzhenitsyn's or Liu Binyan's stature. In this volume, Paul Pickowicz describes a rare piece of oppositional history written by a Chinese villager: a dissenter's history of rural life in northern China from the 1930s to the late 1980s. Part memoir and part history, the document is handwritten; the author, peasant Geng Xiufeng—a "rural intellectual" (*nongcun zhishifenzi*), one-time minor official, and party member—believes that government policies long ago turned from the true path of socialism. Geng begins his memoir with the forthright statement that his initial interest in agrarian socialism was inspired by neither the policies of the Communist party nor the writings of Mao Zedong. Geng, who intends that his history be published, has repeatedly and publicly objected to what he considers the efforts of state agents to usurp credit for the work he and others had done to promote agrarian socialism. "Time and again," Pickowicz writes, "[Geng] irritated petty state authorities by insisting that the official party view of the history of cooperative formation in Hebei was incorrect." As in the case of Huang Shu-min's (1989) political biography of a party secretary in Fujian Province, one gets the strong impression that local support for the Communist party has always been conditional. Geng's manuscript provides a decidedly unofficial view of recent Chinese history and an alternate vision of what rural China could have been.

People like Geng no doubt existed in the Soviet Union as well as in China, although their opposition might have been less forthright than his. As Pickowicz points out, Geng's opposition has not gone unnoticed: he has been marginalized, labeled a crank, and ridiculed by local officials. More recently he has been described by some local authorities as a "Soviet-style dissident." In earlier decades, the marginalization of such dissenters could have had far greater consequences.

As I noted previously, perhaps the most telling criticism of the totalitarian model is that it does little to illuminate "actually existing socialism." If one accepts the model, it becomes difficult, if not impossible, to understand how alternative versions of the past, the second economy, and nepotism could emerge. As reliance on overt political terror and mass mobilization declined in many socialist societies in the 1970s and 1980s, clientelism and elaborate subcultures of instrumental-personal ties developed, making it possible for people to circumvent formal regulations and acquire everything from better housing to the latest rock music videos (see, e.g., Walder 1986:5–14). Citing these developments, many observers have rejected the term *totalitarian*. Walder prefers *neotraditionalism* because, he argues, it better captures the "formally organized particularism" (1986:7) of Chinese society after the 1950s. Václav Havel, writing of Czechoslovakia in the 1970s, uses the term *post-totalitarian,* which he contrasts with the totalitarianism of "classic dictatorships" (1985:24–27). Others write of bureaucratic centrism, and some retain the totalitarian label (Haraszti's "totalitarian socialism," for example), wishing perhaps to highlight the fact that political control continues to be highly centralized and fundamentally noncompetitive.

Havel (1985:28) provides a vignette that captures important elements of the culture of state socialism—perhaps especially "late state socialism." The manager of a fruit and vegetable shop places in his window the slogan "Workers of the World Unite." Why, Havel asks, does he do this, and what is he trying to communicate? In Havel's view, "the greengrocer is indifferent to the semantic content of the slogan," but the slogan is not meaningless. It proclaims, "I, the greengrocer XY, live here and I know what I must do. I behave in the manner expected of me. I can be depended upon and am beyond reproach. I am obedient and therefore I have the right to be left in peace." This message, according to Havel, is addressed to the greengrocer's superiors, neighbors, and customers, and it shields him from potential informers.

In China, the issues and periodization of socialist culture are different, but Havel's insights are relevant. When, we may ask, did people in China shift from displaying a picture of Mao out of devotion to doing so as a prophylactic of the "leave me in peace, I am reliable" kind?[11] What do such shifts indicate? In the 1960s and 1970s, Havel says, Czechoslovaks had to act as though military occupation was fraternal assistance, as though the lack of free expression was the highest form of freedom, and as though the destruction of culture was its development (1985:30–31). The party state, he writes, "pretends to pretend nothing," and individuals must give this lie credibility by behaving as though there is no pretense (1985:31). As Humphrey points out in her chapter on Mongolia, "there is a shared sense that the official truth is not true" (cf. Link 1992:6–10, 176–91).[12] In Soviet Georgia, Jones relates, official history became suspect as "official reality" became unreal. In such circumstances, personal memory becomes more reliable than the official narrative, which is so often contradicted by experience.

It is important to note that during some periods of intense political and economic mobilization, silent disagreement and pretending not to pretend have been impossible. Schwarcz argues that during China's antirightist campaign of 1957, and again during the Cultural Revolution of 1966–76, millions of Chinese were robbed of their silence. Confucianism, she points out, teaches that it is possible to maintain inner autonomy through self-cultivation, but in Mao's China "this spiritual practice was increasingly difficult to maintain [as] intellectuals were repeatedly required to castigate themselves, to incriminate themselves and their colleagues" (Schwarcz 1991c:104).

In such environments, Humphrey notes, everyone has a double life. Anyone can be an informer; the victim can also be a victimizer. In ways that many who have never lived in a statist society may find difficult to comprehend, "the fundamental lines of conflict run right through each person" (Havel 1985:70). Jan Gross (1988:120) has argued that under Stalin, the pervasive fear of the informer enhanced the perception of the state as omnipresent and therefore omnipotent. This perception was created not because the state was necessarily powerful but because the instruments of coercion were privatized; in effect, terror and compliance were produced by making denunciation available to everyone (Gross 1988:120).

The chapters in this book support the view that as the party overreached itself, a process of delegitimization gained momentum. In controlling one domain of social life, party leaders and their agents left another to blossom; unintended effects flowed from mandated policies. In the end, the party state and its exhausted, confused, increasingly cynical officials could deliver on neither the party's threats nor its promises. Ordinary people, however, continued to operate "as though" the system worked, and the party state was not completely bereft of either its positive or its negative inducements. But with increasing frequency the party state had to share the stage with the informal economy and the personal network.

As I have already noted, in the post-1989 era it has become fashionable to see state socialism as a house of cards. Why, we now ask, did it not fall sooner? In claiming greater territory for itself, the state, it has been argued, destroyed or disabled competing institutions, structures, and practices. Gross refers to this as a process of "spoiling," and to socialist states as spoiler states; what cannot be controlled, he argues, must be destroyed or disabled (1988). Gradually, the enormous public/official sphere, perhaps because it colonizes so much but delivers too little, becomes suspect, corrupt, and alienating. At the same time, institutions, associations, and alliances that could fill the void—what some refer to as civil society—have been destroyed or rendered ineffective.[13] Many people retreat into private life. In China, for example, the late 1980s and early 1990s were marked by a craze for *qigong* (breath and body control) and by a voracious demand for romance novels.[14] In Eastern Europe, summer villas, rock music, private writing, and alcohol offered opportunities for escape or introspection.

There is nothing inevitable, of course, about the collapse of state socialism. In a recent article titled "What Happened in Eastern Europe in 1989?" Daniel Chirot summarizes the economic factors that led to collapse, arguing that investment and production decisions were based largely on political will, making it impossible to determine which firms were profitable and efficient (1991:216–217). But why, he asks, did the collapse occur in 1989? Why did these systems not last longer or change in less dramatic ways? After all, these societies experienced no catastrophic economic declines. Chirot answers his question by arguing that state socialism in Eastern Europe fell when it did because ordinary people and their leaders "lost confidence in the moral validity of their social and political systems" (1991:221; see also Ash 1990; Gellner 1991). But why did they lose confidence?

In a recent book, Michael Burawoy and Janos Lukacs argue that "the production regimes of state socialism engender dissent" (1992:114). By engaging in the practices that build socialism, people are regularly and often dramatically reminded of the gap between what is and what should be (1992:127). Echoing Havel, Burawoy and Lukacs argue: "Socialism becomes an elaborate game of pretense which everyone sees through but which everyone is compelled to play" (1992:129). In the end, the rituals that are meant both to construct and to celebrate socialism become its undoing.[15] Ernest Gellner makes a similar argument: "The salvation doctrine of Marxism is centred on the economy. In various ways, this was probably its undoing. It meant that a promise of collective salvation was formulated in terms which were only too clearly open to testing; and in the end, the verdict of history and experience damned the theory" (1991:504–5).[16]

New States and "New" Histories

Today in Eastern Europe, Mongolia, Georgia, and Russia, the task is to rebuild the public domain in a new image. Can this be done after the ravages of the "spoiler state"? The past is crucial to this rebuilding process. In chapter 8, Jones argues that a number of factors account for the intensity of what he labels "memory politics" in Eastern Europe and the former Soviet Union. Looking back at the Soviet period, he describes an apparent contradiction between, on the one hand, republican state structures that encouraged the development of national—in his case, Georgian—constitutions, emblems, hymns, and approved Soviet-republic histories and, on the other hand, domination from the center, which was intrusive and harsh. Georgian memories of a pre-Soviet past survived in the interstices of history, where they were kept alive in ritual, in oral literature and song, in monuments and public buildings, in poetry and historical novels, and in films.

The sense of alienation that people felt and the similarities between Soviet and nationalist conceptions of time were also important factors in the development of memory politics. Jones observes that "like Soviet propagandists, nationalists see past time as bound by and as part of the present." The constitutional and political privileges that were granted to a "titular group" in each republic have also intensified ethnic struggles. These privileges, Jones argues, contribute to the view that a unique relationship exists between the territory of a republic and a particular ethnic-national group. In post-Soviet Georgia, new official histories and new minorities are being created as the former "titular group"—the Georgians—make exclusive claims to "their" historical homeland.

Hayden, too, is concerned with questions of memory politics. In his chapter on late- and postcommunist Yugoslavia, Hayden demonstrates how hidden or secret histories and memories of atrocities provide a powerful framework for the "totalizing nationalisms" of Croatia and Serbia. In recent years, new categorical histories, based on reconstructions of a "forgotten past," have come to play a central role in Yugoslavia's violent politics. These histories, Hayden argues, allow emerging political leaders to claim legitimacy on the basis of the opposition's past record of immorality.

In contrast to Georgia, where a golden, pre-Soviet era has become an integral part of a new national charter (Georgians, it appears, have "forgotten" the Soviet period), Croatian and Serbian nationalisms are constructed upon the bitter and, in some cases, long-suppressed histories of the Second World War and Yugoslavia's own civil war. Charges and countercharges about moral culpability for past actions constitute the raw materials out of which these nationalisms are being created. Hayden's paper, more than any other in this volume, shows the process by which the revised histories of new national groups create their own counternarratives. In the territory that was once Yugoslavia, as in other societies where national ambitions have been recharged, the creation of "our past" often involves the negation of another group's history. Remembering and forgetting are thus locked together in a complicated web as one group's enfranchisement requires another's disenfranchisement.

MEMORY, OPPOSITION, AND HISTORY

The chapters in this volume show that personal memory can be constrained and reshaped by official campaigns of coercive forgetting and, further, that shared memory is considerably more problematical under state socialism than might first be assumed. Party apparatchiks never managed fully to domesticate the past, but at times the technology of amnesia was disturbingly effective.

Given that under state socialism resistance is often passive and the sharing of memory—of past experiences—hesitant, it is difficult, some might say foolhardy, to deploy the language of opposition. Nevertheless, the contributors to this book show that oppositional narratives were created by Chinese rural historians, émigré Croatians, dissenters such as Yugoslavia's Milovan Djilas, and Chinese intellectuals as they first whispered and later shouted their unauthorized memories to foreign colleagues. Evidence of opposition is also found in the hidden histories enshrined in Georgia's national epics, in the unapproved memorializations that transform Chinese ritual and opera into protest, and in the orally transmitted religious histories of Mongolia. It is also clear, however, that new concepts are needed to capture the subtleties of opposition and compliance as experienced under state socialism—and it is here that we enter the domain of the evocative transcript, silent disagreement, passive resistance, and erupted memory.

The colonization of public and private space is one of the hallmarks of state socialism. Nonetheless, as the essays in this volume demonstrate, agents of the state were never able to stifle all forms of opposition—especially those enshrined in memory. These alternative representations of the past, we are learning, have become central to the new histories that are now defining national struggles in the postsocialist world. In this book we have focused most of our attention on memory, but as national and ethnic conflicts embroil many parts of the world, future studies may find the processes of forgetting more compelling.

─────── Notes ───────

1. Exceptions might include Stalin's Soviet Union in the 1930s and Pol Pot's reign in Cambodia in the 1970s.

2. See, for example, Campeanu (1988); M. Djilas (1957); Haraszti (1979, 1987); Havel (1985); Konrad and Szelenyi (1979); Rev (1987); and Staniszkis (1991).

3. For discussion of "everyday forms of resistance," see, for example, Scott (1989, 1990); and Colburn (1989a). For discussions of opposition, resistance, and subversion under state socialism, see, for example, Anagnost (1989); Rev (1987); Rofel (1989); Sabel and Stark (1982); M. M. Yang (1988); and Zweig (1989b); for further discussion of this literature, see Verdery (1991b).

4. For critiques of the "romance of resistance," see Abu-Lughod (1990); and Turton (1986).

5. For discussion of process, practice, and agency, see, for example, Giddens (1979); Moore (1987); and Ortner (1984).

6. See, for example, Hanson (1989); Hobsbawm and Ranger (1983); and Lewis (1975).

7. For a discussion of the effectiveness of the "technology of amnesia" in China, see Fang Lizhi, "The Chinese Amnesia," in *The New York Review*, September 27, 1990.

8. For examples of such silent remembrances, see, on remembering the American liberation of Pilsen, *New York Times*, April 11, 1990; on a tribute to Stalin's disappeared, "Gulag Cemetery," *New York Times*, August 27, 1990; and on silent vigils, Kligman (1990:401).

9. On shared, social, or collective memory, see, for example, Benjamin (1969); Bloch (1925); Bodnar (1991); Burke (1989); Casey (1984); Connerton (1989); Halbwachs (1980); Hill (1988); Hosking (1989); Le Goff (1992); and Rappaport (1990).

10. On intellectuals under state socialism, see, for example, Barme (1989); Goldman, Cheek, and Hamrin (1987); Haraszti (1987); Konrad and Szelenyi (1979); Lee (1991); Link (1992); Simmonds-Duke (1987); Siu (1990); Siu and Stern (1983); Szelenyi (1982); and Verdery (1991a).

11. Since 1989, Mao buttons and pictures are once again being displayed (see *New York Times,* February 19, 1990; *Christian Science Monitor,* February 22, 1990). Now, however, they appear to have become a sign of dissent or "ambiguous protest" against the present leadership, or to be used in much the way a St. Christopher's medal might be used in a Boston taxicab.

12. In *Evening Chats in Beijing* (1992), Perry Link provides an interesting discussion of "official" and "unofficial" modes of expression in China during the late 1980s (cf. Weller 1993:chapter 12). "Both kinds of language are fully 'real,'" he argues, "and are equally essential to getting along in Chinese life" (Link 1992:7); but he goes on to note in a later chapter that the distinctions between the two are very clear. The official language "consists of standard phrases, slogans, and ideas that one uses not to express one's own thoughts or intentions . . . but through judicious manipulation to advance one's interests or to defend oneself" (1992:176). Link believes this bifurcation of language produces a profound identity problem for Chinese intellectuals "with their well-rooted cultural assumptions of the unity of language, morality, and public service" (1992:191).

13. On civil society, see, for example, Gellner (1991); Gramsci (1971); Habermas (1989); Keane (1988); Kligman (1990); and Lapidus (1988).

14. See, for example, Barme and Jaiven (1992:324, 374–85).

15. Burawoy and Lukacs write: "The very conditions that are hidden through participation in capitalist production, in socialist production become the focal concern of the players. The compulsion to participate in the socialist game is potentially explosive—the pretense becomes an alternative turned against reality" (1992:129). In their view, state socialism becomes the brunt of critiques because it is seen not to live up to its own values and goals.

16. In a recent book, Robert Weller makes the argument that official socialist language offers a "thin interpretation" that is easy to control but is neither powerful nor compelling in its appeal (1994:chapter 12).

2

Remembering an "Enemy"

The Bogd Khaan in Twentieth-Century Mongolia

CAROLINE HUMPHREY

ALTERNATELY CONTROLLED BY its huge neighbors, China and the Soviet Union, Mongolia in the twentieth century has experienced episodes of bloody repression and a struggle for effective autonomy.[1] Only since about 1990 has true sovereignty seemed a realistic prospect. Between 1911 and 1921, however, there was a brief period of quasi-independence, from the forced departure of the Manchu governors (just as the Qing dynasty was collapsing in China) to the installation of a Soviet-backed revolutionary government in the Mongolian capital. During this period Mongolia was a theocracy, ruled by the head of the Buddhist church. A vast and powerful organization with over 700 large monasteries and about 1,000 small ones, the church in 1921 claimed up to one-third of the male population as lamas (Bawden 1968:160).

At the head of the Buddhist church was the religious office known as the Javzundamba Khutagt, then occupied by its eighth incarnation, who, like most of his predecessors, was born a Tibetan.[2] Eschewing his extraordinarily long title and following their general principle of not speaking aloud the names of highly respected people, the Mongols know him as the Bogd ("holy one").[3] Initially known only as the Bogd Gegeen ("holy enlightened one"), he acquired a new dual status as the Bogd Khaan ("holy emperor") when the Mongol aristocracy made him head of state in 1911.[4] In his role as emperor he took the opportunity to have enthroned with him a queen, the Eke Dagini ("mother goddess"), although this was strictly against his vows as a lama. He remained head of state until his death in 1924.

The fatal weaknesses of Mongolia were its cultural isolation, small population, and antiquated army. The Bogd's power was progressively eroded by treaties between Russia, China, and Japan that compromised Mongolia's sovereignty, and by coups and armed incursions into the country from north and south. His effective authority was finally removed altogether by the revolutionary government of 1921, which accorded him only titular status. Throughout these upheavals, however, the "holy emperor" continued to be quite literally worshipped by the Mongolian people.

There is no standpoint from which an "objective" history can be written of the Bogd Khaan. This situation, which I believe to be true of history in general, is magnified by the nature of the social contexts from which texts about such a figure could emerge. In particular, we must engage with two contexts of domination: a religion in which the sanctity of the institution of reincarnation was an overwhelming preoccupation, and the quasi-hegemony of Soviet ideological thought. Until 1989–90, when the Mongols emerged from Soviet domination, there was no social space in which even to attempt a balanced history of the Bogd.

Each of these ideological contexts developed its own "official" species of history, involving texts of easily recognizable types that followed systematic, almost formulaic, norms for delimiting relevance and constructing time. Apart from their typological and anonymous character, which establishes both types as truly social documents, these kinds of texts are very different from one another, and they have come to have quite different political weights and visibility. The first type—Soviet-dominated histories concerning the period from 1911 to 1921, often written by nameless collectivities—has been published in numerous variants and translated into many languages.[5] The second type—Buddhist historical biographies (namtar)—consists of sacred texts that exist only in the Mongol script, and most people educated since the change to Cyrillic writing in the 1940s cannot read them.[6] In the Soviet period these previously official texts were confiscated. They continued in limited clandestine circulation, but until very recently, to produce such a text openly would have been to invite arrest. A namtar of the eighth Bogd is said to exist in a restricted state archive (Bawden 1961:1). We can imagine what such a Buddhist history of the eighth Bogd would look like, since stereotypical historical biographies exist of all seven previous incarnations (Bawden 1961).

My primary concern here is not with such official histories but with the more fleeting, episodic, and indirect products of the Mongolian historical imagination, many of which are oral rather than written. This is a culture that loves and respects the distant past, but it creates its own history not so much by constructing sequences in a chronology as by citing precedents—snapshots, as it were, rather than a consecutive film. For example, the present celebration of Mongolia's emerging freedom from Soviet domination involves leapfrogging over the centuries to the twelfth- to thirteenth-century "precedent" of Chingghis Khaan.

James Scott (1990) proposed the idea of the "hidden transcript" in relation to history and memory. Despite its value for the analysis of other circumstances, this concept has only limited applicability for encapsulated societies subject to Soviet-type domination. Instead, one of the most prevalent forms of heterodox public expression in Mongolia has been what I call the "evocative transcript." Scott's term transcript admirably conveys the idea of the social reproduction of texts that circulate as the reiteration of previous texts. Any text may suggest all kinds of meanings to people incidentally, but the term *evocative* indicates a text that is *intended* to elicit or evoke a particular interpretation beyond the surface meaning. Evocative transcripts are ambiguous by design. They come to the fore in political quasi-hegemonies, when the previous codes of classes and ethnic groups are suppressed and two pervasive new kinds of discourse are maintained throughout society by force and fear: a highly ideological, stilted, and mostly written official discourse, and "all the rest," which may be oral and informal but nevertheless must maintain a semblance of conformity in public.

Scott proposes that hidden transcripts are produced both by those in positions of power and by those who are dominated. In the former case, the hidden transcripts consist of the real, almost involuntary, expressions of power interests, which emerge in contradistinction to the public transcripts' expression of the dominant ideology of social harmony, paternalism, development, brotherhood, or whatever it may be. In the latter case—that of the dominated group—the hidden transcripts are the half-muted, covert, or mocking forms of resistance to the same ruling ideology. Scott, working mainly with colonial or class situations, sees these two kinds of hidden transcripts as distinct and incompatible. "They are specific to a given social site and to a particular set of actors" (1991:14), and they are hidden in that they exclude specified others. Although there is a zone of constant struggle and dialogue with the public transcript, hidden transcripts themselves are "never in direct contact. Each participant will be familiar with the public transcript and the hidden transcript of his or her circle, but not with the hidden transcript of the other" (Scott 1991:15).

The Mongolian situation suggests that encapsulated societies in Soviet-type systems provide a different case. In Mongolia, the true, naked interests of both the dominators and the dominated in the socialist period were known to everyone and found in virtually everyone. This knowledge was subversive in that it was distinct from sanctimonious official discourse (the "public transcript" in Scott's terminology), but it was not exactly hidden; it operated openly, but through duality and equivocation, and it was a common resource for all, if only in imagination.

Clearly a major reason for this situation is that socialist Mongolia—from about 1921 to about 1990—was held in thrall to a Soviet Union that operated from above and encompassed Mongolia's own internal hierarchy. Even the general secretary of the Mongolian Revolutionary Party knew the experience of the bullied subordinate. This structural encapsulation, and the appointment of Soviet "advisors" to rule (covertly) every important institution in Mongol society, from factories to schools, meant that all Mongolians in "power" also experienced the insult of subordination in their own spheres. The freest person might seem to have been the poorest and most downtrodden nomad, who had nothing to lose. No one was free, however, since all the "nomads" were, by the late 1950s, made to become specialized livestock herders in collectives and state farms.

Mongolia in 1911 was a relatively culturally homogeneous society with a distinctive life-style. But that virtually everyone could experience being both the dominator and the dominated derives not so much from a common culture as from the structural processes of Soviet-type socialist society after 1921. Certainly the "dictatorship of the proletariat" in Mongolia was nothing like the propagandistic version from Moscow, if only because there was no obvious proletariat in Mongolia at the time of the revolution; one had to be either found or invented. During the Soviet-dominated period, various social groups served this purpose, beginning with freed serfs from the previous feudal regime, then women, then the "lower class" of the lamas in the 1930s, and most recently, anyone with a working-class, especially rural, background.[7] But that these choices were consciously exercised from "on top" and seem to have taken their cue from Moscow does not make the social process any less real.

Mongolian society was repeatedly turned on its head as the emergence of each new kind of "proletariat" was coordinated with purges of the previous elites. New groups flooded into party and government positions as old ones were eliminated or sidelined.[8] The rhetoric of socialism encouraged the plucking out of people from obscurity to participate in the drama of power. Unlike the serf of earlier times, who could never have stood as an equal next to his ruling prince, the subordinate in the socialist context could sometimes take advantage of the ideology and claim for a historical instant the preeminent standing of a "worker" (or, even better, a "woman worker" or an "ex-lama who has seen the error of his ways").

In the Soviet-type command economy, the structure of domination does not consist of a focal nexus surrounded by a subordinated mass; rather, domination resides in a series of equivalent positions in nesting hierarchies, such that a similar domination may be exercised at each level. Even at the bottom, in the remote enclave of some herding collective, the brigadier could subordinate his workers by the same principles, and with the same equivocal relationship to the ideology of "discipline," that obtained at structurally higher levels (Humphrey 1983:258–66). Thus someone who might seem a naive rustic on his visit to Ulaan-baatar might be no stranger to power and its transcripts back in his native mountains. The system imposed a structural unity, a principle of nesting domination, on individuals and groups that were otherwise different from one another (for example, in native region, education, or religious attitudes).

There must have been some people who were always on the fringes of this hierarchy and who therefore remained strangers to the experience of dominating others. But the possibility for dispossessed and alienated people to unite and produce hidden transcripts of resistance was limited; it was countered by the general cohesiveness of Mongol society and by the tendency of the Soviet-type system always to gather up those at the bottom and insert them into the system by all possible means. Frequently, these very people, being distanced from previous elites, were most suitable (by "class background") for promotion into the ranks of the officials in the next generation.

The anthropological implications of what I am proposing—the presence of both subordination and domination in almost everyone's life—are different from those of the colonial or class situations discussed by Scott. In those cases, the hidden transcripts have their locus in social gatherings where people of a certain category can express themselves to one another. In other words, the producers and receivers of the hidden transcript belong to the same social category and share a social space: the planters' clubhouse where they can discuss what they would like to do to the bloody natives, or the midnight arson expedition in which the apparently docile servants revel in setting fire to the landlord's mansion.

In Soviet-dominated Mongolia,[9] such like-minded gatherings no doubt existed, but they were not peopled by the kinds of stable and enduring groups with their own social space that Scott rightly insists are necessary for the production of hidden transcripts.[10] Furthermore, they were constantly subverted by the knowledge that virtually everyone had a double life, that anyone could be an informer, and that the weapons of the "weak"—rumor, gossip, and innuendo—were those of the "strong," too. Even today in Mongolia, although there is a public sphere of governmental reports, decrees, newspapers, and so forth, the whole society is more "private" and oral than one would think possible for a modern state.[11] For example, it is normal for certain important political events in the government and party not to be announced, yet people do hear about them.

A walk down a street in Ulaan-baatar consists of stopping every few yards to exchange news with acquaintances, whether a well-placed official or a lowly watchman—anyone may have something interesting to impart. The short gaps between these conversations are often spent assessing the reliability of the last one. It is impossible to make a simple correlation between the official ideology and the public realm, or between resistance and the private realm, since almost all social life is necessarily played out in conversations that are somewhat public and somewhat private.

This observation implies that the main form available for the expression of the heterodox is not, as in colonial and class situations, the hidden transcripts produced within social circles of the like-minded. It is, instead, the throwing into the social arena, as it were, of texts that are memorably ambiguous. Even if the situation is one of confrontation (that is, the producer and the receiver of a text are opposed to one another), both parties make an implicit appeal to "someone else"—the bystander who is the bearer of a common morality. A bystander may or may not be physically present; nonetheless, such a third party is implicated in the form of the evocative transcript, which requires there to be a judge: the one who laughs at the joke, perceives the double entendre, or retells the story—in other words, a postulated representative of Mongolian cultural values.

This sort of confrontation is different from the direct dualistic conflict described by Scott (1991:7–15)—the betel juice spat on the dress of the European woman in the bazaar, or Mrs. Poyser's outburst to the Squire: "We're not dumb creatures to be abused"—in which either radically different cultures or different class moralities within a single culture are opposed to one another. In such cases a common understanding cannot be presumed, because Mrs. Poyser has never experienced anything like the Squire's position of power. But in the Soviet-type system, everyone understands the arbitrariness of any individual's position in the hierarchy of power, and everyone knows, therefore, that morality rests elsewhere. This is why evocative transcripts make an appeal outside the dualistic system of dominator-dominated—a comeuppance by means of the subtle, coded invocation of the values of the common bystander. The evocative transcript thus has a tripartite structure involving the two opposed parties and an implicit third. The role of this third party is taken on by the people who turn the incident into a "story" or "transcript"—who remember it and repeat it and interpret it. Usually we know only this social version, refracted and re-formed by numerous tellings.

It is this public circulation that makes the evocative transcript a separate phenomenon from the private, unapproved, and painful memories—repressed only to return—that are so eloquently discussed by Vera Schwarcz in chapter 3. The kind of stories that concern us here may, on the other hand, be a stage in the process by which personal recollection is transformed into rethought history, which Andrew Lass analyzes in chapter 5. There is also a sense, I think, in which people may "relive" evocative transcripts through ritual and in other ways—but a fuller exploration of this topic would require another paper.

It might be argued that all texts have an evocative or ambiguous aspect; that is, implicit as well as explicit meanings can be found in them. What I am trying to express by the term *evocative transcript*—a provisional term intended to cover a range of different types, such as texts that are masquerades, or decoys, or provocations—is not that one may discover covert implications in any text but that some texts are deliberately designed to evoke a dual reaction, and this reaction is directed, not fancy free. Such texts often come to have an almost riddlelike character in which one sense depends on what it is publicly possible to say, while the "solution" rests on knowledge of analogy and precedent. (It is worth pointing out that riddles are an important part of Mongolian oral culture.) Let me give an example of the kind of story at issue, although this one does not concern memory of the Bogd. The Mongolian writer and scholar Rinchen is said one day to have met the career politician Tsedenbal, who was to become the prime minister of Mongolia. Tsedenbal said, "I am thinking of learning a foreign language. Respected teacher, which one do you think it would be best for me to learn?" Rinchen replied, "Thinking of your dinner, it would be best for you to learn German." This reply is a dig at Tsedenbal: the listener appreciates that Tsedenbal would not learn a foreign language for disinterested reasons ("dinner" in Mongolian implies job, pay-packet, and perks) and understands an implicit reference to the fact that Mongolian prime ministers have always learned Russian. Rinchen's reply also appeals to the common plight of Mongolia: because Russian is by far the most obvious language to learn, Rinchen implies that Russia is not where our interests lie. Russia will fail us; Western Europe is a better bet.

Such apparently trivial moments, and the individuals whose remarks are lit by them as if by a spotlight, are famous in Mongolia and are the subjects of endless retellings and reenactments. These instants throw into relief not just the main actor but also those who are being confronted, revealing them in a certain light—a hue that colors them for years, so long as social memory of that moment lasts.

Trailing after these moments come the refracting snapshots of rumor (*tsuurkhal*) and oblique "sayings" (*yaria, ug*). They are characteristically anonymous and therefore spread easily between people who are unsure of each other; they can always be taken at face value. But it is because there is something beneath face value that they are remembered. I propose that it is through texts, both oral and written, calling upon an unstated stratum of latent morality that much of social memory is transmitted. This transmission is carried out both by those who uphold the official ideology at a given time and by those who oppose it.

Even the official Soviet-style histories are not without hints of other sentiments. For example, if the aim was to cut the Bogd off from a moral continuity in history, it would have been easy and expedient to call him by another term. But throughout the official histories he is referred to as Bogd Gegeen, which results in strange locutions that can be translated as "his Saintly Holiness's clique" or "the hypocritical note from his Saintly Holiness's so-called government" (Academy of Sciences 1973:287).

Such expressions suggest a situation far removed from that discussed by Scott (1991). The point of his distinction between the hidden transcripts of the subordinates and those of the powerful is that their empowering effect comes from their being concealed from the other side. In encapsulated Soviet-type situations, on the other hand, in order to come up with a version that will be memorable and effective even for one's own "side," one has to use language that is, in a sense—but not in a very strong sense—the preserve of the other side.

Consider a joking expression (*ug*) used by the ordinary people to describe the communist bosses (*darga*): they are "oxen sitting in carts." This expression gains piquancy from everyone's knowing that oxen should pull carts, that "carts" is a slang word for cars, and that oxen are commonly regarded as stupid. The expression might seem to be a classic hidden transcript of the downtrodden, but it is not. I have heard the bosses themselves use it, mostly as a way of getting at other bosses, but also in a self-deprecating, or possibly ingratiating, way about themselves.

The confrontational moments recalled in stories, songs, and shared memoirs imply the existence of values alternative to those of the official ideology—but not of a single, coherent alternative. This point is particularly evident when Mongolian people talk about historical events, especially those that allow a great range of evaluations either because they were so one-sidedly interpreted in the public ideology or because the official texts simply left them out. The public history of the Bogd Khaan, the archenemy of the revolution, fits the bill in both ways: it is distorted and it is remarkably uninformative.

Official history books do not dwell on the Bogd, but rather talk about his "clique." His personality and his actions are unexplained; he is not even described as a traitor to his own country like other counterrevolutionaries. It is as if he represents simply the negation of the revolution. The Bogd's evilness could be read into the text because all Mongolian readers would know, from their schooling and daily experience, that his name had become barely mentionable, that his artifacts and memorials had been erased or transformed into something no longer his, and that people had gone to their deaths for the slightest association, even an invented one, with him.[12] Doubly dangerous because his role as a reincarnation both recalled ancient values and conjured the future—the possibility of a ninth incarnation—the Bogd became the black hole of Mongolian history.

Perhaps I should preface Mongolian accounts of the Bogd with some Western descriptions. European judgments of this mysterious personality vary greatly, though they all tend toward the sensational. A. M. Pozdneev, who knew the Bogd slightly and seems to have found him reprehensible, wrote:

> At the present time, the *khubilgan* [Buddhist incarnation] of the Jebtsun Damba Khutukhtu is nearly twenty-two years old; in height he is a little below the average, and he is thin; his face is somehow yellow, without the slightest hint of colour, and still more unpleasant by virtue of the expression of some sort of childish wilfullness and capricious stubbornness which is always present in it, and also from the lips, which are extraordinarily sensuous in their development. (1971 [1896]:368).

On the other hand, the Swedish missionary Frans August Larson, who knew the Bogd well, wrote:

> I found a vast crowd of several thousand jostling, laughing people, packed into every nook and corner [of the Bogd's palace]. I supposed that I should witness some religious ceremony, so you can imagine my surprise when a window in the upper story of the palace was thrown open and a jolly man, dressed in a gown of glittering gold, appeared and flung out a lady's corset. It flew over my head and I caught it. My impulse was to throw it back at him, but before I could do so someone snatched it out of my hand. . . .
>
> He disappeared from the window. The mob called him back. They cheered when he returned with his arms filled with Western ladies' dresses. These he threw out one at a time . . . and hats which must have been designed to match each costume were tossed out as if they were so many cakes. The Living Buddha even tried one—a concoction of straw and ostrich feathers—and thrust his head through the window for the admiration of the crowd. . . .
>
> After he was crowned Emperor he soon selected ministers and officials. His government ran smoothly. The best blood of Mongolia flocked around him. This was a prosperous time for Urga [Ulaan-baatar]. Life was very gay, and hope ran high. It was a good season and wealth

abounded. Mongolia prospered as she has never prospered at any other time during the years I have lived among her people. . . .

He was always very kind to me. . . . He was a sick man when I took my friend Sven Hedin to visit him. He was nearly blind and his heart had been broken by the turn of affairs in Mongolia. But he did everything in his power to make Hedin's visit to Urga a success. He was not only the Living Buddha who gave absolution for their sins twice weekly to the Mongolian supplicants, but a great man who recognized genius in other men when he met it. (1930:113–134)

In some Western accounts, such as that of the Hungarian engineer Joseph Geleta, an orientalist romanticism is apparent. The Bogd Gegeen appears simultaneously attached to and removed from his people, narcissistic and two-faced:

The monastery in which the Bogdos lived is held in great reverence by the people. It lies on the banks of the Tola River and the palaces which it comprises look like the embodiments of some fairy-tale. . . . On the most important religious festivals the Grand Lama sat enthroned in the temple, blessing the congregation, not with spoken words or by raising his hands but with the aid of a long cord. One end of the cord was held by the Grand Lama, while the other end, which was in most cases outside the temple, was touched in turn by members of the congregation, it being presumed that the cord carried their prayers to the holy man and his blessing back to them. . . .

The Palace is furnished with true Eastern opulence, but there is nothing of the East about its central heating system, its private electrical generating plant, which was installed long before the people of Urga had heard about electricity. When it was decided to convert the Palace into a museum the work was entrusted to me, and so I had ample opportunity to explore the building. In one room all the walls were covered with long mirrors, all of which, I discovered, turned on hinges. On looking behind the mirrors I was amazed to find that the walls proper were covered with finely-executed drawings of a most grossly obscene character! (Forbath and Geleta 1936:259–61)

The eighth Bogd, born in Tibet in 1870, was brought to Mongolia in 1874. Upon his arrival at the Mongolian capital, the boy, like his predecessors, had to visit the camp of the Tushetu Khan, the most senior prince in Mongolia, where the prince and his wife personally kindled a fire and made tea for the child (Pozdneev 1971 [1896]:374). Every year the Tushetu Khan by custom offered the Bogd a "winter present" consisting of a stomach of butter and a sheep's chest and heart (Tomorkhuleg 1990). The significance of this gift is that in the seventeenth century, the first Mongolian incarnation in the line was born into the family of the

Tushetu Khan and thus was a lineal descendant of Chingghis Khaan. The line of the Bogd Gegeens maintained a symbolic fictive kinship with the ancestral emblem of Mongol sovereignty.

The eighth Bogd was the first to combine a religious role with an imperial one. On his accession to the throne, the Bogd successfully brought the Western Mongols and the region of Tannu-Tuva into his state, and his edict of independence aroused declarations of loyalty from virtually all the Mongol regions of China. But after only a few years, this empire began to fall apart: Russia would not countenance the conquests in China, and the Bogd was forced to accept the reimposition of Chinese suzerainty; Mongolia was invaded first by a Chinese army, then by a White Russian one; and finally it was taken over by the revolutionary Mongolian-Soviet coup. Toward the end of his life, racked by drink and, it is rumored, syphilis, the Bogd despaired.

In the rest of this chapter I will discuss ways in which this tragic—or not so tragic—sacred figure has been remembered. Both Stalinist and Buddhist contexts surround the social memories of the Bogd. I shall provide some instances of pre-communist texts, including "hidden transcripts" of the type brought to our notice by Scott, but my argument is that as official, Soviet-type ideology penetrated Mongolian society, such texts were superseded by a pervasive, ambiguous, "evocative" discourse.

The Buddhist understanding of the Bogd Khaan is radically different from the European because it removes the need to reconcile the gap between the man and the role. One man, whose father had been a lama and who was brought up to worship the deceased eighth Bogd, told me why the Bogd's excesses did not affect his standing among the ordinary faithful: "My father used to tell us, 'It is only our eyes which see these bad things.'" This religious view is explained by the Diluv Khutagt, a prominent incarnation from Western Mongolia, in his memoirs:[13]

> The body of my last incarnation was a worldly person who drank, but the body of my incarnation before that was a learned and pious lama who was everywhere revered and invited far and wide to visit monasteries. . . . It may be that in my incarnation of two generations ago, when religious merit was accumulating elsewhere . . . ignorance and error were accumulating in the monastery itself, and therefore, as far as our mortal eyes can see, the vehicle of my next incarnation was inferior to the one which had gone just before.
>
> We must remember that illusion, the distortion of our understanding by material things, is always about us. To speak of 'good' and 'bad' incarnations is a very gross way of speaking. (Lattimore and Isono 1982:141–3)

The eighth Bogd's wild activities tried his religious followers to the limit. Nevertheless, many sources describe the adoring faith of the lay populace and the annual *dansug* ritual in which they begged him with costly gifts not to abandon his transitory body (Bawden 1968:162; Larson 1930; Pozdneev 1971 [1896]:382–3).

Adoration of the Bogd's "bodily vehicle," however, did not entirely prevail. A broad, though covert, opposition to dilatory high clergy had been growing among the lamas throughout the nineteenth century. In 1913 a lama was put to death for having slandered the Bogd. Among several versions of what he is supposed to have said, one is: "Is that miserable old blind Tibetan still alive? What do we call him our king for? I don't care a fig for his orders and admonitions." A similar execution took place in 1921 when a lama called the Bogd "a wretched Tibetan beggar who has wandered here" (Bawden 1968:166).[14] More substantial opposition came from a fundamentalist movement for the reform of the church (Popova 1987).[15] I mention these examples of "hidden transcripts" in Scott's sense (the Bogd's secret erotic drawings are another) in order to contrast them with the multivocal texts characteristic of the socialist period.

The writings of the Bogd himself demonstrate that there were at least two distinct styles of historical-political thinking, one strategic, one religious, during his reign. They can be related to the "two principles"—the mutual legitimation of church and state, formally laid down in Khubilai Khaan's time and revived by many subsequent Mongolian monarchs—now united in the hands of a single man. These styles are relevant to this chapter because the actions of the communist regime served to separate them; both were forced underground, the strategic more deeply than the religious.

As head of state, the Bogd necessarily engaged in international negotiations. The texts indicate that he commanded entirely straightforward and logical arguments in defense of Mongolia's interests. But he also issued edicts (*lungdeng*) in the mythical-prophetic tradition established centuries earlier by his predecessors. A lungdeng was inspired by a dream or a request from the faithful. Sometimes, an old lama told me, the Bogd would rise up from his bed at night and, looking into the sky, decree that it was the Will of Heaven that a certain ritual be performed. His sayings would be dispatched by word of mouth; sometimes the lungdeng were written down, becoming small books that were read out all over the country. One example tells the faithful that a predestined time of evil has come:

> The yellow and the black ones [lamas and laypeople] must exert themselves, they must not smoke or drink or wander from their families. They must do nothing to destroy the peace, must not say bad things about the lamas . . . because from the next Horse Year until the Monkey Year numerous forebodings predict a time of illness, suffering and death. There will be armed fighting, disorders, and disasters of fire and water; cold and hot times will be mixed up. The God [lit. "sky"] of Disease will come down from on high. Even if there is clothing there will be no-one to wear it; of 10,000 people, 9,000 will die. . . . Lamas will join

the military. Lay people will become like slaves. Nobles will become
like dogs. Poor beggars will become administrators. . . . The recourse
is prayer and offerings. . . . If you do this, from the Wood Monkey year
a time of universal peace and happiness will come.[16]

Charles R. Bawden has written, citing such a text, that the Bogd seems to have
been aware of internal weakness and sensitive to impending political change, but
he did not aim at fundamental change in society and remained locked in a timeless
isolation (1968:172–3). Since the Bogd did, in fact, reorganize the Mongolian government, introduce two chambers of representatives, conduct a census, establish
a "reform fund" for social and cultural measures, build schools and a telephone
network, and many times request aid and training from the Tsarist, Japanese, and
United States governments, such a blanket judgment seems questionable.

It is interesting that a seventeenth-century Inner Mongolian lungdeng described by Alice Sárközi (1971) uses some doom-laden phrases almost identical to
those in the preceding quotation. In sum, it seems that the Bogd was juggling two
different political cultures that generated alternative forms of discourse. He used
the more practical form in his capacity as head of state in the international arena,
while he employed the prophetic form in the internal religious-political domain.
Such distinctive styles could be maintained and could generate hidden transcripts
in opposition because the major feudal corporations of Mongolian society were
still intact during the Bogd's reign.

In the decades after the 1921 revolution, all social memory of the strategic
kind of text was deeply repressed, and the documents themselves were hidden in
inaccessible archives. The Bogd was officially depicted as the crazed (but crafty)
puppet of various cliques, only just capable of placing his seal on a document.
His cogent political negotiations on behalf of Mongolian autonomy were systematically occluded in all political discourse, speeches, and textbooks. Either they
were simply left out of the account, or they were interpreted as cowardly plots
to engage the whites, the Western imperialists, or the Japanese against the revolution—it having become an absolute principle that Mongolia's interests lay only
with the Soviet Union.[17] The lungdeng continued to circulate secretly, as they do
to this day, but their status as texts was abruptly changed. No longer unambigu-
ously the edicts of a theocratic sovereign, their connotations became uncertain:
were they masked prophesies about the dire consequences of Soviet rule, or vain
nostalgia for a religious past, or dangerous antirevolutionary rallying calls?

Soon after the 1921 revolution, evocative transcripts began to emerge. In the
mid-1920s, before a definitively negative view of the Bogd had been imposed,
the communist Revolutionary Party employed a Buddhist vision to rid itself of
the Bogd. On the death of the eighth incarnation in 1924, the lamas asked permission to search for his successor. The government, heavily influenced, if not bound,
by Comintern policies (Brown and Onon 1976:111, 127, 167), was committed to
ending the theocracy and establishing a republic. Nevertheless, the party leader-

ship took the following decision, with its strange recourse to traditional rumors and reference to the mythical land of Shambala:

> The Jebtsundamba Khutukhtus [the line of incarnations of the Bogd] have deserved extremely well of our Mongol religion and state, and when it came to the Eighth Incarnation, he freed Mongolia from Chinese oppression and laid the foundation for it to become a state, cherishing and protecting it, and finally demonstrated the impermanence of this transitory world and passed away. As there is a tradition that after the Eighth Incarnation he will not be reincarnated again, but thereafter will be reborn as the Great General Hanamand in the realm of Shambala, there is no question of installing the subsequent Ninth Incarnation. Nevertheless, many of his unenlightened disciples, with their fleshy eyes and stupid understanding, are unwilling to grasp this, so it is decreed that the Central Committee to be newly elected shall take charge of reporting this and clearing it up with the Dalai Lama. Apart from this, all other incarnations are to be treated according to the law separating Church from State. (Quoted in Bawden 1968:262–3)

What this decision did was to put the issue of the Bogd on ice. "Shambala" traditionally meant a future realm for the righteous armies that would defend religion from the infidels (Mahommedans) in an apocalyptic war. At the beginning of the twentieth century, the Buryat agent of the Tsar, Agvan Dorzhiev, promoted the idea that Shambala was Russia, which would restore the Buddhist kingdom. Now, in the 1920s, the Bogd's line of succession had to be cut off, but to do so, the new Mongolian government had to step into religious discourse itself. There is evidence to suggest that this text was not entirely hypocritical: the government was, indeed, planning to build a temple in honor of Shambala (Rupen 1979:157).

The death of the Bogd in 1924 had been greeted with deep public mourning, and his funeral rites were organized by the government and paid for by the state treasury. An old man remembers a song that was sung at this time:

> Our Bogd Khaan, Lord of the Faith, has gone to the land of Shambala,
> We, his many disciples, are left behind in suffering and tears,
> The highest of the high, our Ochirdar Bogd, has entered the kingdom
>   of heaven,
> We, his many thousands of subjects, are left behind and cannot find
>   the reason why.
> (Enkh-Amar 1991)

The institutions of Mongolian society were being swept away. But the new government labored under a massive Buddhist heritage within which its official proclamations had yet to find a distinctive language or legitimacy. Engulfed by the multifarious oral discourse of the people, government texts in this early period of the revolution could only hint at the new atheist viewpoint. For example, in the edict instructing people to pray and fast as the Bogd lay on his deathbed, it was written: "Although this advice is right, we cannot force people and it would be better to let them decide by their own will and belief" (Enkh-Amar 1991). In the coming years of bitter conflict, the party would disown such early texts of the revolutionaries.

As the Bogd lost power, the role of anticlericalism also shifted. Once the occasional expression of discontent, now it was searched out and glorified as the standard matter of the new propaganda. For a few years in the early 1920s, the battle songs of the revolutionary partisans hailed victory in the name of the Bogd;[18] by the early 1930s, the songs apparently extolled only his downfall. But was this really so? Many songs of the period have a earnest, bathetic quality but seem straightforward (one can imagine them being composed by eager Revsomols in the countryside).[19] Others, however, must have sounded ambiguous and "evocative" to many Mongol ears.

> For the sake of black bread,
> We have ploughed across our mountain.
> For the sake of having become a commune,
> We have driven away our Khambo from the throne.
>
> For the sake of grey bread,
> We have ploughed across our hill.
> For the sake of having become Bolsheviks,
> We have chased away our Bogd from his throne.
>   (Poppe 1978:71)

A little cultural background makes clear how dubious is the enthusiasm expressed in this song. Mongols and Buryats, among whom this song was collected in 1931, were herders who liked to eat meat and milk, not bread. Over the centuries (and still today), mountains have been regarded as holy, and ploughing the earth, as sacrilegious or even dangerous because it disturbs the spirit owners of the land.

By the 1950s and 1960s, scholars were scouring the countryside for jokes and sayings they could use to demonstrate the natural abhorrence of the masses for religion and for the high lamas in particular (Bazardorzh 1973; Purevzhav and Dashzhamts 1965). They sought to denigrate lamas as greedy and lascivious ("figures of fun"), and the subject of the Bogd, who was evidently more than this if he was mentioned at all, became virtually taboo in official discourse. Everyday talk shifted into the ambiguous mode. For example, a widely circulated story claimed that the Bogd's sacred cord, by which he conveyed blessings to the people, was attached to his big toe. This claim could be interpreted by sensible atheists as demonstrating the absurdity of superstition and the lackadaisical nature of the Bogd; at the same time, it could be interpreted by the faithful as proof of the Bogd's miraculous powers: even the most insignificant part of his body was capable of transmitting blessings.

By 1928, an atmosphere of fear, rumor, and deep uncertainty prevailed in Mongolia. Figures of high religious status were being attacked, and even they took refuge in the discourse of feigned ignorance. The Diluv Khutagt wrote in his memoirs of an episode in the 1920s: "The Internal Security man said, 'It has been determined by law, as you doubtless know, that the property of rich feudal person-ages is to be expropriated.' I had of course heard of this decree but I said that I had never heard of it, because I was afraid they might ask me from whom I had heard it. I also said that I did not know the meaning of the word 'piodal' [feudal]. . . . There was in fact no word for 'feudal' in the Mongolian language" (Lattimore and Isono 1982:179). The Diluv also—and this must have infuriated the revolution-ary faithful if he did it to their faces—regularly used the new Mongolian word for "revolution" (*khuv'sgal*) in the sense of counterrevolution (Lattimore and Isono 1982:129, 188). He could easily do so with a plausible appearance of naiveté be-cause the word is derived from a verb, *khuv'sga-*, which means "to change from one form to another," and it is simply convention that assigns it to one kind of "revolution" rather than another.

After the move in 1928 to radically left-wing policies (known as the Left Turn), there began a series of public trials. One of these has been described in detail by the Diluv Khutagt, who was accused in 1930, along with two other khutagts and many other people, of joining a plot hatched by the Panchen Lama, then living in China and backed by the Japanese, to overthrow the regime and restore a ninth Bogd Khutagt.[20] Many moments during these trials became legends and acquired a greater meaning than they seemed to have at the time. Even the proceedings themselves took place in an atmosphere of "signs" and suspect actions. For ex-ample, the coughing of the old Yeguzer Lama, who was not well, was interpreted as his giving hints to the accused. "You have the right to sit there and observe what is going on," said the prosecutor, "but not to take part unless called on; so keep quiet" (Lattimore and Isono 1982:195–6).

At the Diluv's trial, the Manjusri Khutagt, one of the most important high lamas in Mongolia, answered everything "in the spirit of the Buddhist scriptures," as the Diluv put it. He used the prophetic, destiny-laden language of the lung-deng. The Diluv diplomatically wrote that this "sometimes made it difficult for one not trained in the scriptures to understand his full meaning" (Lattimore and Isono 1982:198), but in reality it was a form of discourse known to everyone and even used by the prosecutor, though presumably ironically. When asked what he thought of communist doctrine, the Manjusri Khutagt replied that it was the Will of Heaven. He was then asked if he thought that the actions of individual men were also the Will of Heaven. He replied that they were. The prosecutor then said, "If you believe that these doctrines are the Will of Heaven and that the actions of individual men are also the Will of Heaven, why do you not believe in and support Communism? Are you the kind of man who fasts when good things are spread out to eat?" The Manjusri Khutagt did not reply (Lattimore and Isono 1982:198–99).

If this interchange reflects an appropriation of Buddhist logic that silenced the Manjusri Lama, the Diluv's flexibility, in contrast, enabled him to borrow the "humanitarian" arguments of the regime in order to construct a common moral ground from which he could emerge the victor. Before his trial, when his possessions were being confiscated, the authorities made the mistake of asking the Diluv to address a meeting of poor people. They must have assumed that he would appear as a shameful figure, but he spoke as follows:

> According to the law of the Government they are expropriating property. This is not a question of myself alone, but of all high nobles and personages. I am very glad that this has happened. As you know I have always given to the poor. But this was something I could only do locally. Now the Government is taking wealth all over the country to improve the condition of the poor. I believe that by this means I can increase my virtue and therefore have no complaint to make. You should not be alarmed or consider that anything untoward has happened. Therefore, if any of my clothes or possessions are distributed to you, understand that you may wear or buy or sell them freely. (Lattimore and Isono 1982:181)

This speech is a paradigm of the evocative transcript. It infuriated the authorities because they wanted people to think they were taking wealth from a grasping and unwilling clergyman, to the credit of the government. The Diluv, however, evoked the whole issue of the status of lamas' property, which had been freely given to them by believers and which, if only symbolically, they publicly and extravagantly redistributed to the populace (as Larson's account of the Bogd, quoted earlier, describes). For this reply the Diluv became a particular target of Choibalsan, who was soon to become "the Stalin of Mongolia."

During his trial, the Diluv appeared to have been forced to compromise. The authorities simply assumed he was a hypocrite who supported the revolution in public while plotting against it in secret. But perhaps he genuinely did shift his ground, finding in the Buddhist tradition new interpretations that could not be faulted by his oppressors. For example, he writes that when asked whether he thought the new state of affairs was the Will of Heaven, he remembered the saying in old books that changes in the state of a nation occur when the Will of Heaven and the actions of men coincide. He answered, therefore, that the new state of affairs was as much a result of the action of men as it was the result of the Will of Heaven (Lattimore and Isono 1982:202).

On another question intended to trap him, he decided to adopt the matter-of-fact, evidence-of-one's-eyes criterion of the court. Another defendant, a lama called Choijin who was sentenced to ten years' imprisonment and later executed, was not so adroit. Asked whether he thought the Banchin Bogd (the Panchen Lama) was a good man or a bad man, Choijin replied that this counterrevolutionary was not the real Banchin Bogd. The Banchin Bogd was a very holy person who could not possibly be involved in plots against Mongolia. One of the prosecutors said angrily, "You are obviously an adherent of the Banchin Bogd and you should be liquidated by the people!" The Diluv, in answer to the same question, replied that he thought the Banchin was probably a bad man. "How do you know?" he was asked. He replied that he did not know the Banchin personally, but that the newspapers constantly reported that the Banchin was trying to raise troops in China and was looking for Japanese support to invade Mongolia (Lattimore and Isono 1982:202, 206).

These two exchanges show how fatal the direct expression of religious attitudes and values had become, and how the survivor, the Diluv, took recourse in elliptical statements that preserved his integrity by exposing the flimsy speciousness of the plot in which he stood accused.

A comparable transcript concerns the scholar Rinchen, who was imprisoned for several years during the 1930s and 1940s. This story was told to me in the early 1970s by a Mongolian friend, an intellectual and devout Buddhist who was well known as an admirer of Rinchen—a reputation that put him in a perilous position for many years. Such stories, however, circulated generally and were commonly known to people not at all well disposed to the dangerously outspoken scholar.

> He [Rinchen] refused to confess. He was the most brave. He said, 'I did not do anything against the Revolution.' He was put in a cold box. Lost consciousness. Put in a hot box. Again refused to confess. He was beaten. One day he was beaten by two Russians and a Mongol: 'Where are the members of your bloc?' Two teeth were taken out, and now he has new iron teeth and a scar also on his head. The two Russians wanted to shoot him, but he was strong. As he was being beaten, suddenly Choibalsan arrived in the prison cell, with Russians on either side of him. Rinchen rose, covered in blood, and said in Russian, 'Gdye vasha revolyutsiya, tovarishch marshal?' ('Where is your revolution, Comrade Marshal?') Choibalsan looked away to the side. The Russians said nothing and left without a word. Choibalsan took a Chinese cigarette from his inner pocket and gave it to Rinchen. Then he turned and walked out. After this they did not beat Rinchen much. That evening he took the cigarette and gave it to the prison officers. They divided it in little pieces among the prisoners, who were ravenous for a smoke.

Here the shift into the Russian language underlines the sarcastic, evocative quality of Rinchen's blameless question.

In later periods, a historical religious sensibility was largely forced out of the realm of words altogether. For example, people in Ulaan-baatar in the 1970s remembered a certain freshwater spring where the Bogd's wife, the Eke Dagini, used to go to worship. A visit to this spring, which officially could be explained as "medicinal," could also be privately interpreted as a commemoration of the Eke Dagini. Paul Connerton (1989) has noted the longevity of gesture and its role as a bearer of social memory. The gestures involved in "taking the waters" (bathing the head, drinking the spring water) can be seen in this light. In Mongolia such incorporated practices, to use Connerton's term, became highly significant. Clothing, hairstyles, washing, and food all became signs of revolutionary reliability or its converse. For example, during his trial it was suggested to the Diluv that despite the cold he should not wear his lama's outer robe, as though he were going to a religious service, when he was going to court. He complied.

Forced completely underground, religious gestures could become hidden transcripts.[21] But for equivocation, gestures are as good as, if not better than, speech. Publicly taking the water at a sacred spring could be seen not as a religious act but as "taking a cure," and placing stones and other items on a holy mountain shrine could be explained as "clearing up."[22] Indeed, to the extent that people believed in such explanations, these archetypally religious acts acquired a double function. Perhaps some transformations of religious culture take place in this way, as a series of reiterated gestures changes its significance over time.

This sort of religious transformation is a complex matter, and it has two aspects in Mongolia. First, there is a regular procedure by which the commemoration of people who have died eventually transforms them—that is, their souls—into the "spirits" (ezed) of places. Thus the Bogd's wife, whose tall stature and round, moonlike face had aroused the mirth of irreverent lamas when she was enthroned (Shirendev 1990:68),[23] gradually became the disembodied spirit of her spring, and she was remembered in two ways that depersonalized her. One way was simply as a genealogical niche—the daughter of a well-known lineage in the region; the other was as goddess-spirit, a reincarnation of the White Tara. In other words, commemorative gestures can encapsulate a kind of social memory that implies forgetting the real person.

The second aspect of the changing significance attributed to ritual gestures is peculiar to socialist society. Fear of punishment for "backward attitudes" produces a need for equivocation and may have caused people to change the range and type of explanations they gave for their incorporated practices. By the 1960s and 1970s, people visiting the Eke Dagini's spring would often say they were simply "taking a cure." But the bodily reverence evident in their gestures suggests there was more to it than that.

As the official writing of history became increasingly doctrinaire and realist, it acquired a supratruth value. It was not to be faulted or criticized—who could doubt that society under the Bogd Khaan was unfair, and that in 1915 one khutagt owned 2,094 horses while his 878 serfs between them owned only 3,124?—but somehow it lost contact with "the truth." Few people openly acknowledged this change, but everyone knew it. Therefore the party and the Academy of Sciences masterminded a new kind of history: the "artless" reminiscences of simple people.

The very fact that these reminiscences were published, under the conditions of information control of the time, indicates that they had been officially approved.

Memoirs of partisans in the Revolutionary Army could be expected, but a series of reminiscences (*durdatgal, yaria*) of old religious men, who personified everything the revolution was supposed to have swept away, was also published. These people *could* write about the Bogd Gegeen, since he had been part of their lives. One well-known example is *Ovgon Jambalyn Yaria* (Old Man Jambal's Story), which, often using the form of "a saying among the people," innocently gives the lowdown on the Bogd, his brother, and his consorts, along with a mishmash of details of vanished temples, rituals, and what the lamas used to eat, and stories—naming names—of hypocritical teachers and Mongol girls who took up with the Chinese.

Jambal records an incident that happened during the winter of 1920, when the Bogd was arrested by Chinese soldiers on the pretext of protecting him from the army of the White Russian general, Baron Ungern von Sternberg, then approaching the capital. Jambal volunteered to take tea to the captive Bogd. The Bogd asked him to find out from another lama, the Lobon Lama, the supernatural reasons for his imprisonment and what ritual means might correct the situation. The Lobon Lama apparently "put the matter to the Buddha" and discovered that the cause was a hat and other gifts that had been given to the Bogd by one Badmadorj, who was known to have become friendly with Hsu, the Chinese general (Lattimore and Isono 1982:92). These items should be exorcised in an easterly direction at twilight. The Buddha gave detailed instructions for the exorcism ritual, which involved making an image of Badmadorj conversing happily with a Chinese, and burning these two figures together with some hair from Chinese soldiers. If this was done, the Bogd would be freed within fifty days.

Jambal relayed this answer to the Bogd, although he was not sure the Bogd would agree to part with such a fine hat. With some difficulty, especially in obtaining the Chinese soldiers' hair, he helped another high lama perform the ritual. Finally the Lobon Lama was asked again to ascertain the outcome, and he reported that he had once more conversed with the Buddha, who said the ritual had been a success. The Bogd was freed on the forty-eighth day, and he said to Jambal, "It was of great assistance."[24]

It is unclear how one should read such texts. Careful and knowledgeable historians such as Bawden have taken them at face value. He comments on Jambal, "He records many details of the Jebtsundamba's life, with a candour and lack of comment which give a completely neutral colouring to what might otherwise appear a *chronique scandaleuse*" (1966:17). Yet I was taken aback when, in 1990, I was fiercely assured by old lamas that Jambal's story was "all lies, invented. He did not know the Bogd. He told me he was offered money from the Academy. Don't read it, it's dirty talk." Looking at the text again, I can see details suggesting that it was indeed written with one eye on the values of the 1960s, when it was published.

For example, Jambal reports that a certain famous painter received a visit from his older brother at a restaurant, rather than at home, and then sent him away, saying, "There is no need to meet me again," and furthermore, that the painter hardly ever washed his face or hands. The first point attributes to the painter a shocking lack of hospitality and respect, but the second would be a slander worthy of remark only in the post-Soviet era, when washing became a mark of culture (before that, Mongols even disapproved of washing). Taken together, these two comments about the painter amount to calumny, and perhaps they allow us to see the whole text, in the context of the 1960s—and despite its "naive" and "religious" tone— indeed as a *chronique scandaleuse* pushing readers to conclude that the Bogd was vain, lustful, and superstitious.

So these old men's stories, too, can be seen as evocative transcripts of a kind that can only arise when there is a shared sense that the official truth is not true. As if in a strange game of double espionage, the Academy of Sciences adopted voices who represented the very negation of the currently authoritative voice—that of the trained and ideologically correct young specialist—to become the bearers of a quasi-official view of the past. Along the way these old men's stories did tell of many things that were currently suppressed (they were a sort of "ethnography"). It is as though it was necessary to say some things that were "true" in order to suggest something else that was "not true." Unlike the strictly academic publications of the Academy of Sciences, which often were printed in the old script and therefore were inaccessible to younger generations of Mongols, Old Man Jambal's memoirs were printed in Cyrillic for a wide audience. It must have been hoped that newly educated readers, divorced from knowledge about old times, would interpret the memoirs according to modern values. The ploy counted on a dearth of knowledge about the past. Other old lamas, the few who had survived, could have raised an objection to these texts, but they were prevented from carrying out any public intervention. Considering the social makeup of Ulaan-baatar, however, where all the actors in the texts have living relatives, where everyone knows everyone else, and where insults to family members are not forgotten, it is not at all clear how many people were "deceived."

I have used Jambal's narrative as an example of an evocative transcript promoted by socialist intellectuals; now let me conclude by looking at a quite different story about the Bogd that has been circulating for many years among educated, middle-class Buddhists in Ulaan-baatar.[25] Even though this version is tinged with the concerns of a postsocialist society, it retains the evocative characteristics of indirectness and tacit appeal to common values and experiences.

According to this story, the location of Shambala was discovered by the Russian orientalist Roerich during an expedition in a snowcapped mountain range in Kazakhstan. Shambala was inside the highest mountain, which was covered in ice so clear that everything within could be seen. When Roerich looked into the glassy mountain, he saw a big, happy, bustling city—a capitalist society in which all faiths existed in harmony. The poorest person had 1,000 *lang* of silver. Everyone was a khutagt waiting to be reborn when the ice melts, an apocalyptic event of which global warming is the advance sign. Then the reign of Shambala will spread over the earth and the Bogd will return in a new incarnation.

This is a millenarian prophesy masked as "just a story." But many details tell the listener that it is to be taken seriously. For example, Shambala was discovered by "Roerich." Historically, there were two Roerichs: Nikolai, the artist and explorer, and his son, Yurii, the Tibetologist.[26] For many years they worked and traveled together, and it seems that the storytellers did not differentiate them. "Roerich," from the Mongolian point of view, has a unique combination of qualities: he was a Russian who was not only lauded by the Soviets but was also known internationally as a scholar, and therefore what he said must be right; he was an explorer of unknown places; and he was a devout Buddhist who believed in Shambala. Such a man, now conveniently dead, could discover the true place and nature of Shambala and give the discovery a modern legitimacy that no Mongolian lama could.

Furthermore, Shambala is not identified by Mongols with the world of the dead, a place in which ancestral souls are gradually dehumanized till they become spirits. No ordinary deceased person can go to Shambala. It is the world of the future. It is inhabited, Mongols say, by real people, physically just like us (possibly the idea of reviving bodies frozen in ice is hinted at here). The detail about global warming is a different, scientific kind of proof that the prediction will come to pass. For people who lived through the years of enforced Brezhnev-type stagnation, it no longer made sense to locate Shambala, as had been done in the 1930s, somewhere in China. The reality to be overcome was Soviet, and therefore, while Shambala was still Asian, it must be inside the (now former) Soviet Union.

This text, then, is in no sense a naive statement of belief. In Mongolia today everyone has been educated in atheism. Although there are many devout believers, few, if any, come to religion simply and unaware of skepticism. This story allows for such a fact, and it has its roots in Soviet cultural domination. It provokes the listener to think: "Those godless Russians have always been 'right,' but we know that even among them there is a deeper truth than socialism, which the best among them was able to discover because he shared our faith." Like so many of the evocative transcripts I have described, this story requires the listener to think in two ways at once: Shambala is an ancient religious vision, but its existence is legitimated in this story by the very instruments that have dominated Mongolian intellectual life in this century—Russian scholarship and science. Such a story can be evocative because it is a fragment; it does not make sense in terms of any chronology and therefore cannot be interpreted by reference to temporal sequences. The other texts I have mentioned have this snapshot character too, even if they concern people at particular times and places. In history, but not of history, these images lay out riddles for the listeners and wait for a variety of answers to be given.

EPILOGUE

With the end of Soviet domination, oracular texts are gradually being replaced by directness and action. The Bogd, I was told in Ulaan-baatar in the summer of 1990, has been reborn in the holy land of India and his ninth reincarnation is now a middle-aged man. Occasionally someone would express hope that this ninth Bogd would be invited to Mongolia, now that times had changed, but no one said so in a tone suggesting it was likely to happen.

On August 28, 1990, there was a high-level celebration in Ulaan-baatar of the hundredth anniversary of the eighth Bogd's birthday. This meeting was attended by lamas, representatives of the new political parties, and historians from the Academy of Sciences. It was generally announced to the public, but no date or place was given because the authorities feared too many people would come. Articles in the Mongolian newspapers extolled the eighth Bogd as an intelligent and able man. They analyzed his personality, usually favorably ("He was fond of jokes—what is so wrong about that?"). They claimed that the scandalous stories about him that were spread from the 1950s to the 1970s were based on shaky evidence and must be investigated. The Bogd's religious dimension was given little emphasis. Instead, what was resurrected were the most deeply buried of the histories connected with his name: those dealing with his political activities, especially his achievement in uniting the Khalkh (the people of the central provinces) and the Western Mongols and his attempt to preserve their independence from both China and Russia. This focus coincides with the passionate concerns of present-day Mongolia. One article in the government paper *Unen* (Truth) even called for the restoration of the Bogd as monarch and the inclusion of this monarchy in the new constitution. The restoration of a monarchy is scarcely likely to happen, but the Bogd is now no longer seen as an enemy.

What is interesting is that the fate of the history of the Bogd ("criticized till the bones squeak") is now being used to reassess the writing of history in general. According to the new writers, black-and-white judgments promoted by political concerns should be rejected. Instead, the new history should allow distance from the object to clarify a balanced view. This goal is charmingly expressed by a Mongolian historian as follows: "When we see a horse from afar its dapples cannot be perceived, and if its spots are brown it strikes the eyes as generally darkish and if they are fawn-coloured as generally lightish. In this way history slowly makes things clear, they say" (Tomorkhuleg 1990). When the black-and-white versions are finally swept away, so too will be the evocative transcripts.

--------- Notes ---------

I am grateful to John Gaunt and Bayarmandakh for help with the Mongolian information, and to James Laidlaw in Cambridge and all the participants at the School of American Research conference for their comments on an earlier draft.

1. By *Mongolia* I refer to the Mongolian People's Republic, formerly known as Outer Mongolia when it was included in the Manchu Qing Empire. Inner Mongolia (the Inner Mongolian Autonomous Region) is now a province of China.

2. Javzundamba is the first part of the title, and *khutagt* (*khutukhtu*) is the Mongol term for the reincarnation of a *bodhisattva* as a lama. The Javzundamba Khutagt had eight Mongolian incarnations preceded by a line of fifteen earlier holders of the title, going back to the time of the Buddha—but

sources differ on this mythical prehistory (Bawden 1961:2). At the beginning of this century there were around fifty khutagts in Outer Mongolia, of whom some six were powerful figures with especially large estates of serfs (shabi). Several of these khutagts took up political and even military posts in the Bogd Khaan's government (1911–21).

3. A recent newspaper article cites his full title, Javzundambaagvaanluvsanchoijinnyuamadanzanvanchugbalsambuu, (Ishinnorov and Tserendorj 1990).

4. Khaan (written form xagan) means "emperor," while khan (xan) is equivalent to "ruler" or "prince."

5. The major work, authored and published by the Academy of Sciences of the Mongolian People's Republic in Ulaan-baatar in 1969, is the three-volume Bugd Nairamdakh Mongol Ard Ulsyn Tuukh; for translation, see Brown and Onon (1976). The introduction to this work provides an annotated list of previous official histories.

6. There are also some versions in Tibetan. The biography of the first Javzundamba Khutagt (Jebtsundamba Khutukhtu) has been translated into English and published by Bawden (1961).

7. The expression "lower-class lamas" (door angiin lam) refers not to the lamas' socioeconomic background but to their place in the monastic hierarchy. The lamaseries were, in fact, rather meritocratic, and many lamas from poor backgrounds rose through the ranks by passing examinations and so forth. Nevertheless, the party's policy, which was relatively successful, was to attract back to lay life the lamas with the least stake in the church institution.

8. There is no opportunity here to make this argument fully. In my observation, although the sons and daughters of the elite were privileged, above all in education, their social position was not necessarily a route to power, for which a "desirable social background" (i.e., nonelite) remained very important.

9. As in the Soviet Union, the Mongolian Revolutionary Party experienced a Left Turn in 1928 and immediately set about collectivization. This effort was generally unsuccessful and resulted in armed uprisings, notably the rebellion of 1932 in Ar Khangai. Although the uprisings were put down with the aid of Soviet troops, collectivization was judged to be impossible for the time being. Moscow considered the continued existence of the Buddhist monasteries to be a major reason for this failure. Throughout the 1930s, lamas were imprisoned and executed, and in 1938, the monasteries were razed. Thereafter Mongolia was in virtually complete subordination to the Soviet Union. Collectivization was reintroduced in the late 1950s and early 1960s.

10. "The subordinate group must carve out for itself social spaces insulated from control and surveillance from above. . . . Only by specifying how such social spaces are made and defended is it possible to move from the individual resisting subject—an abstract fiction—to the socialization of resistant practices and discourses" (Scott 1991:118).

11. In the capital city, until recently there were no publicly available maps, telephone directories, mail deliveries, or banks as there are in the West. Streets have names and houses have numbers, but no one uses them; people use landmarks instead. Important institutions may well have no name plates. Essentials of life such as food and accommodation are mostly acquired through acquaintances (tanil), not through public shops or bureaus. To live in Ulaan-baatar at all, one must have friendly contacts, and the whole social organization presumes that people belong to some network and acquire their information through it.

12. His burial place was deliberately "unknown" and everyone was taught that his treasures were the timeless heritage of the Mongolian people.

13. The Diluv (Dilowa) Khutagt was one of the major incarnations in Mongolia. Like other high lamas, he was regarded by the revolutionary government as a representative of the old order, and therefore means were sought to get rid of him. At his trial in 1930, it was impossible to prove that he had taken part in antirevolutionary activities, and he received a suspended sentence. He fled immediately to Inner Mongolia. In the 1940s he reportedly tried to reach Tibet in order to get permission for the institution of a ninth Bogd, but war conditions stopped him. When it became apparent that a communist government would take power in Inner Mongolia, the Diluv fled to the United States. His political memoirs and autobiography were drafted there in 1949, although they were not published until 1982.

14. These examples, cited by Bawden (1968), are drawn from official historical sources that in the 1960s would have been necessarily critical of the Bogd.

15. The printing of the reformers' work was forbidden during the Bogd's government (Bawden 1968:171–72), and it has continued to be prohibited up to the present, since a principled, disciplined

church was recognized to be much more dangerous to the communist order than a lax and extravagant one.

16. Extract from *Bogda Jibzun Damba-yin lundun zarlig.* Fond Natsova (d. 103, op. 2), archives of the Buryat Academy of Sciences.

17. Official histories of the Bogd's rule focus on Mongolia's socioeconomic structure, the feudal dues payable, corvée services, and the wretched life of the "masses," made miserable by debt, disease, and, above all, cruel punishments for minor crimes.

18. Our rifles, which really can blast them,
    We held, saying, "They'll do";
    Thanks to the protection of the Bogd Khaan,
    We cut the root of the Baron.
        (Vladimirtsov 1927:9)

19. In the corridor painted brown
    There is a picture of the greatly revered Teacher Lenin,
    May he enlighten the life of the commune,
    And manifest himself in creating [more] communes.
        (Poppe 1978:71–72)

20. The plan to restore a ninth Bogd is not mentioned by the Diluv in his memoirs, but Bawden (1966), citing Russian sources, writes that this was one of the charges.

21. For example, a former lama kept one of the eighth Bogd's lungdeng (not the one cited earlier), which he treated not as a book but as a sacred object. His every gesture revealed his reverence for it. He allowed me to make a copy, saying, "You must treat this with respect. Do not publish it, because people might use that to criticize him. Read it, and keep it in a high place."

22. Such shrines are placed at mountain passes near roads, and I have heard this explanation of the tires and other bits of machinery found on the cairns: "Lorries shed them when climbing up to the pass, and the drivers put them in a heap to tidy up."

23. Shirendev's historical belles-lettres *Serel* (1990) is a literary work, but it was written in the new spirit of openness and may well reflect the actual jokes the author heard when he was a young lama. Shirendev later became a government minister and president of the Academy of Sciences. He was purged from high official posts at least twice in his life.

24. This is an abbreviated account of the episode, which is described in Bawden (1966). Unfortunately, I do not currently have access to the original source, *Ovgon Jambalyn Yaria,* although I translated part of it in the 1970s.

25. I am grateful to John Gaunt for telling me about this story, which he heard in religious circles in Ulaan-baatar in 1991.

26. Nikolai Roerich painted visionary pictures of Asiatic heroes among snowcapped mountains. His son, Yurii (1902–60), wrote numerous works on Tibet and Mongolia. Both spent many years in India, Europe, and the United States. Yurii Roerich returned to the USSR in 1957, becoming head of the History, Religion, and Philosophy of India Sector of the Institute of the Peoples of Asia in the Academy of Sciences.

3

Strangers No More
Personal Memory in the Interstices of Public Commemoration

VERA SCHWARCZ

> Returning, he opened his eyes,
> stood by the side of the road uninvited,
> wrinkled in his old jacket.
> He remembered and recognized the night
> and was not a stranger.
> —Dan Pagis, "Honi"

A CHINESE REMEMBERER who has survived the vagaries of public amnesia is like the Hebrew poet's road-weary traveler.[1] He, too, has turned to face the night that swallowed large chunks of the living past. He is an uninvited guest at official commemorations that seek to perpetuate personal forgetting. A crumpled figure bearing the burden of his own complexity, he would like to come home to memory, come home through memory. But the Chinese intellectual, like Dan Pagis's survivor, must first reckon with exile from the community of true believers. In the lonely place reserved for those who renounce the comforts of monumentalized history, he crafts small bits of ambiguous remembrance.

I met one such survivor of persecution and forgetfulness in the corridors of a former Buddhist monastery in Beijing. It was in early May, 1989—the very month in which hundreds of thousands of students took to the streets to plead for more democracy. Chen Hengzhen, a man in his early sixties, inhabited a world apart from the militant students.[2] He wore a wrinkled blue Mao jacket unlike the Western-style jeans favored by young people. He smiled rarely, while they sang the Internationale with zest. He had broken brown teeth and fugitive eyes, while the students radiated energy and hope. We began to talk at a conference commemorating the seventieth anniversary of the May Fourth Movement of 1919, the first student protest to call for science and democracy.[3] Chen Hengzhen was not a distinguished guest of the conference. He gave no paper. While other participants lectured in grandiose terms about the historic role of intellectuals in Chinese society, Chen Hengzhen had come to talk about his mother.

Sensing a change in the public conventions governing the criticism of historical characters—a shift from the politically correct *pingjia* (literally, "appraise and judge") to more evidence-based *pingjie* ("appraise and recount")—Chen sought to rehabilitate his mother's reputation in the annals of the Chinese revolution. In small group discussions, he recalled how his mother had been an early political ally of Deng Xiaoping, how she had helped found the Chinese Communist party cell in Paris in 1921. He sought to persuade a new generation of historians that forgotten, neglected intellectuals like his mother had played a key role in furthering the cause of social change.

In public, using a party-sanctioned moment for expanded recollection, Chen Hengzhen emphasized his mother's contributions to revolution. In private, in the corridors of a monastery haunted by the absence of its rightful inhabitants, he told a darker tale: "Chinese intellectuals are naive, so hopelessly naive. Especially my mother. She turned me in to party authorities in 1957, you see. In the middle of the antirightist campaign she tried to protect herself. Worried about being attacked for her own past, she turned over some of the letters I had written to her. In the end, she was not spared persecution. She committed suicide in 1960 during the criticism campaign against her. She tried to protect herself and ended by blackening twenty years of my life. I was made a rightist in 1957. . . . Ah, how gullible she was! She trusted the authorities with everything. As if the party were a benevolent, faultless father. She sacrificed her son for this heartless father.

"All to no avail. The authorities still blamed her for withdrawing from the communist movement in Europe. Her academic studies in France were held against her. When she could no longer defend herself, she went mad. Then she took her own life."

On the margins of public commemoration, a wounded son recalls his mother's betrayal 30 years after her suicide. Chen Hengzhen might not have begun to talk about his mother's tragic faith in the party had the party itself not sanctioned more open discussions of the role of intellectuals in history and society. After the death of Mao Zedong in 1976, intellectuals gained increasing space for critical reflection upon public life. Thought control, which had been fierce during the Cultural Revolution, now gave way to a carrot-and-stick approach: those who supported Deng Xiaoping's reforms could talk more freely about once forbidden subjects. Chen himself had witnessed and had been victimized by repeated campaigns against intellectuals during the long Mao era. He was not about to go out on the limb of recollection alone. Once the boundaries of truth telling had been expanded officially from above, however, a flood of memory, pain, and remorse rushed up from below.

This complex interdependence between public and personal recollection in the post-Mao era is also described by Rubie Watson in chapter 4 of this volume.

Using case studies from South China villages, she shows how public mourning spills over into private grieving as individuals seek to make sense of their own losses. What is at work in this process, according to Watson, is a subjective capacity for "moral memory"—an act of recollection that refuses to identify the past only with what is collectively useful in the present moment. Village mourners in her study manage to convey and deepen personal memory (frequently of disillusionment and betrayal) in the very context meant to deflect such remorse.

Intellectuals of Chen Hengzhen's generation are not unfamiliar with the emotions or the strategies that animate mourning laments in South China villages. They, too, have been required to attend funeral after funeral, whether actual or metaphorical, in which their parents, teachers, and colleagues were entombed by party-mandated amnesia. They have become skilled at keeping quiet, artful at saying as little as possible when criticism of other intellectuals or self-indictment is the order of the day.

Some have also managed, like Chen Henzhen in 1989, to inject bits of truthful recollection into the interstices of public commemorations. Although many Chinese intellectuals served the Maoist state through four decades of an ever-shifting party line, not all did so willingly.[4] Dissenters as well as establishment intellectuals learned to speak in the forked tongue characteristic of survivors of political repression. They are masters of what Caroline Humphrey in chapter 2 of this volume calls the "evocative transcript"—of ambiguous statements that seem to comply with official dogma while challenging it at the same time. Having lived compromised lives, they have learned to read between the lines, to write between the lines, to live, as it were, between the lines. The lines, or rather the one politically correct line, is still dictated from above. Around its harsh and ever-changing edges, oppositional memories sprout like wild mushrooms after rain.

In May 1989, shortly after talking with Chen Hengzhen in the halls of the abandoned Buddhist monastery, I had the good fortune to meet Dr. Gao Renzhi, an aging psychiatrist who practices general medicine in a factory on the outskirts of Beijing. A living embodiment of the wounded healer, Dr. Gao is at work on a study of anthrophobia, focusing on the crippling fear of strangers among Chinese adolescent girls. At the same time, he is trying to make sense of his own dread of confrontation with political authorities.

Dr. Gao, like Chen Hengzhen and Dan Pagis's traveler, sports a wrinkled, patched jacket during most of our talks. One of his keen eyes rests firmly focused on mine as we talk about the relationship between personal memory and historical trauma. This is a subject that other, more prominent psychiatrists in China refuse to speak about because it is so uncomfortably close to Freudian concerns and has long been condemned as "bourgeois."[5] Dr. Gao refuses to deny the high incidence of trauma among intellectual-survivors of the antirightist campaign of 1957 and the Cultural Revolution of 1966–69.

His other eye wanders off on an axis all its own. It strikes me as a globe gone wild in a world full of lies. It keeps searching for a way to catch a sideways glimpse of the truth in a world where frontal looks have all too often turned out to be dangerous, illegitimate. The off-center eye is a survivor's tic. I recognize it from my parents' generation. They too got through—through the Holocaust, through starting second families. Each has tried to forget a great deal; each has a remindful tic.

The eye that twitches, the rumpled jacket, the fearful voice that seeks to speak some snippet of truth—these are the marks of the survivor-rememberer. For such a person, memory is not a heroic gesture. It is what slips out in moments when the tyranny of habitual forgetting relaxes a bit. It is what is salvaged from the "ruins of memory." This is Lawrence Langer's apt term for what animates Holocaust testimonies: a modest, difficult effort to rescue individual identity and some sense of moral purpose in the aftermath of utter devastation (Langer 1991:173–176).

Chinese intellectuals who survived wave upon wave of persecution in the 1950s and 1960s (persecution that spilled over into the "spiritual pollution" campaigns that targeted them even in the post-Mao era) have not suffered the same kind of devastation as Jews who went through the reason-destroying concentration camps.[6] Nonetheless, men like Chen Hengzhen and Gao Renzhi have had to renounce their values and their memories repeatedly. What they have managed to rescue—what they are reconstructing now through memorial activity—are but small fragments of a much-assaulted, if not fully ruined, identity.

And yet, with bits of honest memory rescued and shared, these intellectuals have managed to maintain a sense of personal integrity. With a modicum of integrity, in turn, they are beginning to rebuild a more truthful sense of China's collective identity. Recollection, in this context, becomes an instrument in the quest for justice. This quest weighs particularly heavily upon the conscience of Chinese intellectuals. They are the heirs of the long Confucian tradition that mandated a distinctive role for the educated elite.

In traditional China, intellectuals were called *wenren,* literally, "men of the word." In this capacity, they were to speak for the vast wordless masses. Spared from manual labor, intellectuals in traditional China both served the state and articulated the moral criteria for judging its performance. In this dual function they became *daiyan ren*—"carriers of the word"—from the culturally dispossessed below to the wielders of political power above.[7] In communist China, it became increasingly difficult for intellectuals to fulfill this mission. Under attack for their "bourgeois cosmopolitanism," they were repeatedly cast out from the ranks of the "people." It was only after Mao's death in 1976, when Deng Xiaoping began the official rehabilitation of the intellectuals by reassigning them to the "working class," that Chinese intellectuals could begin the difficult task of self-rehabilitation (Schwarcz 1986:248).

The political status of intellectuals was publicly restored for the sake of the modernization drive. It was accompanied by a tacit demand for amnesia about their suffering during the Mao era. Although the face of a scientist with glasses has replaced that of the soldier on the 50-yuan banknote, living researchers have yet to be accorded similar respect. The slower-paced self-rehabilitation of intellectuals, by contrast, depends upon the recovery of painful and compromising memories like the ones that bind Chen Hengzhen to his posthumously rehabilitated mother.

In the course of this memorial recovery, Chinese intellectuals are also rediscovering their role as *daiyan ren*. They are once again speaking out for the people. Using the mirror of their own suffering, they have turned the roving, tic-burdened eye of the survivor-rememberer upon the ongoing abuses of Chinese society. In the words of journalist Liu Binyan:

> We must answer the people's questions. We have no right to be auditors in the courtroom of history. The people are the judges as well as the plaintiffs. We must supply them with scripts. But before we provide answers, we must first learn. We must understand more about social life than the average person does. (Cited in Schwarcz 1991c:248)

This elitist call to conscience is rooted in Confucian notions of responsibility. It was allowed to flower anew—briefly—in the spring of 1979, when the party itself had begun to expand the parameters of criticism in China. That year was also a time of loud, public commemorations of the sixtieth anniversary of the May Fourth Movement of 1919. Just as with Chen Hengzhen and Gao Renzhi a decade later, intellectuals like Liu Binyan (who was also a victim of the antirightist campaign and of the Cultural Revolution) began to gain access to the truth of their own experience only when the party's official propagandists began to license histories that were useful for reform.

The historiography of the May Fourth Movement lies at the very heart of the manipulation of history and memory in China. Precisely because the event has been pivotal to so many debates about the role of educated elites in society and to actual policies adopted by the party toward them, it serves as a good example with which to illustrate the tension between the official rehabilitation of Chinese intellectuals and their more tenuous self-recovery.

If one were to peel away the layers of memory in communist China—to unveil the bitter heart of the onion—one would come upon the following accretions, from the outside in: first, the official memory of May Fourth, intended to enforce loyalty to the party through the retrospective mythicizing of communist leaders; second, the unofficial yet still public memory of the scholarly community as embodied in commemorative conferences sponsored by the Academy of Social Sciences in 1979 and 1989; third, the intellectuals' collective determination to recall forgotten, repressed figures of the cultural movement of 1919; and finally, the personal memories of revolution-wounded intellectuals who seek to retell individual stories that are still sequestered from the public domain.

Chinese intellectuals have managed to maintain some fidelity to all the layers of this memory-onion. Their task has not been easy. Like Chen Hengzhen's mother, they know themselves to be both victims and victimizers. Hence their reliance on "evocative transcripts" and the language of double meaning familiar to Eastern European intellectuals who also survived long years in what the Hungarian dissident poet Miklos Haraszti called "the velvet prison."[8]

Since demarcations between official and unofficial memory have been so slippery in China, intellectuals have had to rely on fragmented recollections of their own experience. In contradistinction to the party's monochromatic *collective* memory of May Fourth, they have produced a *collected* memory of the event of 1919—one that weaves together the stories of individuals like Chen Hengzhen's mother, who do not fit the model of either hero or villain of revolutionary history.

The Communist party, on its side, has been determined to engineer both memory and forgetfulness. As Ci Jiwei, a Chinese scholar at Stanford University, wrote recently: "Memory is the internalization of history. History is the institution for the social regulation of memory. Those who control the means of regulating collective memory direct the course of future history. Not surprisingly, one of the biggest psycho-political projects undertaken by the Communist Party has been the restructuring of the Chinese memory through the rewriting of Chinese history" (Ci 1990:4).

In the face of such an avaricious public past, personal memory has had to develop complicated strategies for survival. Prolonged subterfuge on the periphery of party orthodoxy invariably led to opportunism and self-deceit. At the same time, however, the interstices of official commemoration provided some safe space for individual recollection, just as private plots on the outskirts of collectivized farms provided space for individual gardening. On the margins of the party's "psycho-political project," some intellectuals managed to narrate history on their own terms. They salvaged distinctive, even oppositional versions of the past. These versions, in turn, fueled the passions of student demonstrators in Tiananmen Square in 1989.

What was left unsaid among history-seasoned intellectuals was always more voluminous than what could be articulated at any one conference or around the table of any one seminar discussion. But the privately shared stories of survivors like Chen Hengzhen and Gao Renzhi, like the slowly remembered details of the original May Fourth Movement, serve to expand the Chinese intellectuals' sense of community. Comemoration, in this sense, helps create a more nuanced version of the communal past as well as a more bearable vision of the collective future.

MONUMENTAL MEMORIES

Public commemorations of May Fourth stand in a continuum with a long-lived Chinese tradition of solemnizing the past. From Confucius onward, history was meant to serve a didactic purpose. For example, the carefully edited *Spring and Autumn Annals* of the ancient state of Lu (supposedly edited by Confucius himself), the records of the Han dynasty's grand historian Si Ma Qian, and Si Ma Guang's *Mirror for Government* (written to teach rulers how to extract moral lessons from the past) all sought to instruct and to guide posterity by fostering a scrupulous and reverential attention to the lives of the illustrious dead.

Three centuries before the founding of the first imperial state (in 221 BC), Confucius had already cemented a commitment to cultural transmission through public remembering. When the sage described himself as one "who was not born knowing the past, but someone who loves the past and seeks after it earnestly," he was, in effect, laying claim to the right to use the ancients as a moral precedent with which to judge the present.[9] The *Spring and Autumn Annals* attributed to Confucius set a model for future generations of intellectuals who believed that public morality is best maintained by a judicious apportionment of historical praise and blame.

Si Ma Qian, the Grand Historian of the Han dynasty, continued this tradition in his own *Historical Memoirs* (Shiji). He, too, turned to the past to decipher the moral meaning of the present, thereby elevating the study of history to the highest form of public service: "We reside in the world of the present but set our minds on the ancient Way, that it may be a mirror for us" (Owen 1986:14). By the time the Song dynasty philosopher-official Si Ma Guang penned his *Mirror for Government,* history had become the prominent medium for moral self-understanding in Chinese high culture. The lives of the ancients were researched for details that might instruct the living. From the early religion of ancestor worship blossomed forth a deep cultural preference for historically anchored didacticism. Because the past was replete with filial sons and pious widows, the retelling of their lives acquired a compelling force over the values of subsequent generations.

Initiation into this mode of cultural transmission was never abstract or solitary. Rather it was a ceremonial, communal affair intended to transform individuals into co-creators of tradition. In the words of phenomenologist Edward Casey, Confucian rituals of ancestor worship helped develop a distinctively collective form of commemoration: a "remembering through ritualistic action," a "remembering through/with others" (Casey 1987:235–37). As a result of these memorial practices, the personal past was incorporated into an ever-evolving communal past. Chinese history thus acquired, according to Casey, a quality of "perdurance"—a sense of lasting through time, lasting through conscious connection with others as embodied in a tradition that comes toward us to make us more fully human (Casey 1984:392).

The promise of cultural renewal through collective commemoration requires the individual to transcend personal memories and doubts in the encounter with the edifying aspects of the communal past. What rises up from the distant shores of time is an inspirational archetype. Nietzsche (no friend of historical understanding in its more modest manifestations) called this "the monumental past":

> What good is it for one who lives in the present to observe the monumental past, to be concerned with what is classic and rare in the earlier ages? He will take from it encouragement that the magnificent things that once occurred there were *possible* at least once and therefore may

well be possible again. He treads his path more confidently, because now the doubt that infected him in his hour of weakness—the doubt that he might be willing the impossible—has been soundly thwarted.[10]

The problem with the monumental past, however, is that in addition to being inspirational, it is also coercive. Inspiration, especially at the collective level, invariably carries normative expectations for the individual. In China, where the state has been the main arbiter of communal remembrance, these normative expectations have been particularly obvious. Both imperial and communist China bore the burden of such didactic manipulations of the past.

The state, though never wholly or effectively monolithic, justified itself by monumentalizing the past: the classics of history became monuments, commentaries on the classics became monuments, even the local landscape dotted by ancestral temples became incorporated into the monumental past. Mountains and lakes encrusted with layers of associative poetry and painting became part of the monumental past. Confucian tradition and the Communist party alike insisted that the past was meaningful only if it was "inspirational."

In this monument-ridden universe, dissenting rememberers had to find alternative spaces, create alternative visions of the past. One strategy developed by Buddhist monks and then adopted by Confucian scholars was that of zizan—a self-mocking autobiography penned literally on the borders of inspirational portraits. From the edges of didactic images, intellectuals sought to convey another narrative that left room for doubt, for laughter, for dreams—for all that had been left out of the official portrait (Wu Peiyi 1984:116–17). Whereas the zizan was a strategy for oppositional self-understanding, wild histories (yeshi) were a form of unofficial commentary on communal events. The late-Ming-dynasty scholar Zhang Dai, for example, was one intellectual who resorted to the well-known refuge of wild history (as opposed to "true," or, more precisely, "orthodox" history [zheng-shi]). His reminiscences about life in South China before the Manchu conquest of 1644 were collected in Dream Memories—a moody, meandering text that stands in marked contrast to state-sponsored dynastic annals (Owen 1986:141–43).

Unofficial histories such as Zhang Dai's have a long tradition in Chinese culture. Throughout the imperial era, they provided solace for disenchanted people who felt no echo between their values and the public mores of their time. But yeshi, unlike zizan, were not limited to individual comfort alone. As repositories for alternative versions of the past, they offered the potential for an oppositional vision of the present. Although the state retained a monopoly over public historiography, "wild" voices continued to present moral judgments in the name of a yet uncodified past. In traditional China, the breakdown of dynastic control offered the best opportunity for the proliferation of both wild histories and self-mocking autobiographies. Zhang Dai wrote his moody memoir during the transition from the Ming to the Qing dynasties. Other dissident thinkers used the disintegration of the Sung and Yuan dynasties to record bits of their own remembered pasts that did not fit the paradigm of the old or the rising new rulers (Franke 1961:121–25).

In communist China, the urge to use history to contest the power of present authority has not been totally stifled. Although the sphere of permissible irony and dissent shrank greatly during the Mao era (with the eradication of unofficial publishing houses and private academies that had fostered both *yeshi* and *zizan* in the imperial and early Republican eras), Chinese intellectuals still found ways to use the crevices of the monumental past. Self-conscious heirs of the oppositional tradition, they learned to speak in veiled metaphors. On the eve of the Cultural Revolution this proclivity was especially manifested in the plays and essays of Wu Han, an intellectual who was skilled in the tactic of *zhi sanq ma huai*—literally, "point to the mulberry while cursing the ash." An amateur historian of the Ming dynasty, Wu Han claimed that his work described the plight of virtuous officials in olden days. Yet none of his contemporaries missed the indirect indictment of the autocratic party chief Mao Zedong (Pusey 1969:27–36).

A proclivity for indirection, however, leaves the state in ultimate control of the moral meaning of both past and present. This is a situation Chinese intellectuals have lived with for a long time. For some, it has resulted in cynicism and the morose production of politically correct narratives. For others, it results in prolonged silence broken only recently, often in conversations with foreign scholars. Our success with oral history projects, in this context, may owe itself to people's frustration over endlessly postponed *zizan*. Unable to tell their own stories, Chinese intellectuals whisper them to outsiders. Foreigners provide interstices still denied at home (Schwarcz 1992).

Until the death of Mao in 1976, most Chinese historians found little room to maneuver around the edges of the monumental past. They left risk taking to literary figures such as Wu Han or to the younger generation of history students, who were heirs of the rebellious May Fourth. On the campus of Beijing University, for example, the official historians' vision of the past is incarnated in a large statue of Li Dazhao, the librarian who became a founder of the Chinese Communist party in 1920–21. This statue symbolizes the party's only acceptable verdict on the May Fourth Movement: that it was a brief moment of patriotic mobilization that paved the road for the social revolution led by the Communist party.

The student association of Beijing University, however, guards another vision of the May Fourth Movement, embodied in another monument, this one built by student funds: a bust of Cai Yuanpei, the Confucian intellectual who institutionalized academic freedom at Beijing University on the eve of the May Fourth Movement of 1919. In 1989, during the celebration of the seventieth anniversary of May Fourth, hundreds of visitors came to the Beijing University campus. Very few stopped to look at the monument to Li Dazhao, but none left the campus without paying homage to Cai Yuanpei down by the lake where students walked, kissed, and planned the next movement for democracy.

The monumental past, be it the May Fourth Movement itself or its leading figures such as Li Dazhao and Cai Yuanpei, is so important for each generation of Chinese intellectuals that they continue to contest its meanings in the public realm. And in that realm, the coin of contention is itself monumental. Who will define what Nietzsche termed "the magnificent things that once occurred, that were possible at least once and therefore may be possible again"? And what if the things that occurred were not magnificent and yet must be monumentalized precisely so that they may not occur again?

In the former Soviet Union, a "memorial movement" arose in the 1980s to commemorate the victims of Stalinist atrocities. Aided by the recovery of 612,000 names, the memorial movement brought together families of the victims and their supporters. In August 1987 they organized as Pamiatnik ("memorial," derived from *pamiat,* "memory"—a term also used in the self-appellation of an antisemitic organization). Pamiatnik has been active not only in raising funds for a monument to Stalin's victims but also in increasing awareness of the possibilities for and responsibilities of civil society in the postcommunist period. The monument, when it was unveiled on October 30, 1990, consisted of a simple stone from the notorious Solovietsky Island labor camp. It was sustained by a marble plinth engraved simply: "In honor of the millions of victims of a totalitarian regime" (Keller 1990:10).

China has no such memorial yet. The struggle around the monumental past is still too young, too burdened by the shadow of the brutal crackdown of June 1989. Yet the seeds of a more comprehensive recollection have already been sown. The May Fourth veteran writer Ba Jin, for example, shortly before his death in 1987, wrote an essay asking for the establishment of a Cultural Revolution museum. A victim of repeated persecution himself, Ba Jin knew intimately the vagaries of public amnesia. He knew that in the rush to get on with modernization, party authorities would find it all too convenient to forget what happened—what they had done —in "those endlessly long painful days of torture and degradation" (Ba 1989:381).

The Cultural Revolution museum envisioned by Ba Jin cannot be built until Chinese society is able to challenge and dislodge the party's monopoly on public remembrance. One way to begin that challenge is to draw attention to the enforced forgetfulness that masquerades as commemoration in the public realm. This process of drawing attention to erasures has already begun.

BOOKS OF FORGETTING

Milan Kundera begins *The Book of Laughter and Forgetting* with an archetypal moment in Communist party historiography: the airbrushing of a man out of history. In February 1948, Klement Gottwald steps out onto a baroque balcony in Prague to proclaim the birth of communist Czechoslovakia (a moment not unlike Mao's simultaneous claim of past history and present power in Tiananmen Square on October 1, 1949). At Gottwald's side stands Vladimir Clementis, a noncommunist who lends the victorious leader his fur cap. Four years later, Clementis is charged with treason and hanged. The propaganda department immediately adjusts the old photograph. Where a noncommunist once stood, there is only a bare wall; all that remains of Clementis is the cap on Gottwald's head. And if we missed the point of this opening moment in Kundera's book, the consummate voice of the ironical survivor adds: "The struggle of man against power is the struggle of memory against forgetting" (Kundera 1981:3).

In 1979, the Czech government responded to the publication of *The Book of Laughter and Forgetting* by revoking Kundera's citizenship. Powerless to silence him, the state sought at least to sever his umbilical cord to the motherland. One cannot help but wonder if the same fate awaits China's intellectuals who take advantage of geographical distance from the motherland to catalog her sufferings in the age of party-enforced amnesia.

Writing at Stanford University, for example, the young historian Ci Jiwei has began to detail the Chinese Communist party's "technologies" for eliminating everything but a narrowly construed "correct memory." Foremost among the strategies of forgetting is what Ci calls "the technology of guilt" employed by the Communist party to present itself as the "archcreditor" while everyone else stands in a "debtor" relationship to it. Anyone who lacks a sense of indebtedness to the party is forced to undertake a "ritualized confession" (a process known during the Cultural Revolution as *dousi pixiu*—"fight selfishness by repudiating revisionism"). These confessions are the forcible manifestation of selective remembering. In less pressured times they take the form of *yiku sitian*—"recalling suffering of the old life while meditating on the sweetness of the new" (Ci 1990:6).

Whether the past is sweet or sour, the party insists on reserving for itself the role of chief chef of memory. In China, as in Czechoslovakia, what remains of noncommunists in the party's picture is little more than Clementis's cap: a shadow on the wall, an absence that hints at a former presence. Two photographs exemplify this erasure in China quite starkly: one of Zhou Enlai in Berlin and one of Lu Xun in the company of Bernard Shaw.

The first is a widely circulated image of the young man who became premier of the People's Republic of China. It shows Zhou Enlai in a rowboat in the middle of Berlin's Wannsee park in 1922. The centered image shows a face that is stern, determined, forward looking, as befits the man who became a leader of Chinese communists in Europe and later of the labor movement at home. This one photograph condenses the whole history of Chinese communists in Europe. It condenses it to the point of distortion.

Just how truncated this image of Zhou Enlai was did not become apparent to me until I saw the full version of the photograph at the home of Zhang Shenfu, a cosmopolitan intellectual who had been cropped out of Zhou Enlai's rowboat. On Wang Fu Cang Lane, a side alley in Beijing, the reinstated photograph, along with the octogenarian survivor's voice, revealed a very different history of Chinese communists in Europe.[11] It was Zhang Shenfu who introduced Zhou Enlai into the Communist party in Paris in 1921; it was Zhang Shenfu who became the first secretary of the European branch of the Chinese Communist party in 1922; it was Zhang Shenfu who introduced Zhou Enlai to his position at the Whampoa Military Academy in 1924—a position that launched Zhou on his career as military and political leader in the Communist party.

But because Zhang Shenfu (like Chen Hengzhen's mother) left the party in the mid-1920s—because he was made a "rightist" like Gao Renzhi in 1957—his picture had to be cut out of the party's official history of the Chinese revolution. Only after the death of Mao in 1976 and the public rehabilitation of Zhang Shenfu in 1979 did the parameters of official remembrance begin to stretch in China. When a new generation of party historians sought to write a history of the Chinese communist movement, they found it convenient to exhibit in the National History Museum in Beijing the original photograph of the rowboat in Wannsee Park.

Even restored, however, the photograph was limited in its public meanings. It could not speak fully about the eccentric range of ideas explored by Chinese communists in Europe; it could not tell about Zhang Shenfu's love affair with Liu Qingyang, the fur-bedecked beauty who was the other person in the rowboat in Berlin. This young woman is commemorated in the annals of the communist revolution simply as a "patriotic activist" and the "first woman to join the Chinese Communist party in France" (Li Canming 1987:121–22).

Zhang Shenfu's "rehabilitated" image is not the only one that bears witness to an ongoing forgetfulness at the heart of China's official memory. There are many more. But let me mention just one that involves the simultaneous disappearance of a Westerner and a Chinese intellectual from the Communist party version of history: a photograph of Lu Xun's meeting with Bernard Shaw. Lu Xun, like Zhou Enlai, is an important figure in the public pantheon of the party. He represents the important, if troublesome, "cultural capital" of leftist intellectuals. Hence, Lu Xun's historical image has to be managed with great care.

Just how abusive this "care" turns out to be is revealed by Harold Isaacs in *Re-Encounters with China*. Invited back to China in October 1980, this seasoned journalist sought to take advantage of the new mood of openness after the death of Mao. Looking up friends in Shanghai, Isaacs happened upon a "doctored" photograph. Taken in the garden of Song Jingling, Sun Yatsen's widow, in 1933, the official image shows Song hosting a meeting between China's foremost revolutionary writer, Lu Xun, and the noted playwright Bernard Shaw. Two men have been erased from the picture: Harold Isaacs and the noncommunist literary scholar Lin Yutang. "The two of us," Isaacs writes, "had vanished, brushed away into the limbo of non-personhood as totally as if the brusher had been an executioner seeing to it that we existed no longer, certainly no longer in the garden on that day nearly fifty years ago" (Isaacs 1985:128).

Coming back to China at a time when so many of his former friends were also returning from the wilderness of nonpersonhood, Isaacs is especially sensitive to the party's manipulation of memory. He goes so far as to challenge the affable director of the official Lu Xun museum in Shanghai. She, warned of Isaacs's obsession with the truncated past, greets him with a copy of the restored photograph. On the museum wall, however, the "rehabilitated" image is exhibited with the caption "Shaw, Song Jingling, Lu Xun and others." "My writ of rehabilitation," Isaacs notes, "apparently restored my face but not my name" (Isaacs 1985:130).

Familiar with the bottomlessness of the KGB memory chutes, Harold Isaacs was especially mindful of the technologies of amnesia in China. Few others are able to chronicle so clearly the pitfalls of both repression and "rehabilitation" among colleagues on the mainland. Most Western writers do not know what it means to be erased from Chinese pictures, to be reduced to nonpersonhood. They must rely on Chinese voices to guide them through the wilderness of party-sponsored "memories."

One such voice that reached the West recently is that of the young writer Ah Cheng. In an essay paying tribute to his father, the noted film critic Zhong Dianfei, Ah Cheng reveals the bitterness that accompanies "rehabilitation" from nonpersonhood in China. Individuals are more fragile than photographs. A man airbrushed out today can be reinstated in a newly convenient image tomorrow. But a living, vulnerable artist is not so flexible. He cannot be lifted out of decades of forcible obscurity as if all that past history did not matter. Although Zhong Dianfei himself tried to stretch his work to fit the shifting requirements of political ideology, he failed to satisfy his masters. They declared him a nonperson in the antirightist campaign and during the Cultural Revolution.

The tired father tries to forgive the party when, after the death of Mao, it forgives his trumped-up crimes. The son, however, refuses the consolations of "rehabilitation." When Ah Cheng gets the news of his father's return to party-sanctioned personhood, he is in an art studio in New York. From this safe distance, Ah Cheng chooses to quarrel with his father's acceptance of political rehabilitation in Beijing. New York is the periphery that enables the son to see through the grammatical nicety that removes the adjective "rightist" from the name of his father:

> If I were overjoyed tonight, my past thirty years would be reduced to nothing. As a person, you have already affirmed yourself. There is no need for others to judge you. If the power of judgement is in the hands of others, they may well support you today and deny you tomorrow. Therefore, in my view, rehabilitation has no real significance outside of mere technical convenience. (Ah 1990:313–14)

"Technical convenience" is all that is possible in the public realm where the party's engineering rules supreme. On the periphery of state-controlled remembrance, however, another vision prevails. Ah Cheng in New York, Chen Hengzhen in the corridor of a former Buddhist monastery, Gao Renzhi in his factory clinic, Zhang Shenfu on Wang Fu Cang Lane—each of these intellectuals has managed to salvage some fragment of a forgotten past. Each hopes to use his distinctive bit of the fractured mirror to show China its true face. When and whether such bits of individually rescued remembrance will displace the monumental past still enshrined at the center, only time will tell. But the explosive interaction between historical memory and student activism in the streets of Beijing during the spring of 1989 suggests that state monopoly over public recollection is far from complete.

OPPORTUNITIES ON THE PERIPHERY

Inside China, the closer one gets to Beijing—the geographical center of political power—the more heavy handed becomes the political manipulation of memory. It is not surprising, then, that Chinese intellectuals have had to search for marginal spaces in which they could recover the truth of their own experience. They have had to become, like the Hebrew poet Dan Pagis, weary travelers on the side roads of history. Since the main avenues were full of potholes, memory had to be sought elsewhere.

One such space for China's cultural recuperation that I had the opportunity to witness in the summer of 1991 is Tibet—a place where cultural memory flourishes in spite of political repression because it is nurtured by deep religious faith. On the surface, Tibet is one of the most culturally ravaged parts of China. The vast destruction of monasteries and nunneries, the forcible defrocking of large segments of Tibet's venerated clergy, the repeated imprisonment of her spiritual leaders, and the exile of the people's revered leader, the Dalai Lama, all suggest the painful suppression of national memory.

And yet, in the interstices of party-sanctioned reform, Tibet is undergoing a spiritual renaissance of extraordinary proportions. The opening of a few key monasteries, mostly for tourist purposes, has been accompanied by a massive effort to rebuild hundreds of other monasteries with the Tibetan people's own funds. The large-scale influx of boys and girls into these new institutions for spiritual apprenticeship is beyond anything the Chinese government envisioned in its slow-paced reform of the early 1980s. Although explicit manifestations of religious freedom have been met by brutal suppression (such as the demonstrations in front of the Jokang temple in Lhasa in 1987 and 1989), Tibetans have managed to renew their spiritual life in spite of the Communist party's strict prohibitions.

The deep religious faith of the Tibetan people is something the Chinese Communist party does not understand and therefore cannot control. When Tibetans turn their prayer wheels, when they make offerings to the various deities, when the poorest of the beggar-pilgrims insists on performing ego-slaying practices on the streets of Lhasa—they are engaged in an activity so far beyond the materialism that is the coin of communist orthodoxy that they are, in effect, beyond the reach of the Chinese state.

This distinctive religious tradition has also become a magnet for young Chinese intellectuals and artists who seek some place to come to terms with the ravages of their own history. In the Drepung monastery, for example, at the height

of the *shoten* festival celebrating the emergence of the monks from their summer retreat, I came upon a group of Beijing University students who had walked,
hitchhiked, and hungered their way across China just to witness the rhythms of
spiritual renewal in Tibet. Their mentor was a young painter, Shao Zhenpeng,
who has earned an international reputation for powerful evocations of the spiritual landscape behind the snowcapped peaks of Tibet.

Another young artist, the ethnically Han photographer Jiang Zhenqing, has
focused his lens on the worship-worn stones in front of the Jokang temple and on
the faces of prayer-immersed monks who evoke for him "the eternal fragrance of
Tibetan memory."[12] In a world where remembrance has so frequently been gut-
ted by political persecution, the discovery of Tibet's spiritual tradition is enabling
Chinese artists to recover their own faith in memory. It is not only the geographical remoteness of Lhasa but also its ability to shelter and nurture an alternative
vision of self that is enabling this city to become a place for cultural recovery on
the periphery of China today. In the words of the veteran writer Wang Meng: "Distance itself is the most meaningful enlightenment" (Wang 1991).

New York City is performing a similar function. It too affords geographical distance from China's political center and thus enables young Chinese intellectuals
to discover their own voice. A recent manifestation of this recovery was "Thresh-
old"—an experimental performance put together by artists from Beijing, Taibei,
Singapore, and Hong Kong in June 1990. One year after the Tiananmen massacre,
this broad coalition of Chinese artists gathered at La MaMa theater to create a
piece that they subtitled "A Dance Theater of Remembrance and Forgetting."

Far from the bloodstained streets of China's capital, these young artists tried to
dissect their many-layered attachment to the murderous motherland. One particularly moving piece centered on a young man who dangles from, hugs, then wars
with a crimson rope while, from the darkened balcony, the husky voice of a Chinese woman reads in halting English: "We are born in history. This is an attempt
to escape it. . . . What I forget comes back to me in dreams. Cuts me open like a
knife." Then: "Mother? Motherland?" she asks in a high-pitched voice. The narra-
tor answers herself with a dark, monotonous, "Comrade" (Schwarcz 1991c:85).

This was the same cold-hearted response the Chinese state gave to the student
demonstrators of 1989. They talked about patriotism and the state answered them
with tanks. A year later, the pain of that betrayal is finally given voice on a stage
in New York. Here, as in Lhasa, a geographical periphery offers possibilities of renewed vision.

Inside China, temporal interstices offer refuge not unlike the spatial distancing claimed from abroad. When commemorations of public events take place in
less strident fashion, Chinese intellectuals have managed to recover bits of their
mangled history. Personal recollection in the context of China's public events provides a unique opportunity to correct and enliven public history. Memory, according to Martin Heidegger, is that which keeps us whole in our essential being: "It
is an ingathering of thought. To what? To what holds us."[13] This mutual nurturing

of identity and remembrance accounts for their endurance even in amnesia-laden Beijing. The cohesive power of memory, Chinese intellectuals have discovered, depends on holding on to that which holds us together as human beings—fidelity to the discrete details of the remembered past.

Over the years since 1919, participant-survivors of the May Fourth Movement have managed to inject pieces of actual recollection into officially celebrated anniversaries (*jinian*). In holding on to the remembered past, Chinese intellectuals were able to hold on, even if only fitfully, to a sense of their own identity. They were sustained by the very past they sought to rescue through remembrance.

The thirty-sixth anniversary of May Fourth offers one such instance of memorial fidelity. This was not one of the big anniversaries that are celebrated so loudly in China's public domain. The year 1949 had come and gone, and the Communist party had used the thirtieth anniversary of May Fourth to whip intellectuals into the new "mass line." The 1957 anniversary, with its fierce contention over the meaning of "science" and "democracy," was still two years away. In 1955, a lull from dramatic commemoration provided one survivor-participant, Yang Zhensheng, an opportunity for genuine recollection.

In 1955, Yang Zhensheng managed to withstand the party's pressure to collapse the event of 1919 into the communist-led movement of social mobilization. Propaganda chief Zhou Yang was demanding precisely that in an essay published that year and titled "Develop the Militant Tradition of May Fourth Literature." In this essay, Zhou Yang sought to compel intellectuals to recall only peasant-oriented writers of the past—and thereby to induce them to forget any aspirations for literary independence in the present (Zhou 1955:3–5). Publishing in the same journal as Zhou Yang, Yang Zhensheng set a more modest tone in his "Recollections of May Fourth."

Having been a member of the New Tide society (1918–21) at Beijing University, Yang Zhensheng could and did claim proximity to the event of 1919. He did not dwell on any of the politically correct heroes celebrated by Zhou Yang. Rather, he started with a narrative of his own childhood in Shandong province and the intellectual restlessness of his high-school days. Whereas the younger, more dogmatic Zhou Yang emphasized the retrospective role of communist leaders such as Li Dazhao and Mao Zedong, Yang Zhensheng underscored the importance of young students such as the future literary critic Yu Pingbo.

By 1955, Yu Pingbo had already become a victim of a party-sponsored criticism movement (led by Zhou Yang himself). So it was no small act of moral courage on Yang Zhensheng's part to acclaim the historical importance of his friend from the New Tide days. Recalling the circumstances of the founding of the New Tide society, Yang Zhensheng resisted the teleological thrust of Zhou Yang's vision of a "militant" (i.e., communist-led) May Fourth. Instead, Yang Zhensheng portrayed himself and his fellow students as full of impassioned naiveté.

Being young and impassioned—rather than politically firm and focused, as the party would have its youth depicted retrospectively—Yang Zhensheng and his fellow students had sought only to "tear off the chains from our bodies. Shouting at the top of our voice we stormed the citadel of feudalism . . . though we understood its foundations very little" (Yang Zhensheng 1955:105).

Twenty-eight years after Yang Zhensheng's recollections, Zhou Yang himself had been chastened by history. The propaganda chief of 1955 became a target of the Cultural Revolution, not unlike the intellectuals he had victimized during the 1950s. Zhou Yang, the man known as *gunzi,* the bludgeon, emerged in the late 1970s as a soft-spoken supporter of intellectual emancipation. By 1983, Zhou Yang was no longer interested in the "militant" tradition of May Fourth. On the eve of the sixty-fourth anniversary of the event of 1919, he was writing essays about the need to open up Chinese Marxism to the insights of May Fourth. He was beginning to produce the same kind of "evocative transcripts" that he had frowned upon during the repression of the 1950s. Not unlike Chen Hengzhen and Gao Renzhi, Zhou Yang began to see himself in the light of historical ambiguity. At once victim and accomplice, Zhou Yang now spoke in the voice of one who has learned the opportunities of the periphery.

On May 12, 1983, the recently rehabilitated Zhou Yang spoke with me about his own unfinished dreams in a small room in an alley off the main boulevard of Eternal Peace. Not unlike Yang Zhensheng, who spoke from the sidelines of 1955, or Chen Hengzhen at the Buddhist monastery, Zhou Yang retold history on his own terms. The former *gunzi* (leaning haltingly on a walking stick after a back injury suffered at the hands of Red Guards) now recalled with nostalgia meetings with American scholars in the 1940s. But nostalgia did not reign supreme on this May day in 1983. Rather, Zhou Yang insisted on moving from reminiscences of his own past to a critical assessment of the significance of May Fourth. No longer determined to blend the event of 1919 into the "glorious" tradition of the communist revolution (as he had done in 1955), Zhou Yang emphasized the challenges of an unfinished enlightenment movement:

> All subsequent movements for democracy in China remain indebted to May Fourth. All have been incomplete. Although some intellectuals tried to solve the problem of feudal mentality in the 1940s, they were unsuccessful. Even the Chinese Communist Party's land reform campaign in the 1950s did not tackle the deepest aspects of the culture problem. Courage alone—the Communists' slogan "be not afraid to have your head chopped off"—did not suffice in dealing with old habits of mind. . . . Superstitions persist in spite of repeated efforts to wipe out backwardness and ignorance. Enlightenment thought is still needed, you see, because the power of habits of thought is stronger than other kinds of power. It is invisible.[14]

On the face of it, Zhou Yang was speaking of the shortcomings of Chinese Marxism. He was joining his voice with the voices of several others who, in 1983, were beginning to describe Maoist communism as no better than a "feudal super-stition" that needed to be cured by a strong dose of May Fourth–style critical thought.

But the subtext of Zhou Yang's recollections was more suggestive. When he spoke about the "invisible" power of habits of mind, he was also paying tribute to the tenacity of memory. He was acknowledging the courage of Chinese intellectuals who had remained faithful to an enlightenment-centered vision of May Fourth during the decades in which Zhou himself, in the name of the party, had required a simplified portrait of political militancy. His own situation as victim of the Cultural Revolution had endowed Zhou Yang with new empathy for marginalized intellectuals. In 1983, he was acknowledging their, as well as his own, attachment to history. In Heidegger's terms, Zhou Yang held on to, and was held together by, a hard-won, belated fidelity to the past.

Commemoration of May Fourth offered Zhou Yang the same opportunity for personal rumination as had been claimed by more deeply displaced intellectuals such as Chen Hengzheng, Gao Renzhi, and Zhang Shenfu. Victim and victimizer alike knew that public rehabilitation of themselves and of the event of 1919 did not do justice to the fullness of history—especially its darker side: the invisible tenacity of suffering and loss. The interstices of commemoration thus provided these men with space to remember as well as to mourn their truncated lives.

Without their recollections, China's collective memory would be a far flatter, duller terrain. Insofar as public (national) memory can accommodate and make some peace with their darker vision, it too gains depth and resilience. The body politic, not unlike the individual, is revived as it revives the past.

This close association between memory, mourning, and rebirth is an old one in the Chinese context. It precedes, while at the same time it echoes, the Freudian in-sight that unfinished mourning is a prescription for lifelong melancholia. Although mourning is not always allowed by the Chinese state, as is the case for those killed in 1989, memory has nonetheless begun to do its job of healing. In the cramped interstices available for personal remembrance, individuals recall the past, dwell-ing on the plethora of erasures. To accept this many-faceted loss is not easy. Yet in the contemplation of loss lies memory's greatest gift. This is what Dan Pagis's traveler does when he stops, turns, and becomes less a stranger to his own loss-riddled life.

Thus it is fitting to end this exploration of the intricacies of remembrance in modern China with a few lines by the poet-emperor Li Yu. As the last ruler of the Southern Tang dynasty, Li was taken into captivity by the invading Song in AD 975. In the inhospitable northern capital of Bianjing (modern Kaifeng in Henan province), he wrote his best poems.

No longer an active participant in history, no longer its imperial author-codifier, Li Yu consoled himself with snippets of recollection. In exile, Li Yu became more intimate with his past. From abroad, he turned to face his home-land—never forgetting that it was lost to him forever, and that he was responsible for this loss. Like Chen Hengzhen, Li Yu was no stranger to the history that befell him. Like Dan Pagis, the poet who survived the Holocaust yet refused to lend his memory to a mythicizing of history, Li Yu merely mourned:

> The past is fit only for grieving,
> Its traces rise up before me, hard to brush aside . . .
> My golden sword lies buried deep in loss,
> My youth turned to weeds.
> (Liu and Lo 1976:131)

--------- *Notes* ---------

1. Dan Pagis was a Holocaust survivor. Born in Radautz, Romania, in 1930, he made his way to Israel after the war. By the time of his death at 56, Pagis had become one of the outstanding voices in modern Hebrew literature. For an exploration of Pagis's poetic journey through the landscape of remembrance, see Ezrahi (1990:335–63).

2. To protect the identity of this vulnerable informant, I have changed his name and some of his identifying characteristics. The record of our conversation, however, comes directly out of my field journals of April–May 1989; I recorded it shortly after the encounter described.

3. For a fuller discussion of the various academic conferences held in Beijing to commemorate the seventieth anniversary of the May Fourth Movement, see Schwarcz (1991a:109–23).

4. For a fuller discussion of intellectuals who sought to or were forced to serve the Maoist regime, see C. Hamrin and T. Cheek, eds., *China's Establishment-Intellectuals* (1986), especially pages 3–20 and 247–57.

5. Arthur Kleinman has been investigating the fate of psychiatry and psychiatrists in China for more than a decade. His book, *Social Origins of Distress and Disease* (1986) describes a few case studies of doctors under duress. The introduction refers to the investigator's own encounters with traumatized mental health workers who have not yet been sanctioned to talk about their own pain in public. Thus they are forced to spill out their stories at night in the dormitories of foreign visitors. Some of these issues are further developed in Kleinman's essay "Remembering the Cultural Revolution," presented at the April 1991 meeting of the Asian Studies Association. I am grateful to Dr. Kleinman for ongoing conversations that have alerted me to the inner dilemmas of psychiatrists in China.

6. For a preliminary contrast of the memory of survivors of the Cultural Revolution and of the Holocaust, see Schwarcz (1991b:10–13).

7. For a fuller discussion of the ways in which the traditional roles of Chinese literati affect the consciousness of contemporary Chinese intellectuals, see Schwarcz (1986:248–252).

8. For a discussion of the various applications of Haraszti's metaphor of the "velvet prison" to the predicament of Chinese intellectuals, see Barme (1989).

9. This discussion of the Confucian commitment to memory draws upon Stephen Owen (1986), especially his commentary on verse 19 of chapter 8 in the *Analects* (Owen 1986:13). For a fuller discussion of the uses of history in China's public culture, see "La référence à l'histoire," a special issue of *Extrême-Orient, Extrême-Occident* edited by Yves Chevrier (1986). This issue includes very suggestive essays on historical myths and the myth of history, on the meanings of "historical truth" in Chinese culture, and on the function of historical references in the inner life of Chinese intellectuals.

10. This quote from Nietzsche's "On the Use and Disadvantage of History for Life" is drawn from Krell (1990).

11. For a fuller discussion of the interviews with Zhang Shenfu and the political context that led to his erasure from the annals of the Chinese revolution and his subsequent rehabilitation after the death of Mao Zedong, see Schwarcz (1992, especially chapter 3).

12. This expression comes from a catalog accompanying an exhibition of Jiang Zhenqing's photography held in Dalian from August 24 to September 1, 1991. In the catalog, Jiang quotes this fragment from a poem by the veteran writer Wang Meng, titled "Reveries of Tibet":

> Caidanzhuoma's singing voice,
> Is as sweet as days gone by.

Memories of Tibet,
are always fresh.
Even when her people,
are far, far away.
Distance itself
is the most meaningful enlightenment.

13. This quotation, from Martin Heidegger's 1952 essay "What is it we call thinking, and what calls for our thinking," comes from Krell (1990:263).

14. Personal interview with Zhou Yang, May 12, 1983.

4

Making Secret Histories
Memory and Mourning in Post-Mao China

RUBIE S. WATSON

THE LINK BETWEEN MEMORY and mourning is a powerful one. In Chinese society, before the Maoist cultural agenda was put into place, funerary rites involved a process of memorialization. They offered an occasion for retrospection and introspection as well as an arena within which justice could be sought, grievances aired, and moral blame apportioned. Untimely death, especially violent death, required extraordinary ritual attention. The "restless ghosts" that violence produced had to be acknowledged so that they could be settled, or at least managed. Violent death was neither ignored nor denied but was managed as it was memorialized (on death ritual and ghosts, see, e.g., Harrell 1986; Watson 1982; Watson and Rawski 1988; Weller 1985; Wolf 1974).

In the following pages I describe two ethnographic examples in which connections between memory and commemoration and between mourning and injustice are particularly dramatic. I then turn to post-Mao China and a necessarily more speculative discussion of the treatment of violent death—especially deaths caused by state-sponsored violence.[1] How, I ask, have the victims of state-inspired violence, China's "new ghosts," as some have labeled them, been remembered and "managed"?[2] What cultural resources make it possible for ordinary people to counter official amnesia and so remember the forgotten, unmourned dead that such amnesia produces?

Writing of a particularly well-documented attempt at officially inspired obliteration, Anne Thurston (1987) describes the last months, death, and secret cremation of Liu Shaoqi.[3] During the winter and early summer of 1966, when the Great Proletarian Cultural Revolution was gathering steam, Liu served as the second-ranking member of the Chinese Communist party, president of the People's Republic of China, and Mao's heir apparent. In August 1966, however, Liu was demoted.

One year later, Liu and his wife, Wang Guangmei, were led to separate "struggle sessions" in two dining halls at Zhongnanhai, the residential compound for high-ranking Chinese officials. From this point onward, Liu and his wife were kept separated from each other and from their four children and were placed under house arrest (Thurston 1987:126). Meetings and communications among members of the family were not allowed. The struggle sessions continued, and Liu's health deteriorated. In the autumn of 1968, Liu was finally transferred to a hospital, where his mistreatment continued, and a year later he was flown to a special prison in Kaifeng, where he died on November 12. "At midnight," Thurston reports, "in the deepest secrecy, Liu's remains were transported by jeep to a nearby crematorium," where he was cremated under a pseudonym—no occupation was recorded on his death certificate (Thurston 1987:153). His family was not told of his death until 1972; the people of China were informed only in 1979.

After learning of his death, Liu's children began a search for his remains. "In mid-1976," Thurston writes, "they were told that in a certain room in Babaoshan [a Beijing crematory and columbarium] was an anonymous box that might contain their father's ashes. Through subterfuge and carefully disguised, because the children of Liu Shaoqi remained pariahs in revolutionary China, they gained admittance to the room" (Thurston 1987:151). Their search was in vain, however, and it was not until 1980, 12 years after his death, that Liu's ashes were returned to his family. There are many victims of China's revolutionary violence, however, whose remains, like those in the unidentified box at Babaoshan, continue to be unclaimed and thus unmourned (Thurston 1987:153).

In a personal account of her experiences as a Rebel Red Guard, Lo Fulang (1989) tells of the treatment of "counterrevolutionary" dead in Sichuan. In attempting to collect or steal—it is unclear which—weapons from the local military command, Rebel Red Guards were fired upon by soldiers; eleven of their number were killed and many others wounded. The dead were labeled counterrevolutionaries and, according to Lo's account, their bodies were heaped before the gate of the military command post. "Many parents," Lo continues, "never even dared to claim the bodies of their children. Those who did . . . had to hold funerals in secret because public ceremonies for counterrevolutionaries were forbidden" (Lo 1989:134; for similar examples, see Gao Yuan 1987:24, 59–60; Yue and Wakeman 1985:190).

It was common practice not only in Sichuan but also in other areas that people who died while still charged with counterrevolutionary crimes received no memorial service, and if they died while separated from their families, "the ashes were often never returned" (see, e.g., Thurston 1987:151). In the case of suicide, Thurston notes, "the traditional memorial service for the dead was often replaced by a struggle session against [the deceased]. For suicide during the Cultural Revolution was taken as evidence of guilt, as a betrayal of the revolution, of which the suicide itself constituted proof" (Thurston 1987:151, 138–45; see also Wakeman 1988:260; Yue and Wakeman 1985:184).

There may have been—no doubt in many cases there was—private grief; but as in the Rebel Red Guard case just described, there were times when even spouses, parents, and children were not allowed to share their private mourning. Others chose not to display evidence of mourning, thereby "drawing a clear line" between themselves and the victims. The logic was brutal: enemies of the people are not people, so their deaths need not and should not be mourned.

If millions of Chinese can be declared nonpersons and their deaths can be ignored, it may not be surprising to find that events can also become nonevents. For many years the famine of 1959–61 and its twenty-eight million dead received no official recognition (see Bernstein 1984). Today this period is known as "the three bad years," although in the West it is often called the "Great Leap Famine," a designation that clearly connects it to the failed policies of Mao's Great Leap Forward.[4]

The periodization of the Cultural Revolution itself has been a matter of some dispute. At one time it was believed to have lasted only three years, from 1966 to 1969. But as former leaders like Deng Xiaoping regained their authority and purged the radicals, the Cultural Revolution was declared a disaster (the precise wording was "the ten years of great disaster") and dated from 1966 to 1976. This latter periodization is now generally accepted. For over a decade, however, the events of the years from 1966 to 1976 remained fragmented, making the killings, torture, forced migrations, and internecine warfare of this period seem like independent, unrelated events. Without a vocabulary to name, classify, and so analyze their experiences, victims and victimizers alike remained confused and fundamentally isolated in the aftermath of their ordeal.

Socialist China is not the only society that forgets or tailors histories in order to serve the interests of present-day powerholders. As Simmonds-Duke (1987) argues, it is not only state socialism that has official memory lapses. The detention of Japanese-Americans during the Second World War, for example, did not enter the history textbooks of American high-school students until the 1980s. In East Asia, Chinese and Koreans have been fiercely critical of Japanese accounts of the 1930s and 1940s. They argue that the people of Japan have a responsibility to remember the devastation imperial forces created and must not be allowed to fall into a self-serving amnesia.

In recent years much has been written about the relationship between history and power, memory and suffering, the past in the present. In *How Societies Remember*, Paul Connerton argues that "the control of a society's memory largely conditions the hierarchy of power" (1989:1). Katherine Verdery shows how, in Ceausescu's Romania, the state controlled time through its ability both to redefine the past and to expropriate the time and efforts of its citizens (1991a:242; see also Simmonds-Duke 1987). This control over memory and time is never total, however. Unapproved memories or understandings of the past create and are created by subordinated groups. In highly centralized societies, attempts are made to deprive citizens of these unapproved memories, or at least the ability to propagate and so convert such memories into alternative histories. It is the state's attempts to privatize memory, and so ultimately to obliterate it, on the one hand, and the attempts by ordinary citizens to make sense of their own experience by sharing and so "publicizing" it, on the other, that are the twin foci of this chapter.

In the following discussion I examine the process by which personal experiences of traumatic events are given meaning and are transmitted under conditions of official hostility or denial. How do people "remember" the unmourned dead of the Cultural Revolution or the 1989 Beijing massacre? How are shared memories and secret histories of these events constructed and passed on to the next generation? In what ways are memories, oppositional histories, and official histories similar, and in what ways are they different?

I am concerned in part with questions of resistance, subversion, and opposition in the context of socialist regimes where a powerful, state-sponsored cultural apparatus exists to forestall the development of alternative views. While evidence of resistance under state socialism may not be difficult to find, we should not expect the expression of disagreement and resistance to be everywhere the same.[5] In countries like Soviet-dominated Mongolia, for example, as Caroline Humphrey shows in chapter 2, where centralized state organs produced a powerful monopoly over public and private spheres, disagreement and dissent were not shouted but whispered—and even those whisperings were intentionally ambiguous.[6]

In a recent article, Susan Gal argues that the logic of what she calls real socialism "was to maximize the control of the centralized political apparatus over the production of everything—cultural values as well as material goods" (1991:441). For Gal, understanding state socialism involves determining not only which social groups exercised control over public discourse but also how effectively they monopolized that discourse (1991:454). Verdery argues that "the sphere of symbolization and cultural production" must be at the center of any analysis of socialism, because it was through this production that socialist leaders hoped to form consciousness and so transform society (1991b:428; see also Binns 1979; Burawoy and Lukacs 1992; Gellner 1991; Kligman 1988:7–9; Lane 1981). Because this "new consciousness" supported the ruling elite's own legitimacy and, to a considerable degree, their control, leaders were zealous in their guardianship of the means of cultural production (see also Wagner 1987).

"Unlike the western European societies," Verdery writes, "that benefited from several centuries of slow evolution in which consciousness came to be formed more through practice than through discourse . . . eastern European communists came to power with the intention of rapidly revolutionizing consciousness and with precious few means to do so" (1991b:430). In achieving this revolution, control over the mechanisms as well as the agents of cultural production was essential. In such an environment, intellectuals were necessary but dangerous, and differences of opinion were no small matter.

Mao's own views on revolution through class struggle place cultural transformation at the very core of his revolutionary agenda. In an article comparing cultural revolution in China and Russia, Maurice Meisner characterizes the Maoist version of Marxism-Leninism by its "voluntarist faith" in the power of "proper consciousness" to "mold social reality." According to Meisner, "for Mao, history was determined by conscious human activity, and . . . from that belief flowed the enormous Maoist concern with developing and maintaining a 'correct consciousness,' the stress on 'ideological remolding,' and the emphasis on techniques of 'thought reform' " (1985:282).

Throughout his life Mao remained wary of China's educated elite, and, in contrast to Lenin, "retained a Populist-type faith in the spontaneous creativity of the masses" (Meisner 1985:287). Class struggle, education through labor, and reliance on "natural redness" were the weapons of social transformation in the Maoist arsenal. Mao vehemently rejected traditional Chinese culture and, in Meisner's words, believed "that a new culture as well as a new history could be written on 'blank' sheets of paper" (1985:289; for other views of Mao's approach to cultural revolution, see Saich and Ven 1994; Schram 1973, 1989; Starr 1973).

In China, intellectuals have suffered not only from Maoist antipathy but also from the contradictions inherent in their own self-definitions. For centuries Chinese intellectuals have exhibited a general contempt for traditional popular culture, which they have combined with a self-assumed responsibility to interpret and reform that culture (for further discussion, see Barme 1989; M. Cohen 1991; Goldman, Cheek, and Hamrin 1987; Judd 1990; Siu 1990). The mantle of moral standard bearer, self-appointed improver of the masses, and loyal servant of China's rulers—of "remonstrator rather than opponent," as Andrew Nathan (1989) puts it—has always created tensions.[7] Under Mao, these tensions intensified and became explicit, producing agonizing consequences not only for individual intellectuals but for Chinese society as a whole.

In China, both the party and the literati claim to be the true, rightful producers of Chinese culture. Until recently, the contest has been one sided, and Maoist versions of cultural revolution have dominated. Competition notwithstanding, there is considerable common ground between party and intellectual conceptions of cultural production. Arrogant dismissals of "feudal superstitions" have led to attacks on "traditional culture" by both the party and the new literati. These attacks involve a denial that the past is relevant in the present. They have led to the emergence of an "un-civil" society, an example of the "spoiler state" in which party organs attempt to monopolize the cultural as well as the economic realm by destroying or disabling competing organizations, many of which have their basis in traditional practices and beliefs.[8]

I do not mean to suggest that Chinese intellectuals have been silent about party excesses, but rather that their oppositional discourse, perhaps by necessity, has tended to be highly elitist and therefore ultimately divisive. In China, as in many other societies, there is a long tradition of expressing protest by subverting orthodox historical and ritual forms (see, e.g., Barme and Jaiven 1992; Goldman 1981:25–47; Wagner 1987, 1990; Weller 1993; see also chapter 3, this volume).

Strict adherence to the letter of mourning obligations, which excused a prolonged withdrawal from active duty, was often used by imperial officials to register if not dissent, at least the lack of consent.

There is, in fact, a rich vocabulary for such subversions. For centuries Chinese literati have been "pointing to the mulberry and reviling the ash," a hidden form of censure in which a piece of writing can be read, if one is educated in the right idiom, at different levels. There are also the didactic historical allusions found in memorials and petitions presented to the emperor, which point out, albeit obliquely, miscarriages of justice. A form of criticism using irony (*zawen*) was put to particularly effective use by the twentieth-century writer Lu Xun, who employed it to ridicule social and political practices in the China of his day. More recently, the "literature of the wounded" and the related reportage movement have exposed the terrors of the Cultural Revolution and the suffering of the Great Leap Forward (see, e.g., Link 1983; Liu Binyan 1983). And, in the post-Tiananmen period, artful strategies of dissimulation have proliferated (see, e.g., Barme and Jaiven 1992). With few exceptions, however, these forms are aimed at highly literate audiences. Understanding often hangs on erudite allusions, linguistic puns, and insider information known only to the most educated.

In *Ways of Lying*, Perez Zagorin writes about the elaborate rules for dissimulation to which people in early modern Europe resorted "as a refuge from the repressive power of states and churches" (1990:8–9).[9] In some periods, esotericism and elitism, he argues, offered a privileged space within which dissent could occur. "Esotericism, the conception of secret knowledge to be revealed only to an elite and harmful if communicated to the masses," provided an important, if somewhat tortuous, avenue of communication for the dissenter (Zagorin 1990:11). In China, where the intellectual environment remains hostile to contending views, dissimulation and the elitism of intellectuals continue to be intimately intertwined. Much protest in China remains a highly secretive discourse managed by and for a small group of intellectuals.

If, as is often suggested, both the range of human experience that can be publicly expressed and the avenues for expressing it are highly limited under state socialism, one of the ways in which ordinary people can voice their dissent is by a kind of guerrilla action in which the officially sanctioned is subverted. In a way similar to that by which thousands of small acts of foot dragging and sabotage may transform a productive factory into an unproductive one, the grand ceremony— the orchestrated event—may be undone by many small acts of unapproved symbolization and remembrance. Sometimes, as we shall see, these small acts blossom into full-throated protests.

In the 1980s and 1990s, China's public transcripts have been forced to share the stage with hidden ones.[10] In a recent article, Vera Schwarcz (1989) describes a ceremony in which official celebration was transformed into unauthorized remembrance. On May 20, in the midst of the 1989 democracy demonstrations in Beijing, Schwarcz joined a group of Chinese scholars at a ceremony honoring the 56-year career of the philosopher Zhang Dainian. Everyone knew, Schwarcz writes, that they were really celebrating Zhang's eightieth birthday, but such personal celebrations had to be disguised in socialist China.

As the participants paid tribute to Zhang's integrity, they seemed to be speaking not only of Zhang's survival but also of their own. In praising their teacher's endurance, they were remembering the past while at the same time encouraging each other to outlast yet another crisis—everyone expected that martial law was about to be imposed (Schwarcz 1989:129). Zhang himself echoed what many Chinese intellectuals have expressed on other occasions and in other words: "I have done nothing special over these 56 years. I just went on living and somehow managed to reach 80. . . . After 1979 [the year of Zhang's political rehabilitation] I regained my courage and my energy. I tried to think more independently after I turned 70. But it has been too little, too late. Most of my life I have spent obeying and so did not accomplish enough. Still, I expect to go on with my work" (Schwarcz 1989:129; cf. Liu 1990).

It is this often transitory commingling of private and public, this attempt by ordinary people to find personal, unapproved significance in public, state-sponsored ceremony that is so important in understanding the dialectical relationship between commemoration and protest in socialist China. In an account of the subversion of state commemoration, A. P. Cheater (1991) argues that the death rites of important Chinese leaders provide a stage upon which political tricksters can play. State funerals, Cheater writes, afford people opportunities "to manipulate ambiguous symbols in ways not originally intended by those in power" (1991:67). Public mourning in China, as in many other societies, is concerned with legitimation and succession; it is also, as I discuss later, concerned with the disclosure of personal and social injustice and memories of communal violence.

The work of Joseph Esherick and Jeffrey Wasserstrom (1990) further testifies to ways in which Chinese commemorative ceremonies can be converted into political theater and a celebration of approved *and* unapproved memories. Public funerals, they argue, provide opportunities for people to usurp state rituals by "improvising upon an official script to make it serve subversive ends" (1990:839). The authorities cannot prohibit such ceremonies, nor can they fully control who participates or what messages are conveyed. Zhou Enlai's and Hu Yaobang's funerals in 1976 and 1989 were classic examples of such usurpation, and I will discuss them later.

For Paul Connerton (1989), it is in the realm of commemorative ceremonies— ritual performances that evoke and reenact the past—that one must look for the transmission of what he labels "social memory."[11] As I noted in chapter 1, representations of the past include much more than written histories. "History," according to Maurice Halbwachs, "is neither the whole nor even all that remains of the past. In addition to written history, there is a living history that perpetuates and renews itself through time" (1980:64). For Halbwachs, living history is intimately tied to a process of remembrance that he calls collective memory.

Shared memory is diffuse and multilayered; it is also, in an important sense, unauthored and unauthorized. Memory, as Paul Fussell shows in his book *The Great War and Modern Memory* (1975), can create a set of images that cast a spell over a century. Remembrance ceremonies, soldiers' tales of the trenches, photographs and films, poetry and memoirs all portray not a patterned history, not a tightly organized story with a beginning and end, but a series of evocations or re-presentations (see also Graves 1929; Halbwachs 1980:52). They allow us to "reexperience" events. Memories tend to be transmitted via complicated overlays of images, words, songs, music, and movements.

Because performative domains like drama and ritual are such powerful media for producing multiple messages and combining expressive forms, they are in some respects ideally suited to the transmission of memories. Memories are communicated as an integral part of everyday life (from parent to child, friend to friend, neighbor to neighbor), but sometimes specific remembrances are focused and collectivized by artists. By *artists,* I do not refer primarily to members of a nationally prominent, intellectual elite. As I use it here, the term encompasses a wide range of specialists, including storytellers, poets, novelists, singers, photographers, filmmakers, painters, spirit mediums, actors, exorcists, and charismatic leaders.

In the following pages I draw on two examples from rural Chinese society to show how memories can be transmitted and secret histories constructed through mourning and commemoration. In the villages of Guangdong province, a funeral is a time not only for grieving but also, as I pointed out earlier, for remembering the life of the deceased and for taking stock of one's own past. During these funeral rites, women mourners sing laments for the dead and also for themselves.[12] Although the appropriate sentiments of homage and sadness may find expression at funerals, these songs may also serve as vehicles for personal protests. In a lament for her mother-in-law, a woman chastises the deceased (E. Johnson 1988:154):

> In the past you loved only your older daughter-in-law
> You just regarded me as a blade of grass.
> My parents died when I was very small.
> I was brought up by you.
> You cared for me and raised me.
> Now your other daughter-in-law is bad.
> But you didn't treat me well.
> In the past you raised me as your daughter.
> Today you know I am not a blade of grass
> But that I am a good daughter-in-law.

In a lament for her father's sister's husband, a woman unfavorably compares her own husband's behavior with that of her dead kinsman (Johnson 1988:155):

My *daaih gu jeuhng* [father's sister's husband]
You are at peace
I have come today
I am calling *daaih gu jeuhng*.
I have come to call *daaih gu jeuhng*.
My *daaih gu jeuhng,* you are at peace today, *daaih gu jeuhng*.
You have a son and everything is fine.
My *daaih gu jeuhng* could never eat all his food,
Could never spend all his money.
I met *daaih gu jeuhng* at the head of the street.
He asked me whether I was well.
How could I be well? I have only forty dollars a month.
If I were like other people I would have a good fate.
I should have children pulling at my blouse,
Children clinging to my legs.
If my children were still alive,
I would have three pulling at my clothes on the right,
Three pulling at my clothes on the left.
My *daaih gu jeuhng* also had a second wife.
He as a husband treated them both equally.
Towards the second he showed no special favor.

In 1977, a mortuary ritual (*da jai*) was held to placate the soul of a woman who had committed suicide in the village where I was living (Ha Tsuen, Hong Kong New Territories). At a certain point in the ritual, a group of women gathered at one side of the makeshift altar and began to cry and then to wail. There was no lamenting because, as they told me later: "We don't know how to do that any more." When I asked why they all came together to mourn in this way, one young woman explained: "We remember auntie's sad life and then we think of our own problems and we cry." Elizabeth Johnson quotes a Chinese proverb that expresses similar sentiments: "We use the occasions of other people's funerals to release personal sorrows" (1988:135).

I do not propose to make a direct correlation between these village laments and the national protests that have occurred in socialist China, although the parallels are intriguing. What is important for the purposes of this discussion is the way in which personal memories of injustice are made public in a ritualized context of mourning and remembrance. A lamenter can express sentiments and publicize memories that she could not express in daily life (at least not without risking censure). In other words, the ritual creates a context within which remembrance is encouraged: in contemplating the life of the deceased, each lamenter also calls up her own past. This process involves the translation of personal experience into an idiom—in this case, the lament—that can be shared.

David Coplan captures, I believe, the complicated interlinkages that popular art forms create when he describes the performance of South African migrants' songs as "at once deeply cultural, widely shared, and highly individual" (1987:418). In China, as elsewhere, ritual, poetry, and song offer a special arena within which individual suffering can be given public or cultural significance. In the Guangdong example, the medium of transmission and of transformation itself is the lament within the rite; the mourning woman uses an accepted cultural form to express felt injustices of the past. The lamenter publicizes her personal memories and so shares them with her audience. Whether these laments can be read as a hidden history of the lamenter, of her family, or of village women in general is a complicated issue and must be left for another discussion.

In many respects, my second example of ritual and shared memory is strikingly similar to the kind of communal memories Richard Madsen (1990) has written about in his description of the politics of revenge in rural China—except that the memories I will discuss are located not in everyday politics but in the realm of community ritual. In many parts of rural China, a cyclical ritual of purification and renewal (*jiao*) was held. These elaborate rites, performed at regular intervals, involved all households in a village and may have encompassed an entire *xiang*, or district.

John Mathias (1977) and James Watson (n.d.) describe *jiao* rites for two communities in rural Hong Kong. In the Hong Kong village of Ha Tsuen, where I have conducted field research since 1977, the *jiao* is celebrated every ten years and involves a set of rites that lasts for five days and six nights. The villagers maintain a vegetarian regimen during this period and import religious specialists to conduct the complicated and lengthy rites. Gods and goddesses from local temples are invited to watch the proceedings from a makeshift shelter facing a huge opera stage. Operas (see chapter 6, this volume) are often associated with *jiao* observances and are performed for the enjoyment of the deities and their hosts, the villagers.

The *jiao* is a complex event, and no single description can capture the multiplicity of its meanings and symbolic representations. In his discussion, James Watson stresses "the close relationship between the performance of *jiao* rites and the reenactment of past conflicts." According to Watson's informants, the *jiao* placates the spirits of those who died untimely deaths in the host village and its surrounding territory; the rites settle restless spirits and cleanse the region of baleful influences. Ha Tsuen's geomancer argues that his community's *jiao* originated many centuries ago as a means of placating and honoring lineage martyrs killed in the feuds that once characterized this region.

In Ha Tsuen, each *jiao* cycle begins as a group of lineage elders congregates at a small hill near the village where they propitiate the spirits of local heroes (*yingxiong*), who, it is believed, fell on that very spot defending their homes against a rival lineage. During the *jiao*, priests visit this and other battlegrounds, as well as the sites of suicides, road accidents, homicides, and other untimely (or "bad") deaths. At each site, offerings are made and spirits are soothed. At one level, the *jiao* may be read as a record of past violence or as a kind of performative inscription of community history. It involves the construction and maintenance of a set of shared memories and may be characterized, I believe, as a secret or hidden history of communal violence. Such a history is not preserved in written texts. Commemorated incidents of violence do not appear in genealogical accounts or in state-sponsored gazetteers. They are, however, remembered.

In many societies, spirit possession offers similar opportunities for remembrance (see, e.g., Kim 1989). In his study of Latin American shamanism, Michael Taussig examines "the way that certain historical events . . . become objectified in the contemporary shamanic repertoire as magically empowered imagery capable of causing as well as relieving misfortune" (1987:367). Referring to the work of Silvia Bovenschen and Walter Benjamin, Taussig writes of the "experiential appropriation" of the past and its "anarchical and rebellious . . . rejection of chronology and historical accuracy" (1987:367–68). Ritualized remembrance does not produce a historian's history, nor does memory "recall" the past. Like history, memory is a construction; it is created from a "lived history" out of which people seek "to preserve and recover an image of the past" that is charged with shared meaning (Halbwachs 1980:69).

At this point I turn to the public memorialization of Premier Zhou Enlai, one of the most dramatic examples of *unauthorized* remembrance and protest in Maoist China. Zhou was a loyal communist, widely respected by his fellow Chinese; unlike Mao himself, Zhou had come to represent the acceptable face of Maoist socialism. By 1976, however, the still reigning radicals had nearly succeeded in making Zhou into a nonperson through their control of the media (Goldman 1981:229). A Beijing resident recounted his feelings of anger at the time of Zhou's death in January 1976: "They wouldn't let us mourn him. . . . We couldn't even wear black armbands. . . . A directive came that we weren't even to hold our own memorial meetings in our own work units" (Thurston 1987:7; see also Cheater 1991:72–78; Lo 1989:241–42).

As people took their mourning into the streets, however, they did remember Zhou Enlai. Thousands lined the route along which Zhou's body passed as it made its way from the Beijing Hospital where he died to Babaoshan where he was cremated. There was to be no public viewing of his remains but, under pressure, party leaders were forced to concede, and Zhou's ashes were placed in the Workers' Cultural Palace (formerly the imperial ancestral temple) for three days, during which people could pay their respects. According to Zhou's wishes, his ashes were scattered across China.[13]

At the time of Zhou's death, people laid memorial wreaths at the Monument to Revolutionary Heroes in Tiananmen Square, they wept, and some even wore the forbidden armbands (see, e.g., Cheater 1991:72–78)—yet Zhou Enlai, as Thurston writes (1987:8), "remained insufficiently mourned."

On March 23, 1976, two months after Zhou's death and just before Qing Ming, an annual festival in which for centuries Chinese people had visited and cared for the graves of their ancestors, a single wreath with an inscription commemorating Zhou appeared at the foot of the Monument to Revolutionary Heroes. During that first day a second wreath was added, but by the following morning, both had disappeared. Throughout the next week, more wreaths appeared and were removed. Finally, on March 30, a group of People's Liberation Army (PLA) soldiers marched across the square to the monument and placed a wreath dedicated to Zhou and bearing the insignia of their unit signed by 24 men. Later, another wreath, signed by 24 mourners from the Beijing Municipal Labor Union, was added to the first. That evening the wreaths, which Thurston describes as "a call to mourning," were protected by a group of PLA soldiers (1987:4; see also Wakeman 1985:151, 1988:260). In a sense, these incidents began what was and continues to be an unofficial, hidden, but nonetheless widespread sharing of loss. These wreaths may be said to have inaugurated the first halting attempts to construct an unauthorized representation of the Cultural Revolution.

On April 2, Beijing work units received a directive forbidding participation in Qing Ming activities in Tiananmen Square. During the 1950s, Qing Ming had been redefined by the party as a time to remember revolutionary heroes (see Whyte 1988), and the directive warned people against returning to the "old feudal practices" when Qing Ming was a "festival of ghosts" (see Thurston 1987:12). People were told that they would be punished if they participated, but large numbers refused to heed the warnings. On April 4, the day of Qing Ming, people continued to lay wreaths in memory of Zhou at the Monument to Revolutionary Heroes. Eulogies and poems were read and, because there were no loudspeakers, transferred line by line throughout the crowd by relay.

While the people thronging the square criticized the radicals (although rarely by name), they also supported Deng Xiaoping. Deng had been purged during the early years of the Cultural Revolution, but in 1973 Zhou had brought him back to the capital where he had to face yet another round of criticism from left-wing radicals. Now, on April 5, 1976, police and militia forces began to clear the square. In the melee many were injured and some were killed; the exact number has never been publicly acknowledged. This scenario was to repeat itself with terrible consequences during the memorial rites for Hu Yaobang in 1989.

The tragic events of June 4, 1989, bring together all the elements I have discussed: commemoration, mourning, ritual, theater, protest, and violence. Although it is perhaps premature to speak of an official history, it is possible to discern an official account of the "counterrevolutionary rebellion," as the events of 1989 are styled by party authorities. But before turning to those accounts and to the oppositional forms that counter them, a brief sketch of the relevant events is necessary.[14]

The unexpected death of Hu Yaobang on April 15, 1989, drastically altered the carefully orchestrated schedule of events that both party officials and students had organized to commemorate the seventieth anniversary of the May Fourth Movement. In 1987, Hu was ousted as Communist party general secretary, in part for his toleration of a previous student protest in 1986. According to many commentators, Hu's death did not create, but did accelerate, an ongoing process of political discussion and protest in China.[15]

The public response to Hu's memorial rites was perhaps less spontaneous than the demonstrations associated with the mourning of Zhou Enlai, but it is important to note that both involved highly dramatic subversions of state ritual (a kind of ritual hijacking) and a level of public participation that astonished even the most active protesters. There are, however, important differences between these two events. During the mourning of Zhou Enlai, people appear to have been actively engaged in a personalized form of mourning as they struggled to remember and so make sense of the Cultural Revolution. During the mourning of Hu and the demonstrations that followed, personal memorialization mingled with and seems eventually to have been overtaken by feelings of present injustice.

In the immediate aftermath of Hu's death, meetings were held at Beijing University and students marched to Tiananmen Square, where they placed wreaths, banners, and posters at the Monument to Revolutionary Heroes. According to Li Qiao and other participants in and chroniclers of the demonstrations, there were demands at this point for a reevaluation of Hu's achievements, an acceleration of democratization, increased efforts to control corruption, and a dialogue with officials (Li et al. 1990:21). On April 19, demonstrators clashed with the police at Xinhuamen, the main gate to Zhongnanhai (the walled compound where most state leaders reside).

On the morning of April 22, Hu's memorial service was held in the Great Hall of the People, located directly across the square from the Monument to Revolutionary Heroes. Despite warnings to clear the square, thousands of students were cheered by Beijing residents as they marched to Tiananmen on the day and evening before the service. In the early hours of April 22, security forces entered the square to take up positions surrounding the Great Hall (see Li et al. 1990:26–27). At this point a spontaneous sit-in began, and as the memorials to Hu were presented inside the Great Hall, loudspeakers broadcast the ceremony to the demonstrators outside.

On April 26, the *People's Daily* published an editorial claiming that the demonstrations were riots instigated by a handful of troublemakers (later to be designated "black hands"). At a press conference on the same day, an organization known as the Temporary Students' Union demanded a dialogue with state officials and called for press freedom. In an effort to dispel the impression that their mourning activities had turned into a riot, student leaders stressed that their goals would be achieved by nonviolent means. On April 28, the Autonomous Students' Union of Beijing Universities, an unofficial association, was founded.

On May 3, 100 Beijing journalists held a meeting supporting the students and criticizing press censorship. The following day a huge procession of students, journalists, and workers marched to Tiananmen Square, an event that was reported by the Chinese press. In a speech to representatives from the Asian Development Bank, Zhao Ziyang, general secretary of the Chinese Communist party and a prominent reformer, declared that China was stable and that the students' just demands should be met, thus supporting those who argued that the student movement should be seen as patriotic.[16]

On May 12, student leaders announced a hunger strike, and on May 13, a Student Hunger Striker's Association was established. Two days later Mikhail Gorbachev arrived in Beijing accompanied by a huge entourage of world journalists and television reporters. By that time tens of thousands of Beijing residents were demonstrating in support of the hunger strikers.

On the following day, at a meeting in his home, Deng is reported to have proposed the implementation of martial law. At this point Zhao is said to have stated that he could not continue as general secretary; but his resignation was not accepted. The All-China Federation of Trade Unions donated 100,000 yuan to the students on May 18, as the official media freely reported the growing demonstrations in Beijing and other parts of China. An inconclusive and acrimonious meeting between Li Peng and student leaders, including Wu'er Kaixi and Wang Dan, was televised on the eighteenth.

On May 19, students announced the end of the hunger strike. At a midnight meeting called by the Central Committee, it was agreed that martial law would go into effect on May 20. Once martial law was declared, troops were ordered into the city, but residents threw up roadblocks in an attempt to obstruct the soldiers. The crisis heightened as workers at the Shoudu Iron and Steel Works went on strike. The following day, in an open letter, students demanded that Deng Xiaoping and Li Peng resign.

By May 25, the demonstrations were beginning to wane. Wu'er Kaixi and Wang Dan announced that the protests would end on May 30, but on May 28 a group of hard-line, radical students decided to remain in the square until June 20, when the Standing Committee of the National People's Congress was to meet. By now most of the students in the square were from the provinces, for many Beijing residents had returned to their campuses or homes. At this point (May 29–30) the Goddess of Democracy statue was erected in the square as it became increasingly clear to everyone that a power struggle was going on among top party leaders; one faction, represented by Wan Li, announced support for martial law but noted that the student movement was patriotic, while the other faction, led by Li Peng, declared that "people in the leadership" had created confusion. On May 31 and June 1, large crowds returned to the square. On June 2, soldiers marched to areas near Tiananmen, and again Beijing residents attempted to prevent their deployment. At 6:30 P.M. on June 3, an emergency notice was issued informing residents not to go into the streets.

On the night of June 3 and in the early morning of June 4, tanks, armored cars, and troop carriers entered the city center. As the soldiers advanced, thousands of people were injured and killed. Troops encircled the square, and in the early hours of June 4, students at the Monument to Revolutionary Heroes were escorted from Tiananmen after a truce was negotiated between the demonstrators and army commanders. There was heavy loss of life along the avenues and alleys leading into the square and in the Muxidi district of Beijing. At the time of the massacre the Chinese Red Cross estimated the number of dead at 2,600; later, in August, Amnesty International gave a figure of "at least" 1,000 dead (1989:1).

How are the histories and memories of June 4, 1989, being constructed? How have the dead been remembered? Official versions in the form of reports, media broadcasts, books, and commemorations of the army dead were quickly produced. A report by Chen Xitong (1989), the mayor of Beijing, to the National People's Congress is perhaps the most complete statement of the government's position.[17] In this book-length study, published by the New China News Agency on July 6, Chen characterizes the demonstrations as a "counter-revolutionary rebellion" instigated and fueled by "a tiny handful of people" aided by hostile forces outside China. Zhao Ziyang, he argues, committed a serious mistake in supporting the demonstrators, thereby encouraging the turmoil. While upholding the patriotism of the students, Chen argues that a handful of people used the hunger strikers as "hostages" to blackmail the government. He reaffirms the integrity and honor of the army and blames the Workers' Autonomous Federation, in particular, for inciting Beijing residents to attack the soldiers. He puts the death toll of soldiers, police, and public security officers at "several dozens" and claims that 6,000 were injured. Chen reports that more than 3,000 civilians were wounded in the operation and that 200, including 36 students, died.

Part of Chen's report is devoted to a detailed chronicle of events in the square on the morning of June 4. According to his account, troops reached Tiananmen at 1:30 A.M., and by 5:00 A.M. students were leaving the square. "During the whole operation no one," he maintains, "including the students who refused but were forced to leave died." The square, he notes, was finally "returned to the people" on the morning of June 4. Chen reiterates Deng's four cardinal principles (uphold the socialist road, the dictatorship of the proletariat, the leadership of the Communist party, and Marxism-Leninism–Mao Zedong Thought) and charges that the rebellion was instigated by the forces of bourgeois liberalization and capitalism.

Throughout the report three themes are particularly stressed: only a "tiny handful" of intellectuals and workers fomented the rebellion, the square was not the site of a bloodbath, and soldiers ("soldier-martyrs") were killed in putting down the rebellion. Repeatedly Chen separates the vast majority of student demonstrators from the "small group of troublemakers" (black hands, hooligans, counterrevolutionaries) who took advantage of the student protests.

In contrast to this master narrative, unofficial versions have been transmitted through smuggled letters, clandestine interviews, speeches given outside China,

reports published in émigré journals, and commemorative ceremonies and performances marking the anniversary of the massacre in Hong Kong, Europe, and the
United States.[18] The accounts of those who participated in the protests stress
the just cause of the demonstrators, portraying them as the real inheritors of
the patriotic student movements of an earlier era (on this point see Wasserstrom
1990). They highlight the wide support for the protests among Beijing's population and express outrage at the obduracy and harshness of the leadership. In
many accounts, official corruption is a major theme. The hunger strike and the
meetings between student and government officials take center stage in these reports. Whereas official narratives provide details of time and place, oppositional
accounts tend to emphasize matters of principle.

What are the mechanisms through which official and unofficial narratives of
June 4 are being created? After a rather sluggish start, the cultural production
apparatus of the party began to pump out its version of events. The dissemination
of these accounts followed well-rehearsed lines of communication between leaders
and "the masses." The usual channels—print media, radio, television—were utilized as media personnel were brought into line or removed from their positions.
Later, political study groups were reinstated on a compulsory basis. Much was
made of reclaiming the sacred space of the square "in the name of the people."

Television coverage focused on the "hooligans" who had been arrested and, for
a brief moment, a woman who had turned in her own brother (a student leader)
to the authorities. As early as the morning of June 4, violent scenes of attacks
on military personnel with accompanying texts that stressed the army's ability to
quell disorder (luan) were being broadcast (see, e.g., Foreign Broadcast Information Service (FBIS)-CHI-89-106, June 5, 1989, p. 84). Beijing Television Service
recounted incidents in which soldiers were murdered and burned by "ruffians."
The report eulogized the soldiers: "Their heroic acts and glorious exploits have
won fervent praise and strong support from the masses of students and citizens.
They are worthy to be called soldiers who are sons and brothers of the people
under the leadership of the party and worthy to be called the staunch pillars and
iron wall of our socialist People's Republic of China" (FBIS-CHI-89-106, June 5,
1989, pp. 88–90).

Gruesome pictures of dead soldiers were prominent in many official representations of the "turmoil," as were televised meetings between mourning relatives
and leading political figures.[19] On June 9, Beijing Television Service reported that
Deng Xiaoping, Yang Shangkun, Li Peng, and other leaders met with a group of
PLA officers who had enforced martial law in the capital. At this meeting Deng expressed his condolences to military and security forces and asked for a moment of
silent tribute for their fallen comrades. And on June 18, Beijing Television Service
reported that Yang Shangkun, representing Deng, had again met with the families of soldier-martyrs whose individual names were announced as each family
member was introduced. The report concluded by informing the audience: "The

martyrs' families thanked the party, the PLA, and the people for bringing up and educating the martyrs, saying that because their children died for the motherland they died gloriously for the right cause" (FBIS-CHI-89-116, June 19, 1989, p. 39– 40). In constructing these soldier heroes, officials were attempting to salvage a badly tarnished image of the army as servants of the masses. This campaign portrays the army, guided by the party, as saviors of society from the abyss of chaos.

The equation between the demonstrations and social chaos that officials emphasized at every turn has been accepted by many Chinese, especially in rural areas. Other people, notably in Beijing and other major cities, are openly skeptical of this official account. It may well transpire that the process of willful forgetting serves the present leadership's interests better than a fully fashioned campaign of remembrance. By January 1991, Yuan Mu, a leading spokesman for the government, was reported to have said on Chinese television that he hoped people would gradually forget the "June 4 disturbance" (see New York Times, January 8, 1991, p. 4).

How do observers, mostly ordinary people, and the participants themselves counter this forgetting? How do they remember the spring of 1989? There are many obstacles to the construction of counterhistories of the June 4 massacre, including official intimidation, imprisonment, torture, and execution. The dissident movement is dispirited and dispersed, with no recognized (and recognizable) leadership. Although much has been made of the fatalities on both sides, the civilian dead are anonymous. Significantly, no list of named dead has been published by either side.[20] The dissident movement itself has not singled out any civilian casualties for special recognition or honor. This "forgetting" reminds us that there is no simple process of transformation by which personal memories are shared and shared memories converted into alternative histories.

Chinese state authorities have politicized mourning and death to such an extent that they seem able to deny both when it is in their interests to do so.[21] Writing about the treatment of the dead in the Soviet Union, Christopher Binns (1980) points to a revolutionary penchant for heroic death. "In Belorussia," he notes, "in just five years 6,000 memorials and obelisks . . . thirty-eight parks and 600 gardens in memory of the dead of the second world war were constructed" (1980:180). Binns accounts for this "excessive" remembrance by arguing that these memorials encourage patriotism, but more importantly, he maintains, they celebrate the transcendence of death by immortal deeds. In societies where belief in an afterlife must be refuted, such memorials give people hope that, as an inscription in Leningrad's Piskarev cemetery phrases it: "No one is forgotten and nothing is forgotten" (see Binns 1980:180, n.14). In fact, many are forgotten, especially those deaths for which the state itself is responsible.

During the Cultural Revolution, people were sometimes forbidden or, out of fear or ambition, chose not to mourn victims of the terror. Beginning in 1978, however, and continuing until 1981, when Deng Xiaoping had consolidated his position, a limited and officially condoned mourning became possible. There were a few highly visible memorial services for victims of state-inspired violence, including Liu Shaoqi (see *Renmin ribao* [People's Daily], May 15, 1980, and May 18, 1980; Whyte 1988) and Zhang Zhixin, one of the most famous execution cases during the Cultural Revolution (see Liu Binyan 1990:147–49; Thurston 1987:36). There were also quiet and often more private observances: when I visited a Buddhist temple in Shanghai in 1986, I was told that many masses, paid for by "foreign relatives," were being performed on behalf of Cultural Revolution dead.

More calculated acts of defiance took place as well. At the Fourth Congress of Writers and Artists in 1979, the names of over a hundred writers who died during the Cultural Revolution were read out (see Liu Binyan 1990:140–41; Thurston 1987:133). Liu Binyan concluded his speech at the congress in these words: "The article I just published is enough to label me 'rightist'; if I write a hundred articles like that, it will be nothing but a 'rightist' label over and over again. So why not go on writing?" His audience laughed (Liu 1990:140).

As Liu Binyan notes in the same book, however, the remembrance, the mourning, the analysis of what had gone wrong, and the attribution of guilt remained frustratingly unfinished. Liu argues that officially sponsored investigations of "criminals of the Cultural Revolution" were never actively pursued, and after 1981 the leadership and the party pulled back from discussions of the "ten years of great disaster." According to Liu: "It was established that the Gang of Four was counterrevolutionary, but Mao, who started the Cultural Revolution, was not touched. The chaos had been created by leaders of the Central Committee in the first place, many of them had been in seats of power during the Cultural Revolution, and now they were given credit for ending it and were as firmly installed as ever" (Liu 1990:149, 215). It appears that forgetting was better and certainly less dangerous, at least for some, than remembering.

In constructing their official account of the spring of 1989, party leaders created individual martyrs (heroes in the communist tradition of model worker, soldier, peasant) with whom they presumably believed ordinary people could identify. Accompanying this positive impulse was a negative one: ordinary people were not allowed to mourn those whom the ruling elite sought to forget. In such circumstances the mourning of victims and the memories of the events that produced their deaths must go underground. State authorities fear that public commemorations will continue to be hijacked by the citizenry for the expression of unapproved memories, grievances, and protests.

Wishing to take no chances with further subversions of official commemorations, the Central Committee of the Chinese Communist party declared (as reported in the *Beijing Evening News* and by Reuters on October 11, 1991) that "fancy funerals" for leaders henceforth were banned. According to the Reuters report, "when senior officials of the [Communist] Party and state die, their funerals must follow the principle of simplicity." Further, it was decreed that dead leaders would be cremated and their ashes buried, no tombs were to be built, and, in an apparent reference to Zhou Enlai, no ashes could be scattered. Finally, family members were warned that they were not to interfere in the writing of official biographies. Clearly, China's aging leaders are not blind to the powerful and uncontrollable political mix that mourning, commemoration, and protest are capable of producing, as they themselves prepare to leave the political stage once and for all.

As yet we do not have a clear sense of how ordinary people remember the Cultural Revolution or June 4. Perhaps no single memory community (see Burke 1989:103), no single secret or oppositional history, crosscuts the sectional, class, status, and regional cleavages that exist in China. Some have argued that the party's ability to transform people into nonpersons has so divided Chinese society into mistrustful, fearful camps of alienated but complicit individuals that any form of transcendence is nearly impossible to achieve (see, e.g., Madsen 1990; Thurston 1990; Weller 1993:chapter 12). Maoist attempts to create "blank pages" on which to write a new society, as well as the widely shared dismissal of traditional culture, have made it especially difficult to create a meaningful and unifying medium for sharing unapproved memories and hidden histories. There is, however, a highly successful and perhaps ironic precedent for such sharing.

In China's first nationwide mobilization (the Land Reform Campaign of 1950–52), the party, through its cadres and revolutionary work teams, created a public structure for remembrance that was to be a core element in all future movements. To "speak bitterness," to recount out loud and in public personal experiences of oppression, was a liberating experience for China's rural villagers and urban workers. Like the laments of village mourners, "speaking bitterness" was at once highly controlled and yet emotional, as memories of suffering and loss were both released and deepened.

Like many other nation-states, the People's Republic of China was formed by a process of remembering and forgetting (see Connerton 1989:14–15). In providing for the expression of heretofore private memories and hidden histories, party cadres created in every village and workplace throughout China an approved history of oppression and a powerful weapon of class struggle. This public remembering turned "my past" into "our past" (see chapter 5, this volume), but it did so through a process of violent exclusion in which "speaking bitterness" became intimately intertwined with the exercise of class vengeance. Because of the violence of the revolution, Richard Madsen explains, China's social landscape was littered not only with approved memories of the past but also "with dangerous memories of arbitrary injuries endured and inflicted" (1990:187).

The Cultural Revolution contributed mightily to this littered landscape and, as Arthur Kleinman writes, produced a delegitimation crisis; millions of people were forced to carry their pain and suffering in silence (1986:123, 130). The memories of the "ghosts" of China's shared violence and state-sponsored vengeance have yet to be laid to rest. These memories, like those of the betrayed son Schwarcz describes in chapter 3, have not yet found a meaningful history within which they can be articulated, understood, and, like the the memories of the village martyrs memorialized in rural *jiao* performances, managed by being publicly remembered.

———— Notes ————

1. The discussion is necessarily more speculative because little detailed ethnographic work has been done on mourning rites in the People's Republic of China.

2. Geremie Barme and Linda Jaiven begin their introduction to *New Ghosts, Old Dreams: Chinese Rebel Voices* (1992) with a quote from Lu Xun, one of China's great literary figures. Lu Xun wrote the following words after hearing of the execution of five young writers in 1931: "I can but stand by, looking on as friends become new ghosts, I seek an angry poem from among the swords." Barme and Jaiven add: "In early June 1989, at least a thousand . . . 'new ghosts' were created" (1992:xv).

3. It is indeed ironic to refer to "well-documented obliteration." It is perhaps a special characteristic of state socialism that the lives of those the state seeks to annihilate—to airbrush from history and existence—leave a paper trail that belies their obliteration. Thurston and others (see especially Dittmer 1981) rely on interviews, official records, and the writings of family members to retrace Liu's last months.

4. For examples of official and unofficial treatments of the period of the Great Leap Forward and the Great Leap Famine, see Bernstein (1984) and Goldman (1981:43–60).

5. On resistance in capitalist and colonial societies, see, for example, Colburn (1989a); Foucault (1978, 1982); Ong (1987); and Scott (1977, 1985, 1989, 1990). For discussion of resistance under state socialism, see, for example, Colburn (1989b); Rev (1987); and Sabel and Stark (1982). For discussion of resistance in China after 1949, see, for example, Anagnost (1989); Cheater (1991); Esherick and Wasserstrom (1990); Rofel (1989); M. Yang (1988); and Zweig (1989b).

6. The state's monopoly, of course, is never total. In recent years there has been much discussion of the degree to which state socialist regimes have achieved control over the public and private spheres (for China, see, e.g., Shue 1988; Siu 1989a, 1989b). Summarizing recent work on Eastern Europe, Verdery argues that inherent contradictions in state socialism compromise the state's capacity to control the lives of its citizen-subjects (1991b; see also Burawoy and Lukacs 1992; Gross 1988; Haraszti 1979; Kligman 1988:7–9; Rev 1987).

7. As Nathan (1989) points out, even in post-Mao China many intellectuals continue to look for reform from above. In this regard, the extensive Chinese literature on "neoauthoritarianism" is interesting (see, e.g., three special issues of *Chinese Sociology and Anthropology*, 1991; see also the *Christian Science Monitor*, May 15, 1990, p. 5; *Far Eastern Economic Review*, March 9, 1989, p. 12).

8. For discussion of the "spoiler state," see Gross (1988) and Verdery (1991b). Verdery describes the internal logic of a "spoiler state": "Because a social actor's capacity to allocate resources is relative to the resources held by other actors, power at the center will be enhanced to the extent that the resources of other actors are incapacitated and other foci of production prevented from posing an alternative to the central monopoly on goods" (1991b:421). For discussion of civil society in Eastern Europe, see Gellner (1991) and Kligman (1990). For a fascinating contrast to Maoist views of the past and of "traditional-peasant" culture, see Kligman (1988) on Romania. Kligman writes that in Romania, "rights to the past are critical to territorial claims by the state . . . [and] such rights are, at least in part, 'legitimated by the historical fidelity' of the peasant" (1988:257). There are, of course, interested constructions of "the peasant," but the link between legitimacy and continuities with the past is strikingly different from the Maoists' more thoroughgoing rejection of "tradition."

9. On dissimulation, see also Strauss (1952); for criticism of Strauss, see Zagorin (1990:9–10).

10. See Scott (1990) for discussion of public and hidden transcripts.

11. On "social memory," see Benjamin (1969); Bodnar (1991); Burke (1989); Casey (1984); Connerton (1989:6–40); Halbwachs (1980:52); Hill (1988); Le Goff (1992); and Rappaport (1990).

12. There is considerable evidence for the widespread use of funeral laments in Guangdong (see, e.g., E. Anderson 1975; Blake 1978; Chang 1969; E. Johnson 1988; Watson 1982) and in other areas of China (see, e.g., de Groot 1892[I]:10–11, 1892[II]:801; Ebrey 1991:83n; Gamble 1963:253; Lin 1947:104, 130).

13. For accounts of Zhou's mourning, see Cheater (1991:72–78); Liu Binyan (1990:124–25); Thurston (1987); Wakeman (1988:260); and Yue and Wakeman (1985:339–48). The difference between the treatment of the remains of Zhou Enlai and those of Mao Zedong is interesting. Zhou's

body was cremated and his ashes scattered. Mao's body was embalmed and placed in a specially built memorial hall near the Monument for Revolutionary Heroes in Tiananmen Square (see Wagner 1992; Wakeman 1988).

14. For a chronology of the 1989 demonstrations beginning in April and ending on June 4, I rely on Landsberg in Saich (1990), Yi and Thompson (1989), and Yu and Harrison (1990) unless specified otherwise.

15. See, for example, Manion in Oksenberg, Sullivan, and Lambert (1990); Niming (1990); and Chong (1990).

16. During this period and continuing until June 4 there were demonstrations in other Chinese cities as well. For accounts of events outside Beijing, see *Australian Journal of Chinese Affairs* no. 24, 1990.

17. For officially sanctioned eyewitness accounts, see, for example, *Beijing Ribao,* June 10, 1989; and Beijing Television Service Series on the Tiananmen Incident 24 June 1989, FBIS-CHI-89-142, July 26, 1989, pp. 8–11.

18. For unofficial accounts, see Barme and Jaiven (1992); Oksenberg, Sullivan, and Lambert (1990); Yi and Thompson (1989); and Yu and Harrison (1990).

19. For an English-language representation, see *The Beijing Riot: A Photo Record,* New Star Publishers, 1989.

20. A partial list of the dead and imprisoned has been published by the United States–based human rights group, Asia Watch.

21. For a description of the clash over what constitutes proper mortuary rites in present-day China and the personal distress that such a clash may produce, see Jankowiak (1988:4–9).

5

From Memory to History
The Events of November 17 Dis/membered

ANDREW LASS

"History" is something we do to the collective memories of the civilization, just as memoirs and autobiography are something we do to our own memories. The historian processes the past and attempts to definitively master its dangerous forces. Such acts of making memory into history are interesting in themselves. . . . The past shows its true dominion when it breaks into the present, at precisely those moments before we can control it with the fixed ceremonies that constitute a "history."
    —Stephen Owen, *Remembrances: The Experience of the Past in Classical Chinese Literature*

What is at stake is not only the distance that shelters the author of autobiography from his experience but the possible convergence of aesthetics and of history.
    —Paul de Man, *Autobiography As De-Facement*

I

For once it is entirely appropriate to start with myself.

Beyond the now fashionable insistence that anthropologists account for their place within the fieldwork experience (one is already implicated in that "other" reality one seeks to define), there is the simple fact that for me the "events of November 1989" in Czechoslovakia meant a very dramatic turn in my life. A few months later, on March 14, 1990, I landed in Prague to find many friends and their families waiting for me at the Ruzyně airport. I had returned from "exile" in my native United States (the America I had been born in and which I had made, once again, my home) to the city where I had grown up.

For 17 years I had lived with my memories of Prague and of my place in it, carefully retracing the steps of a boy who had lived the most formative years of his life in this mysterious city, in a country that never ceased to remind him that he was "that American." I had given my memories a Proustian significance, for

I had both re/constituted a narrative space in which I could, at whim, choose to "take a walk" and developed an obsessive curiosity about the very experience itself. In contrast to many Czech émigrés, for whom exile seemed to reinforce the value of "being Czech"—which so often meant a nostalgia that hinged as much on an identification with a discourse on Czech history and culture as it did on personal recollections—my interests were consciously split between these two kinds of historicities.

If my own life had historical depth, it was clearly because I had grown up in a place and time that seemed to resonate with history every step of the way—but the actual history and culture were never "mine." On the contrary, I could never understand the obsession that appeared to imbue the "natives'" concern with history and the role that elite culture played in it. To me it seemed to be so provincial. But then again, did not "they" feel the contingencies of their lives to be fully implicated in the life of "their" nation, something I could neither feel nor claim? And if nations constituted themselves in part by casting their histories, often invented for that purpose, as tradition, how (or is it "why?") exactly was the past—in the singularity of the events and the universality of their relevance—transcribed into the particularity of individual lives, into the constitution of their identity? What is the relationship between memory and history?

Recent theories of national awareness have offered new and important insights into the mechanisms that create a particular kind of individual identity, one that is typically characterized by a heightened historical consciousness. Benedict Anderson's work (1983) has explained the role of the printing press in creating the "imagined community of nation-ness" and helped us understand why linguistic and cultural literacy became an essential component of citizenship in which, to borrow from Walter Benjamin (1969), the art of mechanical reproduction has resulted not only in the mechanical reproduction of art but in the mechanical reproduction of people. In a similar vein, Ernest Gellner (1983)—for whom nationalism is a function of industrial society—has argued quite persuasively that the egalitarian principles underlying modern ideologies are, like the high social mobility of industrial society's citizens, a necessary precondition of an economic system that thrives on growth and requires a large number of mutually interchangeable individuals. Hence the idea of universal access to education and the state's centrally administered education system, which is based on and therefore reinforces cultural and linguistic uniformity.

More recently, Paul Connerton (1989) has emphasized the importance of repetition in the establishment of history and tradition. Whether through commemorative celebrations or the bodily habits of everyday life, our identities as well as our conceptual frameworks derive from the fact that they are never just "for the first time." The cumulative effect of repetition is behind our cultural habits. Social memory is always already fully a part of how we are.[1]

History and culture, both stories and commodities, are, through the institutionalized means of dissemination, re/presented as components of everyday life with the added distinction of the past tense. And so, to cross Prague's Charles Bridge through the act of recollection is to pass statues that both commemorate and illustrate significant tales of yesteryear. The historical monuments, like personal names, tie the past to a place and therefore to the person who moves through it as he moves through his life. From the very beginning, the historical individual's biography has historical significance.

It was not at all surprising, therefore, to find that so many of the symbolic acts that maintained oppositional histories took place in public spaces—as if these locations could have a memory of their own. Thus Wenceslas Square in Prague became the staging ground for all official parades of the last 40 years. At its top stands an equestrian statue of the patron saint of Bohemia. It was on the steps leading up to the statue that the student Jan Palach torched himself to protest the Soviet-led invasion of 1968. He became the martyr of the opposition, and it was on the twentieth anniversary of his death in January 1989 that Václav Havel was taken into custody and to his last imprisonment. It was here as well that so many of the November events of that year were staged, and it was on those steps that presidents George Bush and Václav Havel laid wreaths to commemorate the "velvet revolution" on November 17, 1990. The statue has retained its significance as an "active" monument as well as a tourist attraction. And now, thanks to the media blitz, its image, like that of the Berlin Wall or the towers of the Kremlin, is as familiar as that of the Eiffel Tower.

To oppose the status quo in a public place, then, is to invoke history and therefore to engage, from the very beginning, in rewriting it. The logic is that of history as discursive practice: as the public spontaneously tore down and replaced the official monuments of communism (the images of Lenin and Gottwald were quickly swapped for those of Masaryk and Havel), the secret police immediately started to burn and shred their secret documents—in secret, of course.[2] Evidently, these Czechs took their history personally and dealt with its concretizations first.

In an effort to understand the problem of history and historical consciousness, we have gained much insight on how modern society produces historically aware individuals—that is, individuals who may perceive themselves as agents of history. We also know more about the importance that history, as a type of discourse, plays in a modern society's self-conception. In brief, we can easily imagine how the historical event becomes an individual's memory or see a logical connection between social organization and individual action. But what of these individuals as the actors of history? Certainly, as agents of change their actions will also be guided by the force of habit; the new order that the "velvet revolution" advocates is, after all, informed by the old order from which the opposition first arose. In Czechoslovakia, within months the events of change seemed to lose some of their initial significance as people noticed that the new structures resembled the old ones. And so not only does the past affect the making of the present, but also the memory of the past casts a dark shadow on the significance of change.

Against this tide there is another one at work. New history is written. Events that appeared contingent as they took place must now become necessary as they take on a significance in the new society's historical emergence. The question, then, is not only "how will society remember its actions?" but also, "how will it make of individuals' experiences, society's history?" In short, what is involved on the way from memory to history? As the monuments are torn down and official histories discredited, the unofficial histories are brought to life and the process of rewriting is begun. Eastern Europe turns to the "invention of tradition" once more.

II

In his short and incisive study *The Reality of the Historical Past,* Paul Ricoeur (1984:1) notes that "the recourse to documents marks the dividing line between history and fiction." The historian is indebted to the past, constrained by "what once was," and the idea that the document is actually a trace through which the past can be recovered gives this constraint objective form. "Inasmuch as it [the trace] is *left* by the *past,* it *stands for* the past, it 'represents' the past, not in the sense that the past would appear itself in the mind (*Vorstellung*) but in the sense that the trace takes the place of (*Vertretung*) the past, absent from historical discourse" (Ricoeur 1984:2).[3]

The past is known indirectly. This kind of referentiality distinguishes historical knowledge from any other (according to Ricoeur's view at least) and, paradoxically, provides both the grounds for its objectivity and the realization of its inexhaustibility: the past, as we know it, is always open to corrections. Yet the history of historical discourse reveals a complex genealogy, and the separation between reality and fiction can be seen as one of its ambiguous outcomes. The very fact that the historical trace has on so many occasions been deliberately forged illustrates both the fictitiousness of history and the objectivity of historical reality as a cultural construct.

On the other hand, the effectiveness of historical novels depends on there being already in place a distinction between history and fiction: they are made "believable" by staging the imaginary world with references to an already accepted, "real" historical world. This is what Roland Barthes (1986) calls the "reality effect." Even a superficial look at the rise of historical discourse throughout the nineteenth century reveals that while history, as the scientific investigation of the past, develops as a discipline (with all that this term implies), its impact is always poetically mediated. The role of the arts in representing historical realities is all pervasive, as is the value placed on art as the historical expression of the national ethos. Monuments to famous poets later become the focal points of political demonstrations. For example, the statue of the Czech romantic poet K. H. Mácha in the Petřín gardens in Prague was the meeting place for the expression of antigovernment sentiments throughout the 1960s. As political in their alleged reference as they may be, historical monuments are, after all, commissioned as works of art.

The point is that, at least in the case of Czechoslovakia (though I firmly believe this to be the case to some degree in other places), historical change often speaks with poetic license. The political "thaw" that resulted in the Prague Spring of 1968 was experienced first and foremost as a cultural revival: I have often heard it said that all those Russian tanks came to close down the Writers' Union (as fiction, this certainly makes for interesting history). And it was, once again, the arts, and artists, writers and journalists, who kept the opposition alive—both at home and in exile—throughout the last 20 years.[4]

This interrelationship between the political and the aesthetic in historical consciousness that is discernible at the level of social practice—and I shall return to this relationship at the end—finds its counterpart in the rhetorical aspects of historiography itself.[5] Thus, as Ricoeur points out, if historians are indebted to the past (and limited by the existence of documents), they are equally constrained by the figures of speech (metaphor, synecdoche, metonymy, irony) from which they will construct the narrative structure most suitable to "represent" the past. And as Hayden White has pointed out, there is no escape from this tropics of historical discourse, "for it is by figuration that the historian virtually constitutes the subject of his discourse" (1982:106). The historical imagination, constrained by the documents that aim to "speak up" for the past, provides us with a plot, an image of the past that is representational by definition (iconic) yet lacks an original model. It remains an interpretation.

III

I have offered this rather condensed reminder of some of the debates that have focused on the indeterminate nature of historical discourse in order to provide a backdrop to the more specific problem with which I began. The historical trace and the gateway to the past that it maintains have emerged from my discussion as the guarantors of history's veracity. And the very possibility of forgery, as well as the readiness with which objects of historical significance are destroyed at times of political upheaval, only confirms that historical factuality is a foundational feature of historical consciousness. (The importance placed on the science of paleography further emphasizes this point.) Yet these examples also foreground the extent to which facts themselves are culturally constituted and socially implicated. This is particularly so in the case of history's most valued source, the eyewitness. Methodological concerns regarding the "objectivity" of the personal account notwithstanding, an individual's narration is valued because it authenticates what it provides: the what and how of past events. The witness's eye is also the eye of memory.

As we have seen, Ricoeur distinguishes between presenting (*Vorstellung*) and representing (*Vertretung*) and—in the latter sense—speaks of the "taking-the-place-of" character of the historical trace. "It characterizes the *indirect* reference specific to knowledge through traces and distinguishes from any other the referential mode of the history of the past" (Ricoeur 1984:2). Thus, when later on he quotes Paul Collingwood's "All history is the re-enactment of past thought in the historian's own mind" (1984:8), Ricoeur immediately issues a warning: "Re-enactment does not consist in reliving but in rethinking, and rethinking already contains the critical moment that forces us to take the detour by way of the historical imagination" (1984:8).

The sense that the past recollected has a distinct quality of being relived is lost to history. The presence of the past—this experience—is retained only as fact that corroborates the content, or the actual events from which the stories of history are spun. The role of the eyewitness is, then, a fundamentally ambiguous one, privileged and yet partial. Something must happen to my recollections in order for them to be history's thoughts. What makes history thinkable? Is it the distance that "pastness" implies? Or, on the contrary, is it the distancing act of thinkability that assures the past its pastness as something that is rethought rather than re-lived, i.e., that is remembered rather than recollected? The distinction between the two is Hegel's.[6] Recollection (*Erinnerung*) hands its content over to remembrance (*Gedächtnis*)—a content on which the latter depends—only to be defaced in the process. In this sense, then, recollection is a personalized act that involves the presence of the past. Yet the recollected may be "placed in memory" only as a meaningless string of names, faceless and available to all to call upon and repeat as fact, like a poem that we "know by heart" but which need not mean anything at all in order that it may be remembered. In the act of committing violence upon recollection, memory rescues thought from the self.

I have chosen the term *violence* in order to bring attention to the experiential side of the construction of distance that accompanies the transformation of memory into history.[7] As Emmanuel Levinas suggests, "violence does not consist so much in injuring and annihilating persons as in interrupting their continuity, making them play roles in which they no longer recognize themselves, making them betray not only commitments but their own substance" (1969:2).

Something happened to me as I prepared for my "return" trip to Prague. A few days before I was to land there, I received a phone call from an acquaintance at the *New York Times*. She wanted to join in on this return, to follow me around and write an article about this dramatic event. "I wouldn't interfere, I promise. If you could, occasionally, just sit down with me and explain what was going on in your head, I would just be like a fly on the wall." The events in Prague had transformed the value of my story: virtually overnight my life took on a historically recognized significance, and now it looked as if it was to go public.

The phone call left me angry. Did this mean the end of the return as planned? In the weeks before my departure, the intensity of my memories had already begun to wane. As if overshadowed by the anticipation of the reality they would have to confront, memories were becoming impossible to recall. And now, I wrote in my journal, did I wish "to have my memories turned into commodities? . . . Won't having to articulate them be tantamount to not having them at all?" What blindness of insight would protect me in the end? What happens to memories when they go on public display? Why must I confront the "narrative truth," the "true" story of history—as if we hadn't all been forced to embellish our lives with lies and find safety and complacency in their "feel" once we had made them fit? Is the "truth" of investigative reporting an act of disrobing that makes hiding, pushing the "back stage" even farther back, a necessity—a condition of the new lie whose sharpness is as disquieting as that of the invasive pen or the journalist's eye?[8]

IV

Barely had I landed in Prague before I was listening to my friends' "life histories." Was the shoe on the other foot? I was never sure, for while I was conscious of influencing their narration with questions that were clearly informed by my professional interests, they were just as eager to tell me their stories. My desire to capture the ethnographic nitty-gritty of history as experience was matched by their desire to confess it. The often encountered resistance reported by oral historians ("the interviewee hesitates and is silent, protests that there is nothing to relate which the interviewer does not already know") was missing (Connerton 1989:19). If preserving the feeling of nostalgia was most on my mind and made me resist letting go of my recollections, for my friends, to the contrary, the very act of reminiscing meant the possibility of explaining historically significant events in terms of their own "whereabouts."[9]

What follows is an excerpt from a lengthy conversation that took place in Prague on March 14, 1990—within hours of my arrival—with my long-lost friend Kateřina and her husband, Jiří.

> J: Some nonsense about "so what don't you like here?" and then they ask you "so why don't you do something about it"? There's really no answer to that or there wasn't any answer. This conversation with our friends from France, they sat here around the table, got me thinking that I'll have to start doing something. Just that passivity which we all let ourselves be manipulated into and that suited the leadership here so much, that was not enough. . . Virtually everyone here was passive, except for a few dissidents whose names you probably know by now the way we do . . . and it is a coincidence that we had decided then (but a lot of people did) that somehow the "time was right" (even if it's a cliché) after that October thing when the celebrations of the republic or whatever took place.[10]
>
> Well, on Wenceslaus Square there was a crowd of people and they got mildly beaten up and nothing happened really and the Voice of America, which we were listening to, was broadcasting something from it, from the demonstration, and you could hear someone calling

"where is everybody?" and suddenly I felt very much addressed by this. Because I was at our summer place, well sort of . . . passively and then three days later a bunch of friends, we met here and we all in unison said "okay, but next time not without us." Coincidentally, "next time" was the march on November seventeenth for the Opletal thing.[11] So we went with Kateřina, it turned out to be the decisive action and, perhaps because the time had ripened, there were incredible amounts of people there. The communist organizers had underestimated this, after all it had been an officially organized march to honor the memory of . . .

AL: Do you think it could have played a role that others had heard the radio broadcast?

J to K: Kateřina, do you think that many people were affected when they broadcasted on Voice of America that October, how should I put it, when on Můstek at the demonstration someone called out "where is everybody?" Do you remember it? When they said there were five hundred people there or five thousand people, I don't recall what number they quoted, and you could hear the "where is everybody, where is everybody?" Do you remember it or am I the only one to remember it? Maybe it wasn't so important!

K: On the contrary, that was another time. That was when there was that trial, but I can't remember with whom, perhaps with Havel or with someone, and somebody there had already said that he expected many more people there and that no one was there . . .

J: Well, then you had it from somewhere else, I heard it here . . .

K: But I'll tell you this much, on the twenty-eighth of October we were at our summer place and we left for there with the knowledge that some demonstration and a massacre are going to take place and basically we had a bad conscience that we should have already been there but because we had to be at our summer place, we had some repairs arranged ahead of time and really . . .

J: Oh, bull we had to . . .

K: Well, we left, but from hour to hour, because we knew that the demonstration was supposed to be at three o'clock, so I, as I was weeding, was saying "so now it probably began, what does it look like, and those poor souls. . ." and, basically, what later happened on the seventeenth we thought would happen on the twenty-eighth. And in the evening we followed and turned on [the radio] and we were very disappointed and disillusioned that no one, that there were not that many people there.

J: That suddenly we were the totally average ones, those who were in their summer residences . . .

AL: That there were more of you who were not there?

J: Yes, exactly.

K: And also because, we told ourselves then, it can't go on like this, we have to do something, okay? This was the last thing that we didn't participate in.

J: And that evening Jan was here, if you recall, and he came with it on his own, we had agreed on it, and he said "NO! And next time I'm going."

K: All of them, for sure. Jiří's mother said, "we're going there," well all those who up until then didn't go for a variety of reasons. Because for me . . .

AL: Was it because of the habitual, systemic passivity?

K: I wouldn't say that, I didn't agree with many of the things, because for instance those who went there to get beaten up were of several groups. One was Havel's, that was okay, and then there were young people going there who evidently got a kick out of it. And people who really didn't know why they're going there and just plain went there.

J: People just went to watch!

AL: Wasn't there just a lot of show in all of it?

J: It was different on the seventeenth . . .

K [responding to my question]: No, there wasn't.

J: We didn't participate in much of it.

K: Oh yes, they did go just to look, just to look.

J: I know a brother from . . . he's the kind of kid, a typical example, runs a vegetable store or something, which is a kind of caste successful under socialism, rich, an entirely different class from us and he would go there and with his kids watch how the demonstrations were suppressed by the armed forces, which is enough of a reason for me not to go there.

K: Yes!

J: I don't know, but it was us, the "working middle classes," as we called it, basically we were missing at all those demonstrations, the large crowd was missing there until the seventeenth of November.

AL: Tell me one thing, you both said that there were more of you who agreed that you were passive and that you won't stay that way any longer. Do you think people came to that conclusion independently, or that it was because you met and spoke about it, or both, or that you had all heard the radio broadcast.

K [in reference to the radio broadcast]: Absolutely not!

J: People's anger finally hit that point. I think that something like that exists, that the stupidity of that Jakeš for instance, that they all heard that speech of his.[12]

K: And there was a video cassette to go with it.

AL: So it did play a role that something circulated here.

J: Yes, yes!

AL: What people had in common, that they all heard this cassette or what?

K: An important role was played by . . . well, Havel explains this somewhere in his memoirs. He programmatically began at a certain point to go to theaters to see his friends. And he discussed this with the other Chartists whether that was a good idea or not because those theaters were also opportunistic and continued to stage plays. Nevertheless, when he came they were friends with him and so on, and he in fact started to work on this group in a programmatic way.

And then, when they locked up Jirous . . . I don't know whether that says anything to you: Jirous is an art historian and he's weird, he is a madman and he says of himself that he's bonkers and he is nuts. Well, and then they locked up Jirous, Havel said "you should do something about this" and the actors told him then, "come on, he is such a nut, because of him we're not going to get involved, but if they locked you up, Václav!" and they said that in December and then in January they [the police] actually locked him up . . .

AL: Oh, that's when I was in Germany and there was a lot of protest. My friend organized a demonstration of actors in Berlin. They did a public reading.

K: Well, and they locked up Havel and he himself says, I don't know, I think somewhere in Lidové noviny [daily], that people began to feel bad about not coming out in his defense. So that the theater where he was, that means here "On the Balustrade" where he had been their playwright and this is where he came from, it was his tribal stage, there was a bunch of his friends there, so they started it and actually stood behind him and first wrote that letter and others started to join them, and then others and others, okay? Here you've got it all in the Lidové noviny, so if you look through it, it's all mapped out there exactly, in fact, from January how that whole last year progressed.

Several themes that are relevant to the present discussion emerge from the conversation with Jiří and Kateřina. One is that the issue of moral responsibility—the need to move away from the passive complacency and opportunism that characterized the nation and that was a central target of Havel's writings—is given as the primary motivating force that drew them into action. It places their "whereabouts" within the context of the unfolding of events that could therefore be understood— and not merely after the fact—as historically important. Part of the biographical narrative centers on this need to "find one's place" within the larger scheme of things, and it is not without interest that part of this identifying process concerns social differentiation. The passivity of those like Jiří and Kateřina, who were caught by history in their summer residences, is marked off from the vulgarity of dishonest participants ("a kind of caste successful under socialism, rich, an entirely different class from us") who went to Wenceslaus Square for the spectacle.

My wish to know more about the influence of the broadcast from Voice of America (my interest lay in pinpointing the role of mass media in the November events) resulted in a dialogue between Jiří and Kateřina. At that point memory took central stage. (Jiří: "I don't recall the number they quoted. Am I the only one to remember it? Maybe it wasn't so important!" Kateřina: "That was when there was that trial, but I can't remember with whom, perhaps with Havel. . .") The failure here, in Hegel's terms, lies with remembrance, not with recollection. It is those facts that lie outside the individual's immediate experience—the actual numbers, names, and dates, the "list of names" that comes from beyond the self—that have "slipped the mind." And yet these "absent" facts still manage to exert their pressure. If Jiří is the only one to remember it, then maybe it wasn't so important! And, in the end, oppositional history takes over. The chronology of events now has its heroes (Havel, Jirous) and references (*Lidové noviny*), and Kateřina turns to tell a story initially lived and retold by others ("well, Havel explains this somewhere in his memoirs"), which she adopts and presents with a dramatic twist as if, for a brief moment, she had been an eyewitness (Havel said "you should do something about it" . . . and the actors then told him "come on, he's such a nut . . . but if they locked you up, Václav!").

It may appear as if our examples have taken us full circle. I began with a discussion of the feelings of violence and the sense of loss that accompanied the transformation of my personal recollection into memorable facts. My friends, fully aware of themselves as historical beings, presented their "life histories" in terms of already established, historically marked events, to the point of reenacting and appropriating another person's recollection. As Paul Connerton rightly points out, oral history implies a type of narrative, a pattern of remembering, that is not characteristic of all individuals but rather of the elites familiar with this narrative form and aware of themselves as historical actors. "These writers of memoirs see their life as worth remembering . . . conceive their life retrospectively, and frequently . . . envisage it prospectively, as a narrative sequence in which they are able to integrate their individual life history with their sense of the course of an objective history" (Connerton 1989:19). Later on in our conversation, Kateřina presents herself as playing a "historic" role in the student strikes that followed the November 17 events, although the construction of the narrative—or more specifically, the extent of thematic "borrowing"—maintains an acknowledged "distance" from the elite center of action.

V

"What, in your opinion, is most misrepresented today about the events of November 17, 1989?" Havel was asked in an interview for the Czech weekly *Mladý Svět*. He replied:

> I don't find any obvious lies being told, it's more that here and there
> people are blowing their own horn and describing their roles as being
> more important than in fact they were. Once more, I'd go back to Octo-
> ber 28, 1918, which I've studied more deeply. I've read many memoirs,
> and a huge pile of books and magazines that came out during the First
> Republic. As time went by, the number of authentic eyewitnesses actu-
> ally increased, and gradually, more and more heroes of the 28th of
> October were "revealed." (Havel 1991:6)

A concern with the preservation and disclosure of the "velvet revolution" as
a historical event, and of the incidents that took place on and around November 17, 1989, in particular, was a major preoccupation of the government, the
press, and the media in general.[13] Destruction of both the public symbols and the
secret documents of the recent past was paralleled by the need to memorialize and
publicize the events even as they took place. The very act of transforming memory into history was itself part of the battle. Yesterday's photographs played their
part in today's events, as did the radio and television replays and the newspapers
that, as they fought for their own independence, began to re/present the news. On
December 29, the day the parliament struck out the "leading role of the Communist Party" from the constitution, it also established a commission for the investigation of the events of November 17 (at first infiltrated by members of the secret
police). In June, 1990, the true (or maybe just alternative) story of communism in
Czechoslovakia was told in the form of a narrated exposition in the exhibition hall
U Hybernů in Prague. Panel displays with photographs, film and video clips, and
artifacts (including the riot police helmets, shields, and clubs used in the October and November demonstrations) entertained visitors as they walked their way
from the 1948 communist takeover to the present.

But it was with the celebrations that marked the first anniversary of the November events that the making of a new history took its first critical move. I recorded
my impression of the events in my journal as follows:

> On Saturday afternoon, Nov. 17, 1990, the whole country seemed to be
> devoted to the arrival of Air Force One with president George Bush on
> board. What an ordeal. The day, for me, was spent watching the ordeal
> on TV. The pomp was akin to a medieval ritual, a procession, or better
> still, the initial visit of Captain James Cook to Hawaii (Sahlins, 1987).
> Airport–Castle–Parliament (speech)–Castle (lunch)–press conference
> held against the backdrop of Prague on Hradčanské náměstí. Then a visit
> with the aging Cardinal Tomášek—finally Wenceslaus square.
>   There the two (+ wives) sat in a bullet-proof box in front of the
> Wenceslaus monument. Havel gave an excellent speech in which he
> basically told the people that little has been accomplished as far as their
> attitudes were concerned and Bush gave a silly flowery speech in which
> God blessed Czechoslovakia. George then gave the country a replica of

the Liberty Bell which, as he explained, he would ring three times (to commemorate the victims of communism, to celebrate the people who brought in democracy, and to wish a great future for the children of this country). He then rang it four times (on this evening's TV news it was edited down to three).

The place was swarming with the White House Secret Service and mobs of people, including at the bottom of the square, the "Republicans" (*sládkovci*) who heckled and whistled and held signs OF = KSČ (Civic Forum equals the Communist Party). George then entered the crowd to do the Gorbachev-populist touching of the people thing. . . . He also promised some money and "we will not let you down and shall stand by you in the difficult years to come." With all the people waving US/ČSFR flags it all felt quite familiar. I recalled the slogans of yesteryear: "With the Soviet Union Forever (Se Sovětským Svazem na věčné časy)." I was getting depressed.

In addition to the somber ritual engagement that helped establish this date as a new "victory day" (while also securing its significance by an association with a new and opposite ally), the television that evening showed a documentary film (a BBC/Czech production) in which the viewer was introduced to the story of the Stalin monument in Prague as well as to some of the heroes of the last 20 years. Several things were striking about this film.

In the juxtaposition of a monument's history with personal memoirs, which I gather was meant to be symbolic, very little original material (photographs, film clips) was used. The narration was held together by an image of an oversized bust of Stalin on the back of a truck. We watch it drive through the streets of Prague, unable to get rid of its cargo. At the end of the movie the truck, together with Stalin, finds its place next to Soviet tanks on a train headed east, back where it came from—the Soviet Union. For the Czech viewer, at least, the theme of undisposable garbage is familiar as fiction: the film is simply alluding to a famous story, "Kam s ním?" ("How do I get rid of him?"), by the late-nineteenth-century Czech author and journalist Jan Neruda, in which the hero attempts, in vain, to get rid of his old mattress. Here, then, history is presented as fiction, its narrative structure based on a short story, its "reality effect" on the authentic materials of period films.

Recent interviews with individuals who remember the monument's history are supplemented by a few newsreel clips for dramatic effect. Yet all of this is meant as background—a sort of memory jolt—since the "case of the Stalin monument" is associated with the more distant (and by now nearly forgotten) period of postwar history. The actual thrust of the film rests in several interviews with members of Charter 77, a nonpartisan association of people opposed to the communist status quo.[14] They describe their activities as members of the underground: how they managed to "do it" in spite of continuous surveillance, the disruption in their lives, and the loss of their original careers. And the past itself is brought to life through docudrama: the intellectual window-washer made famous by Milan Kundera's novel *The Incredible Lightness of Being* once again carries his bucket, sponge, rag, and squeegee across the bridge on his way to work; the famous singer rides the tram to the office where she is a secretary; the actress stages a Shakespeare play in her living room with all those who used to attend once again present; and the politician tells of his jogging with the two secret policemen who were assigned to follow him (in this case, all three in the jogging scene were actors). Is history here relived as dramatic performance through a beautifully made, funny, as well as moving film—as art? Has biography become fiction?

When, in the initial move, the relived becomes the rethought, in the final move history comes alive once again. I do not wish to argue that Ricoeur's distinction between *Vorstellung* and *Vertretung* cannot stand up to the facts, but rather to make use of this distinction in order to highlight the subtle yet real difference between two movements that involve memory and history. If the writers of memoirs produce the raw materials—the traces that make history thinkable (for the historians)—the finished product is also amenable to another reproduction characterized by the sense of "lived presence" and typically reified as art.

The opposition between recollection and remembrance (which I have chosen in order to draw attention to the production of historical facts out of personal memory) seems, then, to be modified by additional factors that we have seen recur all along: the public face of art and the artistic modification of the public sphere. If, in the production of history, historiography and its methods hold the veracity of the document foremost in order to stay away from fiction, and if, because of this attempt at rethinking, the "lived" must give way to the "said," what else is it that transpires when, in this process, artistic imagination interferes?

I have already suggested (and argued in more detail in Lass 1988) that the significance of the historical monument or the historical novel or play lies in the concretization or meaning-fulfillment of history that it provides. An indeterminate meaning is particularized as an object that is, self-evidently, "this way." The merely thought can be lived, once again, as history takes on the spatiotemporal horizon of everyday life. In the movement from memory to history, an aesthetic move appears to divert the final product into another kind of object. We have seen how, the closer we get to the center of the "new history," the narrative of personal history becomes stylistically more elaborated and closer to an acceptable artistic mode. Or perhaps we should reverse the logic: the closer we get to the establishing and writing of the history of the November 17 events, the more the personal stories become publicly constituted artistic dramas. If so much of the "revolution" was a matter of spectacle—I have so often heard the period described as a carnival followed by a hangover—then so much of its outcome, of the understanding and rewriting of the past "after the fact," seems to demand the public eye, the spectacle, as its final absolution. Now history can be lived after all.

It remains to be seen how much of Havel's dramatic commemoration will remain once the date of November 17 is—if it ever is—formally established as a state holiday.[15] Or what will remain of all the creative storytelling in the public's mind, or better still, in a child's new schoolbook of history and literature. My point is this: recollection may require effacement in order to become memory—that is, a pure list of names, a function of the abstract, generalizing aspect of language (and thought) as opposed to the particularizing one of proper names—but memory also elicits concretization (as both aide-mémoire and as meaning-fulfillment). Hegel, we are reminded by Paul de Man, speaks "derisively of pedagogical attempts to teach children how to read or write by having them associate pictures with specific words," for unlike recollection and the imagination, memorization "is entirely devoid of images" (de Man 1982:772). Yet, as we have just seen, it is the space between the two that provides the very rupture through which social practice enters the scene. Socially constituted, the concretizations themselves amount to political legitimization. In effect, the cultural monuments function as deictic shifters because—as supplements for the effaced "I" of recollection—they are engaged by the agent of memory, the user, who is once more placed in relation to the past as a specific person within a general societal scheme: as a social actor (a citizen) within (national) history.[16]

What of all those beautiful, moving photographs and film shots from the November events? They played a decisive role in helping to change the status quo. Replayed a year later, they now make up several coffee-table books, one of the Christmas presents of 1990. Photographs of real people made public, they retain the faces but not the names. Yet, like all art, and not unlike proper names, they retain the specific while suggesting the general. It is as if in the act of defacement, it is the aesthetic that returns to the names—devoid of the self and its meaning—a face. A self restored (or is it "illuminated?"), "under control," is consumable by the "universal subject"—it is a self whose face is returned for internalization (a central feature of Hegel's recollection) and for experience, away from the pure gaze of objectivity and abstraction. Mediated by the trained eye of desire, what was originally internalized and then recollected as "mine" can be once more expressed and displayed as "ours."

Clio, it appears, wishes to have everything of our personal lives and seems not at all concerned that some of us experience violence as our recollections are erased by remembrance. One part of our life wishes to join the new history— the revelations that place our memories on the heroic side of suffering—while the other part wishes to remain private. There is the privacy of our recollection, there is the secrecy of our doings. We have seen them all in our discussion so far: oppositional heroes retelling their story, friends wishing to confess. Much remains to be said about those who have trouble recollecting, who wish not to be remembered, who live in fear as their secret past is threatened by illumination.

The interview with President Havel that I cited earlier continues with a question directed at Havel the dramatist: has the new regime destroyed him as an artist because it has robbed him of his themes? "I would know right away what to write about," he is quick to answer. And what would that be?

Today we are seeing remarkable things around us. I would particularly enjoy mapping the basic existential ground—not just fear of the future, or fear of freedom, but we are starting to see fear of our own past. It's a theme that surfaces in the familiar problem of "lustration"—the checking of people's records with the secret police. All of society was caught in its nets. It has torn these nets apart and got rid of them. But now it's afraid to reflect on its own past involvement. That, to me, is dramatically very exciting. (Havel 1991:6) [17]

------- *Notes* -------

1. Anderson's (1983) "meanwhile"—the possibility of parallel temporal awareness that characterizes the rise of the literary novel as it does the modern, historical consciousness—finds its parallel in Connerton's (1989) "before." The former work offers new insight into the origin of "nation-ness" and the rise of historical consciousness that accompanied it. The latter draws attention to the importance of ritual in constituting a personal embodiment of a public past. Yet the idea that the formation of habit constitutes society's mechanism for remembrance only begs the question it is meant to answer. If the body's habit is to be called social memory, how do we distinguish it from a person's (conscious) memories, characterized as they are by the sequence of distinguishable events? And what, then, of history through which society remembers itself? Certainly it is the case that commemorative festivals help establish the historical identity of a society, in part because individuals participate in them and thereby share in the formation of the "habit," but does it not remain essential that we distinguish between these phases? As "memory" becomes a catchall term for a wide range of phenomena that are intertwined in complex and significant ways, its heuristic value only diminishes.

Since these are, indeed, muddy waters, I consider it useful to make the following distinctions. First, the idea that all social being has temporal depth—in effect, Connerton's points—should not be confused with the fact that only some of this "memory" is actually thematized as such, i.e., that people talk of the past and claim to recall it. For the sake of clarity I think of memory as personal, as "that which happened to me," and of history as discursive practice—an objectified, even institutionalized way in which society refers to itself "in the past tense." The biographical and the societal past overlap, and it is the aim of this chapter to address this.

2. Klement Gottwald, also known as the "president of forgetting," was the first president after the communist takeover in 1948 (see Kundera 1981). Thomas G. Masaryk is considered the founder of independent Czechoslovakia in 1918. He became the country's first president. The concretization of history, the transformation of historical relics into national monuments, and their destruction during times of historical upheaval are the focuses of an earlier study (Lass 1988).

3. The German term *Vorstellung* may best be translated in the present context as the performance or realization of the past as a mind-image. *Vertretung,* on the other hand, is best translated as a representing of the past by standing in for it.

4. The battle over censorship was the primary cause around which the antigovernment critique was organized. While this is not a central theme of my present discussion, the fact that the original demand for freedom of speech and freedom of assembly of the 1960s was, by the late 1980s, transformed into the more encompassing human rights issue is essential for placing the changes in Czechoslovakia in their world-historical context. Religion, for example, was not a central theme in 1968, though it certainly became one later. But it was the issue of ecology that marked a dramatic shift in the opposition's value system. This is particularly important to note because, from the 1960s to the present, it was—so far as the general public was concerned—the world of consumerism that dominated people's daily strategies. The government devoted its efforts to satisfying consumer demands and did so quite successfully, not only at terrible economic costs but with drastic consequences for the environment. Yet, as a value worth fighting for, environmentalism was "imported," and it will be the one that will suffer the most resistance from the general public. And, at the cost of oversimplification, it is because the Charter 77 opposition was, by design, nonpartisan and because, once events got going in the street, a deliberate effort was made to keep them in the street and to get them disseminated as quickly as pos-

sible beyond the city (and to the large factories) that the "velvet revolution" was successful and very different from the Prague Spring.

5. I use the term *historiography* here for the sake of convenience, in order to distinguish the discipline of history and historical writing from the more encompassing "historical discourse" on one hand and "history"—the actual chronology—on the other.

6. The distinction is made in Hegel's *Aesthetics*. An insightful reading of this topic is provided by Paul de Man (1982) and duly appreciated by Jacques Derrida (1986).

7. The complicated problem of what may be meant by the expression *violence,* or of the myriad ways in which acts of violence are socially recognized and made part of one's sense of reality, is not the issue here. Most recently, David Riches (1991) has attempted to shed some light on the varied uses of this term in anthropological literature.

8. In an interview on National Public Radio (September 7, 1991) the Russian émigré writer Lev Lovsev stated that he had no wish to go back, not even for a visit; he had spent the last 15 years creating his country in his own imagination and did not wish to suffer the pain of losing that world or having to create it all over again. Dean MacCannell (1989) speaks of the ever-receding back stage of our private lives as we adjust to the public display of what is considered private and "behind the scenes" and is increasingly more valued in the production of the authentic spectacle.

9. All the people I spoke to are university educated and, at this point, play an active role in the changes that followed the November events, though not at a high level. They are not members of the new ruling elite and they always speak of the ruling elite as "they."

10. Czechoslovakia gained its independence and was first established as a republic on October 28, 1918. Except during the last few years, this date was not recognized or commemorated by the communist regimes.

11. November 17 was officially recognized as "students' day" to commemorate the clashes that occurred between university students and the Nazis in 1939. On October 28, 1939, a demonstration in Prague resulted in a confrontation with the German occupation forces. One person was killed and another, Jan Opletal, was wounded and died later (November 11). His funeral on November 15 turned into a massive demonstration. The Nazi government countered on November 17 by closing all Czech universities, executing 9 student leaders, occupying dormitories, and sending 1,200 students to concentration camps.

12. Miroslav Jakeš was the head of the Communist party from 1987 to 1989 and, therefore, the "man in charge." The widespread suspicion that he was literally stupid was confirmed when a tape of a speech he presented at a regional meeting of the party was smuggled out. Widely copied and disseminated—repeatedly broadcast over Radio Free Europe—it resulted in public ridicule because both Jakeš's opinions and language sounded worse than those of a "local drunk" (*místní vožrala*).

13. I have been repeatedly told not to use the term "velvet revolution" (*sametová revoluce*) unless I was being facetious. The opinions on why, however, differed. My friends for the most part agree that it was "velvet" because all Czechs were collaborators and basically comfortable (the "passivity" issue, once again). It was not a "revolution" for that very reason. Or, to put it positively, since there really wasn't any bloodshed and the changes took place peacefully, it was not a revolutionary change. Finally, the term "revolution" has a bad reputation, associated as it is with the now discredited "Great October Revolution." In any case, I should just call it the "November events" or, as some students proclaimed on the first anniversary, the "stolen revolution."

14. Charter 77, founded in January 1977, soon became the center of dissent and the self-proclaimed watchdog for the Helsinki accord on human rights in Czechoslovakia. Many of its outspoken founders—such as Václav Havel—became key players in the events of November 1989.

15. As of the time of this writing (autumn, 1992), and to the best of my knowledge, it has not been so established. How the different associations that have been accumulating as this date repeats itself each year will work themselves out—what shall be remembered, what commemorated, and what associations placed under erasure—is a topic worthy of a separate study.

The point is that not everyone participated in the celebration on Wenceslaus Square or, in spite of the wide publicity the event received on television and in the press, that everyone followed the event from the comfort of home. Many of my friends found the whole production in bad taste. Yet 1990 saw the first changes in political and religious holidays: the end of World War II has been moved back to May 8 (as opposed to Stalin's May 9), and July 4 (United States Independence Day), July 5 (a day celebrating the Slav apostles Cyril and Methodius), and July 6 (commemorating the execution in 1415 of the Christian reformist Jan Hus) have been designated as holidays. Fortuitously, they made for an extended weekend, much to the delight of the public, who left for their summer homes. In 1991, the second anniversary of the November events seemed to pass without much excitement.

16. "The essential property of deixis (the term comes from the Greek word meaning 'pointing' or 'showing') is that it determines the structure and interpretation of utterances in relation to the time and place of their occurrence, the identity of the speaker and addressee, and objects and events in the actual situation of utterance" (Lyons 1981:170). In the present context the monument can be said to reposition the viewer's relation to the past. This theme is more fully explored in an earlier paper on Czech medieval relics (Lass 1987).

17. The fear of the uncovering of past involvement that Havel refers to is certainly not unusual: was not the same phenomenon used as part of the Gestapo's methods? And once the war was over, did people not live in fear of being accused of collaboration with the Nazis? Inciting fear of one's own past—was it not the very centerpiece of the witch hunts engaged in by communist regimes (of which Havel was himself a victim)?

6

Mulian Saves His Mother in 1989

ELLEN R. JUDD

IN THE FALL OF 1989, *The Story of Mulian* was very nearly performed on the sloping riverbank below the historic county seat of Qiancheng in western Hunan. Had it been performed as planned, thousands of local people and their guests could have temporarily displaced gold panners and boat people and occupied both banks and the surface of the river itself to witness and join in ten days of concentrated ritual drama. Higher secular authority intervened, however. On the eve of the opening of the cycle, the performance was moved an hour's drive away to the modern city of Huaihua. There it was staged in a conventional auditorium inside a walled government compound. On the opening day of the cycle, uniformed police equipped with walkie-talkies were stationed at the entrance to ensure that only officially invited drama scholars attended the performance. During the following days the police disappeared and portions of an unofficial audience inconspicuously materialized, but the direct connection between performance and audience had been ruptured. The erasure of the popular audience embedded within Mulian opera hovered over and structured the subsequent performance.

The removal and rupture were intentional political interventions. The Mulian opera cycle is a profoundly political form of popular drama, replete with the pageantry of power and the play of resistance. It has been unofficially prohibited since the 1950s, and the last officially approved performance of the cycle in this region and in the *chenhe gaoqiang* local opera style had taken place in 1946. It was universally expected that the 1989 event would be the final *chenhe gaoqiang* performance of Mulian opera ever. Even if it had taken place in Qiancheng, this performance for the historical (video) record would still have carried traces of state control and sanction. The memory of Mulian opera as it had been in the past came alive in this reenactment of state censorship. If the opera had seemed out of date in socialist or postsocialist China, this reminder of state power was sufficient to rekindle long memories of ambivalence toward the state.

Under the conditions in which the performance actually did occur, the already complex mix of official and popular politics was doubly augmented. First, the danger of openly performing Mulian opera in public resulted in the controversial removal to Huaihua. And second, it was necessary to deny emphatically that there was anything at all political about Mulian opera—a denial that was itself a political precondition for the possibility of its performance after June 4, 1989.

The danger of Mulian opera did not lie in its officially identified locus, the portrayal of "hungry ghosts" and the promotion of beliefs described as superstition. Instead, the danger lay in a certain mode of presentation of the central tenets of Chinese political culture. The thematic and narrative elements of this presentation and their internal conflict and ambiguity will be outlined later, especially in relation to the pivotal concept of filial piety. The elements were presented—or, more accurately, would have been presented—in an intensely heightened context of ritual drama in which the audience would have witnessed the magical dramatic transformation (see Mair 1989) through which the ever-present but normally invisible worlds of heaven and hell appear before human eyes.[1] They would have seen the mechanics of those other worlds and their effects on the world of mortals; dramatic tales of extraordinary virtue and everyday evil, each earning its appropriate retribution; amazing appearances of ghosts (*gui*) and monsters; the anguish of death, bereavement, and betrayal; and the serious play of domestic and political comedy. The most fundamental boundaries, including that between life and death, would have been placed in question both by representations on stage and by the negation of distinctions in the practice of representation.

Through ritual drama of this intense and popular character, personal dimensions of life, death, and the regeneration of life become fused with public dimensions of shared commemoration focused on the same existential themes. The force of shared remembrance (Owen 1986) is inscribed in ritual dramatic form and threatens at any moment to ignite personal and public memory. Mulian opera is both vehicle and instigator of acts of commemoration that cannot be apolitical even under the firmest denials of the state. In tolerating and even encouraging a revival of national popular culture during the 1980s in an apparent search for political legitimacy, the post-Maoist Chinese state has also unleashed the potential for political explosion in the interstices of memory and commemoration. Here lie the cultural resources of a past that may flash up as an image to be seized at a moment of historical danger (see Benjamin 1969:257; Taussig 1987).

MULIAN OPERA

Mulian Saves His Mother (translated in Mair 1983) remains salient in the present as a Dunhuang transformation text (*bianwen*), which is among the earliest extant texts related to performance in Chinese culture.[2] It presents the central narrative of the Mulian story: Mulian (from Mahamaudgalyayana) is a devout Buddhist, but his mother has departed from the tenets of Buddhism and is consigned to the Avici hell where she suffers extreme torment. Mulian achieves arhatship and searches for his mother, journeying first to heaven and then, when he learns of his mother's fate, to successive halls (*dian*) of hell. Even with heavenly assistance he is unable to help her until Buddha, at Mulian's pleading, institutes the practice of holding the *yulanpen* feast on the fifteenth day of the seventh lunar month.[3] Through this feast Mulian's mother and all hungry ghosts are fed. Mulian continues his efforts on behalf of his mother and his merit is eventually sufficient to obtain her reincarnation, first as a dog and then as a woman, before she is finally received into heaven.

The story of Mulian, with numerous embellishments, became a widespread and influential drama cycle in medieval China (see Mair 1986–87; Teiser 1988a). In addition to being a window on Chinese society and culture and on early Buddhist influence, it is a keystone in the history of Chinese drama and is currently the subject of intensive attention on the part of Chinese drama historians (Hunan c. 1985; Li 1989a; Liu Huichun 1988; Wang Xiaoyi 1988; Xue 1988).[4] These historians have at their disposal a variety of texts and accounts, including a 120-play version of the cycle compiled in the Ming dynasty by Zheng Zhizhen. They are also actively collecting, researching, and promoting the twentieth-century versions of Mulian opera still available within diverse local opera traditions, such as this version in *chenhe gaoqiang*. For many of these scholars, the Mulian cycle constitutes a "living fossil" (*huo huashi*) through which they can examine the history of Chinese opera and its regional diversity.

In the official Chinese view, opera of this character is offensive and harmful to the people because it portrays ordinary people in consistently negative terms and it promotes beliefs regarded as "feudal superstition" (*fengjian mixin*).[5] Mao's denunciation of the old opera stage as occupied not only by emperors, generals, talents, and beauties (*diwangjiangxiang caizijiaren*) but also by monsters, ghosts, and spirits (*niuguisheshen*) could hardly apply to any corpus of drama more accurately than to the Mulian cycle.[6] When one recalls the power attributed to the force of ideas in Mao Zedong Thought (see Mao 1966), in addition to the Chinese state's long-standing wariness of potentially seditious drama, the official attitude toward the Mulian cycle is not surprising. A subject of discussion surrounding the Hunan performance in 1989 was whether or not Mulian opera should be openly performed. Very few of the scholars present were prepared to advocate open performance—this view was too vulnerable to the dangerous label of bourgeois liberalism to be expressed widely after June 4, 1989.

For those directly involved in staging the *chenhe gaoqiang* performance of the Mulian cycle, strong and varied motives were at work. The event was mounted with UNESCO backing and an (abortive) hope of capturing the eye of the international scholarly community. It was also an exercise in the commoditization of Chinese popular culture. For Li Huaisun, the central researcher and the scribe of two thick volumes of Mulian drama text, the performance was the product of genuine enthusiasm and the pinnacle of a lifetime of local work in popular drama. He was responsible for most of the local research and scholarly compilation of the *chenhe gaoqiang* version (Li 1989a; compare Hunan 1984). For the older performers, classified as folk artists (*minjian yiren*), this performance was substantially their own artistic recreation of a cycle remembered from the past, and it was potentially a final statement of their artistic legacy in a dramatic form on the point of disappearing.

For the foreign anthropologist, it was the most powerful drama she had seen in 15 years of observing and studying Chinese drama. It was a concentrated symbolic expression of Chinese culture—but less in the three-in-one synthesis of Confucianism, Daoism, and Buddhism into the neo-Confucian values explicitly highlighted than in the play of differing and conflicting versions of the story of Mulian. In the pages that follow, I present the core lines of this multilogue and examine the thematic core of the Mulian cycle and its dramatic expression in a set of parallel narratives. I follow this with an examination of two of the primary means—excess and irony—through which the text and performance subvert their own overt themes, and then with an examination of the political context of the 1989 performance. I conclude with an exploration of the space of subversion opened by a popular drama evoking images remembered or envisioned. It remains unavoidable that the voice which provides the vehicle must be my own.

FILIAL PIETY

It is a point of apparent unanimity that the core of the Mulian cycle and the larger complex known as Mulian opera (*Mulianxi*)[7] is the concept of *xiao*, which is conventionally translated into English as "filial piety." This deceptively simple concept is grounded in practices of ancestor worship that extend back to the dawn of recorded Chinese history. They are deeply rooted in familial relations, the construction of the self, and the exercise of state power.[8] They are inscribed in body and mind through personal memory, funerary rites, rituals of commemoration, and multilayered cultural elaborations of remembrance through which filial piety is represented and recreated (see Casey 1984; Owen 1986).[9] The Mulian cycle is the body of Chinese drama most intensely focused upon filial piety and its commemoration.

Those who are especially concerned with the light the Mulian cycle casts upon the history of Chinese culture emphasize the significance of filial piety as an indigenous theme in this early and exceptionally influential representation of popular Buddhism in China. Release from worldly desire and the cycle of birth and rebirth hold comparatively minor places in the story of Mulian. In the prefatory series of plays (*Qian Mulian*), the figure who ultimately becomes Mulian appears in heaven committing the transgression of longing for the world. He is punished for this lapse by being sent again into the world to be born as Turnip Fu (Fu Luobu), the son of Fu Xiang and Liu Qingti. In the world, he displays Buddhist piety as evidenced in reverence for the scriptures, chastity, vegetarianism, and good deeds, but the dramatic elaboration of his exemplary qualities is focused on his filial piety. Whatever other expectations might exist for the devout Buddhist—perhaps in other worlds—in this world filial piety is represented as essential appropriate behavior for a mortal, and as a quality recognized and valued by otherworldly authorities. But contradictions remain: in violation of his primary filial obligation, Turnip Fu renounces marriage and thereby descendants, and his model expression of filial behavior consists in searching for and saving his mother rather than his father, who is represented in the Mulian cycle as having accomplished his own salvation. These remain as paradoxes embedded within the core of the narrative.[10]

These and other elements, especially the incorporation of Daoist ritual and Mulian's remarkable feats of magic in the course of his search for his mother, have contributed to an interpretation of the story of Mulian as quintessentially syncretic, and specifically so in the sense of combining Confucianism, Buddhism, and Daoism into the three-religions-in-one (*sanjiaoheyi*) of neo-Confucianism.[11] Together with the elements of the three religions of the Chinese great tradition, there are also the popular elements of ancestor worship and shamanistic ritual that contribute to the synthesis and produce a concentrated expression of popular Chinese culture (see D. Johnson 1989; Li 1989b; Teiser 1988a). This is not only a scholarly observation but an active interpretation internal to the contemporary recreation and performance of Mulian opera. Doubts about its political quality could be overridden, in the decade following the reforms of 1979, by a focus upon Mulian opera as a treasure of Chinese national and popular culture. Paired appeals to nationalism and populism legitimate the opera cycle and render it performable. The emphasis on syncretism provides a historical subject of study and highlights the officially acceptable cultural value of the drama. It also evokes an expanded, contemporary syncretism encompassing state socialism and post-socialism. Historical reference in Chinese culture is commonly and conventionally a play of allegorical reference to the present. In the case of performances of popular culture, it has the added dimension of evoking shared, unofficial memories and meanings. It is never simply esoteric.

The figure of Mulian is loosely based on a historical person but has long since become a transformed and transforming repository of popular culture, remembered and realized through embodiment in ritual performance. The feats performed by Mulian in searching for and saving his mother epitomize filial piety in its direct familial sense, but the feats themselves are impossible for any member of the audience to replicate without supernatural assistance. Mulian's neglect of some of his filial duties, as in failing to continue the line of descent, along with the magical quality of the filial behavior portrayed, may generate dramatic and ritual effect through mechanisms of inversion, but the portrayal of filial piety in Mulian opera is only partially presented through the character of Mulian himself. Mulian, of course, is not a mere mortal in the usual sense, and he is far from ordinary even as an opera character. Mulian may be conceptualized as a magical mirror that reveals filial piety and focuses the filial behavior of the more human characters in Mulian opera into a concentrated, reflected overlay of the multiple dimensions of filial piety.[12] Indeed, most of the substance of filial piety is conveyed through characters other than Mulian, whose own filial piety is minimalistically represented by the magical feats through which he pursues salvation for his mother, who has condemned herself by abandoning vegetarianism and committing other violations of Buddhist doctrine.

Filial piety is more realistically portrayed in the actions of other characters in Mulian opera, including those in plays (*Hua Mulian*) that are not intrinsically part of the cycle but that can be, and in Hunan in 1989 were, performed together with it, interspersed with the plays of the Mulian cycle proper. Together this set of plays forms a convoluted dramatic structure in which a (flexible) range of variants is presented, each of which treats the theme of filial piety in some sense, but with different characters and plots.[13] Refracted through the Mulian story at the core, Mulian opera as a whole constitutes an open structure of ambiguity focused on filial piety (compare Bakhtin 1984).

This ambiguity is expressed through the concrete behavior of various appropriately moral persons, that is, those who realize filial piety in their selves and their lives. There is no narrative connection between these characters and their stories and those of the core narrative, and the fragmentation of this loose parallel structure simultaneously conceals and constitutes a richness of meaning. In *Head of Bees* (Mifengtou), a son becomes the object of murderous designs on the part of his stepmother and her lover. The stepmother falsely denounces the son to his father for making advances toward her. The son, unwilling to compromise his stepmother's reputation, is ordered by his unsuspecting father to kill himself. He demonstrates his moral qualities of filial piety by obeying this order despite great anguish. When his father discovers the wrong he has done his son, he is stricken with grief, but it is already too late. In the final scene of the play, stepmother and son meet in the court of the king of hell, where the stepmother is condemned and the son is sent to heaven. The son further demonstrates his filial piety by a show of warmth toward his stepmother, whom he knows to have been the cause of his death. In this narrative, a young man is cruelly tested in a more realistic sense than that faced by Mulian, and is offered no supernatural aid in this world. His worth as a person is shown in his ability to obey familial authority even when it is clearly in the wrong. The intensity of the suffering and the wrong is the subject of extended dramatic elaboration on the part of the son facing death and, later, the grieving father.

A similar tale of exceptional filial piety is presented in *Hou Seven Kills His Mother* (Hou Qi sha mu).[14] In this case the model of filial piety is a daughter who becomes embroiled in a deadly domestic dispute with her stepmother and stepbrother. The stepbrother kills his mother while attempting to kill his stepfather, and then accuses his stepfather of the murder. The daughter saves her father from execution by confessing to the murder. Her conviction is explained as being the result of her mistake in the course of reciting Buddhist scripture: she chanted one character wrong. This is an error that would not be serious for an ordinary person, but it is a grave error for an educated person (*dushuren*) such as herself. Her exceptional goodness brings supernatural intervention to the execution ground and she is narrowly saved, but not before the enactment of scenes of suffering and grief on the part of herself and her father. The play concludes with further supernatural intervention in which the truth of the matter is revealed in a dream to a high official, who can then resolve the case justly.

A slight transposition of the theme appears in the classic *Woman Geng Hangs* (Geng shi shang diao), the performative peak of the 1989 *chenhe gaoqiang* cycle and the play that saw the largest unauthorized audience materialize in the theater. Filial piety for women implies the "three obediences": when young a woman should obey her father, when married she should obey her husband, and when widowed she should obey her son. In this play, the woman surnamed Geng donates a gold hairpin to two men whom she takes to be Buddhist monks. The two are actually confidence men and thieves who have deceived her and taken advantage of her pious generosity. They pawn the hairpin, and the woman's husband sees and recognizes it and demands an explanation. The thieves allege that it was given to one of them as a love token, and the husband is shattered. He refuses to believe his wife's explanation, and lengthy scenes of anguish on the part of the husband (who demands divorce) and the wife (who threatens suicide) are enacted.

By this time a number of frightful hungry ghosts have appeared in the play; this is their most vivid and extended appearance in the cycle. Each tells what drove him to suicide (usually failure in worldly ambition) and to the fate of a hungry ghost who must drive a living mortal to suicide in order to reenter the cycle of birth and death. One hungry ghost, a huge figure with a rope around his neck and long red tongue hanging out, is selected to take advantage of this opportunity. With the (necessary) encouragement of this hungry ghost, the wronged wife takes tearful leave of her young children and proceeds to hang herself from a beam that the other hungry ghosts have pushed onto the front of the stage. She places a black cloth over her head and is, in fact, suspended (with the inconspicuous aid of a body harness) over the audience, to the delight of the chosen hungry ghost and the horror of the audience. The children find the body and convince their father that they saw their mother give the hairpin to mendicant monks, and the husband is devastated. He is also quickly attacked by arriving members of his wife's natal family.

The concept of filial piety is extended in a further familiar and established direction in another *Wai Mulian* play, *The Loyalty of Kuang Guoqing* (Kuang Guoqing guo zhong). Connections between the family as the state writ small and the state as the family writ large were fundamental to the political culture of imperial China and extended to homologies of the relationship between father and son and between emperor and minister—two of the five basic relationships (*wulun*) that each Chinese man was expected to uphold. Kuang Guoqing serves his emperor nobly in resisting foreign invasion,[15] but is slandered as plotting rebellion by a rival at court. The emperor sends his command to Kuang Guoqing to commit suicide, and the loyal official chooses not to resist but to obey the order. Following the extended scenes that mark death and mourning in every play in Mulian opera, the official dies and is immediately received into heaven. Relations of worldly authority and the intersections of these with similarly structured relations of hierarchy in the worlds of heaven and hell are pervasive in Mulian opera. The construction of the exemplary moral self never departs from a reality of hierarchy and the imperative of obedience. Questions of adequate knowledge regarding hierarchies in this and other worlds and prescriptions for appropriate moral behavior in relation to them are the central issues compressed into the concept of *xiao*.

EXCESS

Xiao, or filial piety, is elaborated in Mulian opera in a context of persistent and intense attention to death and the regeneration of life (see Bloch and Parry 1982; Martin 1988). Death, apprehension and fear of death, bereavement, mourning, funeral ritual, what happens to people after they die, and remembrance of the world by the deceased and of the deceased by the living are the substance of all of the plays that compose the cycle. Mulian opera should properly culminate at the feast for hungry ghosts on the fifteenth day of the seventh lunar month, and in at least some parts of China portions of the Mulian story appear in funerary rituals. This wider context adds to the power of the dramatizations themselves, and it should be remembered that the audience ordinarily participates in some of the rituals and does not simply watch a secular performance.

Personal memory and public commemoration of the deceased remain key elements in Chinese culture, elements that were muted and partially appropriated by the early socialist state. In more recent years there has been a resurgence of memory and commemoration of the deceased, especially of those who died in connection with the political transformations of the postrevolutionary state. No widely accepted new forms of commemoration have yet emerged and, at the present time, with or without acceptance of its ritual significance, Mulian opera remains an unparalleled symbolic vehicle through which the problems of mortality and politics can be expressed and confronted.[16]

One might here follow Abner Cohen (1979) in noting the power imbued in symbolism by virtue of its multivocal fusion of existential and political dimensions. The preoccupation with death that is marked to such an extreme degree in Mulian opera fuels the power with which the opera addresses questions of appropriate and moral social and political behavior. The concept of filial piety adeptly hinges these dimensions and grounds the fear of death and the norm of obedience in the construction of the moral self. The particular shape of this fusion is determined by the pervasive presence of the state in Chinese society and culture (see Wolf 1978). Mulian opera provides distinct confirmation of Maurice Bloch and Jonathan Parry's (1982) posited association between rituals of death and the recreation of structures of political domination.

In Mulian opera, especially in its formal structure, one may also discern the play of excess within the space of death constructed by dramatic transformation.[17] This play of excess is evident even in the explicit messages of the core narrative of Mulian's saving his mother. Liu Qingti, Mulian's mother, requires unusual efforts on her behalf because she has been consigned to the utmost depths of hell. Her voyage through hell and Mulian's subsequent pursuit along the same path reveal a sequence of unendurable tortures (including having her eyes gouged out by vultures, attack by poisonous snakes, being impaled by pitchforks, and corporeal disintegration) and the mechanisms through which these are imposed upon her (a hierarchical structure of courts, officials, and underling ghosts).[18] She is shown to merit this horrendous fate—instead of reception into heaven or reincarnation—on the grounds of having forsaken her oath of vegetarianism and having failed in generosity and support for the institutions of Buddhism. The greatest emphasis is placed upon her eating meat, which may be read either as a symbolic concentration of moral turpitude or as a relatively minor matter.[19] Judging from conversations held at the time, both interpretations appear to have been present in the minds of those in attendance at the 1989 performance of the opera.[20]

One consequence of the emphasis on vegetarianism is to heighten the audience's sense of being at risk. Another consequence is an implicit questioning about whether the severity of the punishment is truly merited by the common act of eating meat. Liu Qingti herself strenuously resists at every stage of her descent into hell and shows no remorse. Whether her judgment is deserved or not, it results in terrifying ordeals and in an extreme response from her son, whose merit has won him the help of Guanyin, the goddess of mercy, in reaching the western heaven, receiving enhanced magical powers, and then pursuing his mother through successive halls of hell.[21] The story of Mulian itself constitutes a template of excess at the core of the cycle.

The resonating narratives of filial piety outlined earlier are marked by repeated excesses of filial piety, especially in the instances of obedience to the point of self-destruction in which the authorities themselves (father, husband, or emperor) are profoundly in the wrong. Guanyin herself, according to her mother, is utterly overreacting when she responds to her mother's "single phrase of dialogue" (*yiju xiyan*) by deciding to renounce the world. The movement of this excess is even more clearly shown in the instance of the daughter whose near-fatal error was the mispronunciation of a single character during an otherwise faultless life. The culminating effect of this excess is to place in question the pivotal concept of filial piety and, by extension, all obedience to higher authority.

Filial piety remains a question at the heart of Mulian opera, but a question breathed only on the margins, either through tragic excess, as in the previous examples, or in comic fragments. The question posed and the manner of the posing constitute a structure of conflict and struggle at odds with any interpretation of

Mulian opera phrased in terms of the accomplishment of a synthesis (see also
Overmyer 1990). Rather than a fusion of disparate elements of the abstractions
represented by the terms Buddhism, Daoism, and Confucianism, there is instead
an unresolved and contested conflict between the strictures of filial piety and the
play of resistance to it. In the 1989 *chenhe gaoqiang* performance, resistance was
directly embodied in Liu Qingti's struggles and much more pervasively and in-
sidiously realized in the excess of representations of filial piety and in the play of
clowns on the margins of the story of Mulian.

   This structure of conflicting representations nestling within and on the margins of each other is a structure of ambiguity generating a multiplicity of knowledges. There are the conventional knowledges of appropriate filial piety, the
appropriate performance of ritual, and the pervasive reality of hierarchy. And
there are the subjugated knowledges portraying for human view the hidden workings of heaven, hell, and the ordinary world of mortals. The theme of appearance
hiding truth and the theme of deception, even on the part of the highest authorities (exemplified by Guanyin in disguise tempting Mulian), are pervasive
in Mulian opera. So, too, are the occurrence of error and the inflicting of violence and cruelty—portrayed by characters representing the humblest of social
statuses, such as beggars, as well as close relatives, secular authorities, and even
the rulers of heaven and hell. A vast and complex cosmography, more ambitious
than any mere ethnography, is attempted and realized through the transformation of drama. It is a cosmography in which some elements, such as the story of
Mulian and the presentation of filial piety, provide a persistent and common core,
but which is structured in a profoundly open sense (compare Watson 1985). The
openness is one of conflict, indeterminacy, and the seditious seriousness of play.

THE PLAY OUTSIDE

The play (in all senses of the word) on stage in 1989 was only part of a larger performance—that of performing Mulian opera (see also Ward 1979). And this would
have been so even if the performance had taken place at the more open venue at
Qiancheng. It is intrinsic to Mulian opera that representation is explicitly and im-
plicitly put in question through the magic of performance.[22] There is a constant
play with the negation or transcendence of fundamental boundaries—between life
and death; between heaven, hell, and this world; between appearance and reality;
between obedience and resistance—that is immediately realized through a parallel permeability of the distinction between onstage and offstage. The audience,
even in Huaihua, was drawn into the Mulian play in varied but obvious ways. At a
deeper level, the entire event was itself a play, one that replicated, in structure and
in theme, the internal play of the story of Mulian. The lasting salience of Mulian
opera is as much or more a question of this play of intertextuality than it is of the
complex symbolism of the operas themselves. The cosmography of the internal

play is not simply described or even represented, it is partially realized within the symbolic practice of recreating Mulian opera and its conditions of production.

This realization is most directly evident in the manifest role of the state throughout the event.[23] Mulian opera is currently in a precarious situation because of quasi-official sanctions against its performance persisting from the early years of the People's Republic until after the end of the Cultural Revolution. Following a brief interregnum (1976–78), state policy in the decade from 1979 to 1989 rejected the restrictive policies of the Cultural Revolution and permitted the revival of customary practices, including small-scale performance of Mulian opera. The lowered prestige of the Communist party limited its capacity to discourage spontaneous revivals, even when it suspected a revival's effects, and performances such as Mulian opera may have been more widespread during the 1980s than during the early years of the People's Republic.

In any event, during the 1980s the state had much less interest than before in prohibiting or even discouraging the rediscovery of cultural forms. The larger political shifts of the post–Cultural Revolution era included a retreat from revolutionary politics and their partial replacement by the politics of nationalism and state-building (Chevrier 1988). A corollary of this shift was emphatic attention to China's cultural heritage. To the extent that this shift was oriented toward popular culture, it could be legitimated in terms of the residual political rhetoric.

The same tendency was reinforced by the international milieu. A central policy of the 1980s was that of opening (*kaifang*) toward the outside world. Positioning China desirably in the international arena could be aided by an emphasis on China's cultural treasures, both as a matter of political symbolism and as a matter of economic interest. The latter was once again acceptable as a motivation within China, and the managers of China's official cultural establishment were not slow to notice that popular culture could be a marketable commodity, especially when cloaked in a venerable air of ancient history and esoteric ritual.

China's ancient material culture had already been commoditized for the international tourist business as well as for smaller, more specialized clienteles such as scholars and students. Foreigners now make up much of the audience for traditional opera performances in the major cities. Folk drama can also find a market in some specialized international contexts and can serve as a commodity indirectly through mechanisms of prestige in artistic and scholarly circles. The 1989 *chenhe gaoqiang* performance of Mulian opera was made possible by a grant from UNESCO for the purpose of recording the performance, and the organizers evidently had hopes of finding a lucrative international market for both the performance and the recordings.

The income-generating potential of the event was overestimated, however, and the shortfall was increased by the immediate political context. One of the minor consequences of the crisis of June 4, 1989, and its aftermath was cancellation of the official international status of the Mulian opera performance in October 1989.

Through a variety of channels, drama scholars in China have become part of an international research community examining popular culture in terms that are relatively new in China and that have therefore attracted considerable interest. A few drama scholars have become aware, through Richard Schechner's work (especially Schechner 1985) and through meeting with him in China, of the intersection between drama and anthropology, with the result that researchers in drama are among the most active in Chinese scholarly circles in examining belief and ritual and popular culture from anthropological perspectives.[24] The study of Mulian opera within China has also been significantly stimulated by the study of Mulian opera abroad, specifically by an international workshop on Mulian opera held at Berkeley in 1987 (see Johnson 1989). The influential Chinese representatives who attended that workshop stimulated further interest within China for research on Mulian opera and facilitated official support for the contemporary performance of the cycle (Xue 1988).

In short, the 1989 *chenhe gaoqiang* performance of Mulian opera was directly and indirectly conditioned by national and international political and economic considerations operating through the state. The arrangements for the *chenhe gaoqiang* performance were directly in the hands of state institutions. At the national level, this included the involvement of the Ministry of Culture, central and provincial research institutes (most notably the Academy of Art), and the All-China Dramatists' Association. The greater part of the local organizing was done by or coordinated through the Huaihua Art Center, whose staff were all professionals with state-defined classification and remuneration levels (*guojia zhigong*).

The basis of the performance was provided by a variety of written records (depending on the portion of the cycle and whether it was part of the cycle proper or an added element) collected from or transcribed following the accounts of elderly *chenhe gaoqiang* performers earlier in the 1980s. The core of the cycle was, in this version, a local adaptation of the Ming dynasty Zheng Zhizhen text, while the prefatory and additional portions were based on manuscript prompt books collected from performers. The two volumes of printed text used for the performance represented a selection of fifteen plays, each at least four hours in duration, from a much larger corpus. The selection of the material in the two volumes was attributed to several of the performing artists; Li Huaisun of the Huaihua Cultural Office drafted the text (Li 1989a).

In actual performance, there were substantial deviations from the printed text. Many of these involved shortening the performance—to sixteen sessions of about three and one-half hours each, exclusive of associated rituals—and altering the order of the scenes. The scenes of the central narrative followed the text fairly closely, and only two scenes outside the printed text were added to the performance. There were also some other deviations from the text, for the purpose of devising means of incorporating audience involvement despite the unusual circumstances and for purposes of improvisation in the comic scenes.

The performance was staged by the older artists who had joined in the compilation of the text and by others who were in most cases identified as "folk artists" (*minjian yiren*), a category that is not defined by a relationship to folk art but rather by the social and economic status of not being a state employee (*guojia zhigong*). With the exception of some young drama students who appeared as acrobats, most of the performers were members or former members of the six county-level *chenhe gaoqiang* troupes that had existed until recently. The six troupes were virtually disbanded in 1986–87 following a state decision that drama troupes must be self-supporting. A few performers had continued in one of two small troupes, one performing *chenhe gaoqiang* and the other performing songs and dances (*gewu*). A further dimension was added to the play between performance and performing by drawing onto the stage real Daoist priests for some of the rituals, and real jugglers and similar marketplace *baixi* entertainers for the banquet scene where Liu Qingti celebrates the eating of meat.

The contemporary situation of the troupe members was also complex and the subject of some open discussion along the margins of the event. Some younger members of the troupes—those who had become performers during the Cultural Revolution when folk art and its practitioners were being replaced by revolutionary art—had changed to other professions or turned to working the land as peasants. The older performers who were the practical directors of the drama had, in many cases, retired from the stage before 1986. Others were looking to this performance as a possible reprieve for the *chenhe gaoqiang* local opera form and for their own careers—they had been offered the possibility of a new troupe's being formed at the prefectural level if this performance was a success.[25]

The performers were internally divided, especially between those who had entered the drama world before and those who had entered it during the Cultural Revolution, but it was the earlier generation, with its memories of the older drama, that was the mainstay of the event. Several of the older artists played leading roles in creating and directing the performance as well as actually performing one or more important roles on stage.[26]

Within the ranks of the folk artists there was vocal discontent about the conditions under which they worked to produce the performance. They spent three months, a time they felt to be too short, rehearsing for the performance. Only a few had performed Mulian opera in their youth, so this was a relatively demanding task. During those three months they lived in Qiancheng, sleeping behind curtains on the rehearsal stage and providing their own food. During the performance they were lodged in a guesthouse that they considered much inferior to the hotel accommodation provided for those invited to attend the performance.[27] They received a supplement of five yuan per day while rehearsing and eight yuan per day while performing,[28] and they openly wondered where all the funding provided for the event was going. They had been told there was a substantial deficit (which I believe was the case), but were skeptical about this and, in any event, disappointed in their financial and professional expectations. Nevertheless, they did comply with official demands and responded resourcefully to the shift in locale, even though it constituted a grave reduction in the significance of the performance for them and provided difficult performing conditions. This compliance may be viewed intertextually with the opera itself—as a demonstration of the problematic quality of trust, of the pervasiveness of state-based hierarchy, and of the realization of obedience.

In summary, the context in which the event occurred was one permeated by explicitly defined, state-based hierarchical relations that structured the conditions and relations of performance. These hierarchical relations were not qualitatively different from those of the worldly and otherworldly hierarchies portrayed on stage, and an intertextual play of realization and representation is readily evident. The play outside was additionally structured by the international commoditization of popular culture, as refracted through the official organization of the event. This play, too, finds resonances within the stage portrayal of commercial milieus and relations, although offstage one might also find an element of "modernization." Whether within or outside the operas on stage, there was also a marked sense of conflict and resistance—not a rejection of either hierarchy or commerce, but a contest for position and profit on the part of unequally placed contestants.

IRONY

The thread of political analysis and comment runs through Mulian opera. It is not simply a matter of the messages of inevitable hierarchy, the futility of resistance, and the moral values of obedience and filial piety that are evident and recurrent on the surface of all of the plays. The earlier discussion of excess has indicated that the mode of presentation of these messages simultaneously conveys an undoing of the same messages (see DeBernardi 1987; Fernandez 1984). Here I extend this argument through attention to devices on the margins of the opera that generate similar effects but through different mechanisms.

But first, some comment should be made on the extent to which the political events of the spring—especially June—of 1989 affected the performance and event. The openness of the drama and the character of the event demand that attention be paid to the intertextuality between the politics onstage and those offstage, including national politics. An effort to interpret specific lines of dialogue or specific scenes as direct, overt comments on the 1989 conflicts would be misguided. The performance was presented under two powerful lines of political constraint: first, official sponsorship and control of the event and of the futures of the participants; and, second, the official commitment to maintain the policy of openness (*kaifang*) toward the outside world and the presence of foreign, Chinese-speaking scholars. The entire event was presented within a felt tension between the commitment to carry through with a performance planned under different political conditions and the changed conditions that existed by the time of the performance itself. (It was, in fact, very nearly cancelled.)

The result was silence on contemporary political issues. This did not mean that the event became apolitical or that Mulian opera became anything other than intensely political opera. It did mean that the controversial political elements were presented covertly and greeted without comment. In this, the Mulian opera of 1989 was continuing a well-established political tradition in Chinese popular drama, which has an equally long tradition of being viewed with official suspicion. In this dimension, too, there was a complicated play between appearance and reality, drama and life, and obedience and resistance (see Scott 1990).

The one unmistakable reference to current political affairs occurred outside the performance itself but within the event, and is illustrative of the ambiguity involved. A few days into the performance, a senior figure in one of the sponsoring research institutes arrived. Everyone present knew that he had not arrived earlier because he was under a political cloud and had been officially instructed not to attend. His appearance at the performance and his role in presiding over the meetings at the following scholarly conference were staged as an official signal that scholars were not being repressed.

The warm public welcome given to him by one influential participant after another constituted a different signal. Little was said about the political significance of this occurrence, because it was too obvious to require comment. The lightening of the atmosphere at the event spoke for itself. This was, of course, a matter of offstage political drama and did not necessarily mean that the scholar's troubles had dissolved. Furthermore, the harrowing experiences of many people in the months following June 1989 were not viewed as exceptional in Chinese intellectual circles—all intellectuals of even early middle age had personal memories of a series of similar experiences. Consequently, political references that might initially appear to refer to the specifics of the summer of 1989, and that might indeed have those specifics as one level of meaning, had deeper and multilayered referents superscribed through decades and centuries of remembered history (see Duara 1988b).

Onstage, the questionable political elements in Mulian opera were presented with similar ambiguity, and some of the most marked commentary was on the margins and in comic fragments dispersed throughout the performance (see Babcock 1984; Sutton 1990; Weller 1987). In almost all instances, such scenes were perfectly in keeping with early texts of the Mulian cycle and could be interpreted (or hidden) as archaic. In interpreting the material that follows it is useful to remember that the earliest extant version of the Mulian story portrays Mulian, early in his search for his mother, encountering unfortunates condemned to the fate of hungry ghosts by bureaucratic error in the court of the underworld (Mair 1983:92–93).

Much of the noncomic material in the Mulian cycle is open to various interpretations: retribution is just or fearfully cruel; Liu Qingti's resistance is a sign of her iniquity or an act of courage; and so on. The presentation of the tragic material is emphatic and designed to touch upon deep emotions, and I would judge that it does so very effectively. It does so without providing clear answers, which may be a source of additional power as well as of openness. Teiser (1988a, 1988b) has observed in relation to medieval Mulian opera that one of its most important roles was to provide cosmographic knowledge. I agree with this point for contemporary Mulian opera, but with the additional observation that the "knowledge" provided is at least partly in the form of provoking questioning.

Within the intense feeling aroused by Mulian opera, any consistency is disrupted by a structure of fragmentation in which the play of clowns is especially important. These clowns appear either in separate scenes that are primarily comic interludes or in moments within the central narrative, and the same comic characters may move between the two contexts. The role is explicitly set apart, following the usual conventions of Chinese drama, by a white-painted triangle covering the middle of the clown's face. In some instances the whiteface is simply one more in a larger set of signals marking the character as a clown, but in a few instances it operates as the chief marker. In these cases, such as Liu Qingti's brother (who successfully entices his sister to forsake vegetarianism) or the magistrate who condemns an innocent defendant in *Hou Seven Kills His Mother*, the whiteface is a more obvious marker. It is part of the larger play within the opera in which the invisible world (in the form of spirits or ghosts) may sometimes become visible (to selected characters or only to the audience), or in which people's true qualities are revealed despite deceptive appearances. The visible whiteface of the clown marks (some) evil characters—and it also operates as a signal of revelation. The scenes with clowns are privileged moments of revelation of the iniquities of this world and of the underworld.

One illustrative scene occurs in *Head of Bees,* after the son's suicide by drowning.[29] That tragic scene is immediately followed by a lengthy comic scene between a humble fisherman and his wife, who, at the end of the scene, recover the son's body from their fishing nets. Various stresses of domestic life are touched upon, as is common in Chinese folk drama, and there is also extended comic play regarding death—the tragic theme of the preceding and subsequent scenes, as well as of Mulian opera as a whole.

In the midst of comic counterpoint and the addition of laughter to the emotive mix of the opera, a few other comments are made that would not be possible in the noncomic scenes. As part of their argument, the husband asks his wife what the difference is between "cultural struggle" (*wendou*) and "armed struggle" (*wudou*), and she replies that in "armed struggle" she hits him harder. This unmistakable reference to the Cultural Revolution does not appear in the printed text. Nor does the fisherman's brief comment of disgust at the bereaved father's continued denunciation of his son appear in the text. The fisherman does, however, act as the vehicle through which the truth becomes known and the son's good name is cleared—in both printed text and performed version—through the fisherman's reporting on actions of the stepmother that he has observed. The narrative development is identical in both versions, but the performed version allows the addition of countercommentary. The improvisational character of such scenes, more marked than in the core scenes of the cycle, is a significant structural feature of Mulian opera that allows it to undo—to place in question—the cultural effects generated (and exceeded) within the core of the narrative.

White-faced clowns appear at various junctures as wicked persons bringing harm to others. The means by which they do this are realistic in their diversity but usually share the quality of deception.[30] Two clowns who appear prominently in this manner are those who present themselves respectively as Buddhist and Daoist religious, collecting alms from the pious and generous Woman Geng. Their white faces and clownish mannerisms (both, by convention, visible only to the audience) are all that reveal them as untrustworthy. The ordinarily visible signs of piety occasion the trusting action of a believing, good woman that soon leads to her self-destruction. This is not difficult to construe as countercommentary upon the theme of filial piety, in either its everyday domestic or its political aspect. By being presented in the form of comic fragment, the countercommentary can uti-lize the deceptive appearance of comedy to introduce subversive meaning. The fragment is apparently marginal, especially in the amusing scheming and antics of the clowns, but it is structurally at the very core of the action of this play—the clowns' deception of Woman Geng is the pivotal event that causes her doom.

Similarly, Liu Qingti's younger brother, Liu Jia, appears in whiteface to per-suade his sister to enhance her health by breaking her vow of vegetarianism. He succeeds in convincing her, with the result that Liu Qingti is doomed to the most fearsome depths of hell. And, in *Hou Seven Kills His Mother,* the official who condemns an innocent person to death is played by a clown in whiteface. This structure works to invert the margin of the narrative into a question at its heart, and in doing so draws upon all the emotive energy generated by the surrounding narrative and ritual of death and life. And it does this with a laugh.[31]

Clown scenes and roles are used sparingly but are sprinkled throughout Mulian opera, with the effect of generating countercommentary on all aspects of the purported theme. The important cosmographic aspect of Mulian opera comes under question in the portrayal of the workings of hell. Excess is the main mecha-nism at work here, and the terror that it generates is defused by comic episodes. The most sustained of these, and one of the most amusing scenes in the opera, is one in which two brothers, minor officials sharing charge of an outpost in hell, each seek to gain sole charge of the post by eliminating the other. This scene presents a familiar set of problems of fraternal rivalry, bureaucratic competition, and human betrayal that, by being transposed to hell, renders hell more familiar.

Comedy appears here to make mockery of all the purportedly serious values of Mulian opera. Throughout the scene the brothers are portrayed in foolish excesses of religious behavior, as symbolized by continued, farcical beating of gongs and drums. Their breach of the norms of fraternal respect is demonstrated through ex-tremes of insincerity. The "hundred prostrations" (*baibai*) written and sent by the younger to the elder, and the repeated "kowtows" (*dunshou*) of the elder toward the younger, are each intended, through excess and inversion, to kill the other brother and leave the survivor in sole command of the outpost. The murderous plans are effected through the medium of repeated writing of the words of respect. Super-ficially this is a comic spoof of the reverence for writing and its power in this and other worlds (emphasized in the Confucian tradition), and of the universe of bureaucracy.

This scene can also be read as a kind of instruction to the audience on the de-coding of the opera (compare Bourdieu 1968): excess is dangerous; real meaning lies in inversion of overt meaning; it is possible to laugh at familial, religious, and bureaucratic authority. Let the officials approve of the portrayal of filial piety in all its forms, while the popular play goes on in the interstices. This interpretation is persuasive: it is faithful to the performance and seems to capture the compelling and complex power of Mulian opera. Still, I doubt that the interpretation can be left to rest there. There was no sense of definitiveness in the 1989 performance, and both the performance and the text are more a battlefield of warring interpretations than any peaceful synthesis or even a truce. Mulian opera is a play of unending, open-ended conflict and profound indeterminacy. It is a condition of its continued (precarious) existence in social, political, and economic terms that it is profoundly ambiguous in its political meanings and indeterminate in its effects. There is no reading of Mulian opera that does justice to its complexity and can at the same time claim to present the meaning or truth of the opera as definitive or closed.

THE SPACE OF SUBVERSION

Mulian opera is able to produce its unsettling effects because of its capacity to gen-erate a space of subversion. It is able to draw upon the general qualities of drama to mark off a separate time and space for a performance in which the fundamen-tal tenets of Chinese political culture are at once objectified and displaced. Filial piety is dramatically inscribed in performance at the same time that it is artisti-cally and ritually detached from its ordinary embeddedness in social relations.

The power of dramatic presentation is heightened in Mulian opera by the ritual context and by the exceptional resonance of the drama's themes with deeply felt and shared aspects of the moral self—present, remembered, and imagined. The pervasive violation of boundaries—including that between the "real" and the imagined—and the fragmentation of the performance create a transcendent space and maintain it throughout the duration of the performance.

It is this space—open, ambiguous, and silent—that defines and creates the subversive quality of Mulian opera. Within this space the audience, which would be more properly viewed as participants in a ritual, can actively imbue the per-formance with meaning. A major resource participants bring to this space is that of personal and shared memories focused upon death and the regeneration of life by Mulian opera's thematic preoccupation with filial piety. These memories are evoked by the narratives of the Mulian cycle and its interpolated domestic plays. While Mulian opera is very much open to readings that find hidden transcripts of resistance (Scott 1990) ambiguously present even within printed texts, it is doubtful that this is the main locus of subversion. Instead, following Caroline Humphrey (chapter 2, this volume), I would suggest that ambiguous narratives within Mulian opera evoke problematic memories and heterodox imaginings, and that this is where the subversive power of Mulian opera primarily lies. The memories and imaginings are all the more intractable by virtue of not being inscribed themselves within the opera, which contains instead only the formal means of evocation.

The politics of memory and of the construction of the self play out their conflicts within the space held open by the play on stage. That is why the issue of whether or not to perform Mulian opera was necessarily a political issue in 1989. For ordinary people and for folk artists, there is still the possibility of enacting Mulian opera without official approval. For the intellectuals who formed the actual audience for the 1989 *chenhe gaoqiang* performance, that is not a possibility. For this audience, the space created by the opera can be held open only by the denial of political significance in Mulian opera. This denial, which suits the demands of the state and may have been genuinely felt by some of the intellectuals involved, is critical to the continued political salience of Mulian opera.[32]

Mulian opera is dangerous. The existential and political issues revolving around filial piety are as much at the heart of Chinese political culture now as they were when this opera cycle first took form. And the opera is being revived at a moment of historical danger (see Benjamin 1969:257). The collapse of a vision of a socialist future, which inspired much of recent Chinese history, was pervasive by 1989. This collapse created a renewed opening for images of a remembered past, the temporal mode privileged within Chinese culture (Owen 1986). The remembrance implicit in filial piety resonates with contemporary strivings to redefine Chinese political culture through rethinking and recreating the national past.[33]

Mulian opera does not offer an alternative to filial piety, obedience, or hierarchy, and it does not engage in a sustained critique. It works in the space between didactic narrative and the play of excess, fragmentation, and laughter. In its intensity and indeterminacy, it generates a space of subversion. But it is a space that cannot be named.

——— Notes ———

1. I will use the terms *heaven* and *hell* in lowercase, as the most appropriate terms available in the English language. Heaven has a geographic location to the west and above. Hell has a geographic location below. No Christian concordance or influence is implied.

2. The earliest Mulian *bianwen* date from about AD 800 but are presumably based upon unwritten traditions that are several centuries older. They are attributed to Indian sources but are generally agreed to have originated in China. See Mair (1983, 1989) and Teiser (1988a).

3. The *yulanpen* festival is the ritual culmination of the Mulian ritual opera cycle and is the means through which Mulian ultimately accomplishes his goal of salvation (see Teiser 1986). This has remained an important element in modern funerary ritual, at least as reported for Taiwan. In Taiwan, elements of the Mulian story are performed in funeral rituals and have been the object of detailed anthropological study, especially with respect to the symbolic representation, in these versions, of women as intrinsically polluted, and especially so through the blood of childbirth, from which they can be released only after death and through appropriate ritual action by their sons. Mulian then figures as a model of a filial son who, through his own suffering and purity, redeems his mother and

other hungry ghosts from the torments of hell (see Johnson 1989; Seaman 1981; also see Ahern 1973, 1981a, 1981b; Johnson, Nathan, and Rawski 1985).

The strongest confirmation of the importance of this ritual in the contemporary People's Republic of China is the arrangement of all the officially approved Mulian performances for dates far removed from the date of the Feast of Hungry Ghosts (the fifteenth day of the seventh lunar month), when it should occur in the ritual calendar. This temporal displacement is one of the means through which rupture in the cultural field was created. The resulting decontextualization of the drama did not, however, remove its political force. The elements of the drama that were highlighted as it was actually performed were Liu Qingti's transgressions (portrayed as trivial) and her resistance. In effect, this decontextualization may have removed some of the power of the drama for the audience that was not there. It had little effect on the import of the drama for the audience that was there: middle-aged intellectuals who had all passed through the denunciations and tribulations of repeated political campaigns.

4. I would also like to acknowledge the proceedings of the conference on Mulian opera, held in Huaihua following this performance, from October 31 to November 2, 1989. Many of the papers were distributed during the conference, and I referred to these and to my notes on the oral presentations. Selections from the proceedings may be published in the future.

5. The allegation that Mulian opera portrays ordinary people negatively is accurate in strictly literal terms. There is some doubt, however, about whether the characters should be viewed as simply representing classes or strata. Although a range of settings and social strata is represented, one commentator has pointed out that everything is portrayed from a peasant (or perhaps petit bourgeois) point of view. It might also be added that the opera takes place outside ordinary time and space. Except where the plot is one of deception and betrayal, or where some trace of social inequality occasionally creeps in, there is a tendency for characters to appear in a social status representative of their moral worth. This is a comprehensible dramatic device in an opera cycle much concerned with right, wrong, and retribution. It also makes it nearly impossible for a person of humble social status to be portrayed in a positive light. Almost the only (qualified) exceptions are loyal servants.

6. Although not totally prohibited, the performance of the Mulian cycle has been effectively inhibited, by varying accounts, since 1949, 1952, or 1956. It was staged outside the official ambit during the 1980s but was only officially sponsored, and then only as a subject for research and with limited attendance, in the late 1980s. A performance and conference centered largely on a study of Zheng Zhizhen's version was held in Anhui in 1988. The *chenhe gaoqiang* version under discussion here followed in 1989, and a study of a Fujian variant, in combination with a conference on southern opera (*nanxi*) was held in 1991.

7. Mulian opera (*Mulianxi*) consists of five components: the story of Mulian proper (*Mulian zhuan*), a preface to the story of Mulian (*Qian Mulian*), optional plays preceding the preface (in this case, *Liang zhuan* and *Xiangshan*), plays not related to the story of Mulian that are interpolated into the cycle (*Hua Mulian*), and rituals associated with the performance, which occur at various points before, during, and after the performance of the cycle proper. The narrative that comprises the Mulian cycle in a series of plays (of flexible number) are in *Qian Mulian* and *Mulian zhuan*.

8. On the violence done to human dignity through the exercise of state power in the practice of everyday life, see Scott (1990).

9. It would be difficult to exaggerate the role of drama in rural popular culture in China. As a Chinese experimenter in drama working in a 1930s rural reconstruction project observed:

> According to our experience in Ding County, the knowledge of Chinese peasants, especially that about human behaviour, mostly comes from the stage. There is hardly any view of human affairs or recollection of history which does not derive strength from drama. Seen from a certain position, we could say that drama aids learning that comes from books, but up to the present day in China's villages, drama is simply the peasants' only education. (Xiong 1936: 102–103)

10. Stephen Teiser (1988a) has noted that Buddhism places greater emphasis on respect for mothers than does the official version of Chinese kinship, and Gary Seaman (1981) locates much of the meaning of the Mulian story in the redemption of mothers from the pollution inevitable in motherhood or simply being female. These observations are very likely valid within the context of the larger arguments of which they are part. They do not serve, however, to remove ambiguity from the representation of filial piety in the story of Mulian as performed, and it is this persistent ambiguity that is of concern here. Also see Zito (1987).

11. In the *chenhe gaoqiang* variant of Mulian opera, the dominant ritual presence was Daoist rather than Buddhist. In the 1989 performance of the cycle, these rituals were enacted—in some instances by men described as actual Daoist priests—but the enactments were displaced to the proscenium stage and orchestra of the government auditorium. The enactments included rituals framing the performance itself by capturing dangerous ghosts for the duration of the cycle and allowing the performance to proceed safely (*kaitaixi*), carrying in a local deity prior to the performance (*tai lingguan*), and the concluding *yulanpen*. The priests also appeared performing funerary rituals within *The Story of Mulian* itself. Their movement across the boundary between stage and life was not particular to their persons or their roles. Actors in key roles (Mulian and Liu Qingti) partook of the qualities of the characters they portrayed, and audience members joined in the staged rituals and occasionally in the action of the staged drama.

12. Magical mirrors appear in Mulian opera as a means for seeing beyond deceptive appearance to the truth and as a means of protection.

13. A significant theme in filial piety is presented, in this version, not through Mulian but through the character of the goddess Guanyin, who first appears in *Fragrant Mountain* (Xiangshan), a two-part opera that was performed immediately prior to the first part of the prelude sequence (*Qian Mulian*) to the cycle proper. In this play, the young woman who is to become Guanyin hears her mother lament the fate of being a woman and mother, and vows to take religious orders and renounce the world in order to repay her mother for the mother's suffering in bringing her into the world. Here the redemption of women and mothers that is significantly attributed to Mulian as archetypical son in other versions (compare Seaman 1981) is instead attributed to a female Buddhist deity who appears through the cycle itself as a provider of magical power to Mulian. Mulian, as son, can still be read as a saviour of his mother, but this interpretation is not marked in the 1989 *chenhe gaoqiang* performance.

14. This play is a variant of the Woman Huang story studied by Grant (1989).

15. In contrast, scenes of civil war that were part of the prepared text were not performed.

16. Mulian opera continued to be performed long after its quasi-official prohibition in the 1950s. It was reported to have been unofficially performed elsewhere in Hunan in 1989.

17. There are numerous points of remarkable resonance between Mulian opera and the culture of terror described by Michael Taussig (1987). An adequate comparative exploration is beyond the scope of the present paper, but must nevertheless be remarked.

18. Corporeal disintegration is the most threatening prospect because it brings a final end to the life-after-death of the underworld.

19. Reportedly, when the opera was staged in the past, all in attendance would have abstained from meat until the point in the opera when Liu Qingti holds a banquet and eats meat, at which time the audience would partake of a similar feast.

20. The interpretation that Liu Qingti was condemned by the pollution of being female and a mother is one that would not be definitively contradicted by this version of Mulian opera. References are made to the lamentable fate of being female, but while the theme of female pollution may well be present, it is not marked and it appears overshadowed in this version by other elements in the complex of Mulian symbolism.

21. Mulian is the disciple of Buddha most noted for magical prowess.

22. Chinese culture is self-conscious and sophisticated regarding representation onstage or offstage. For a contrasting Western view of possible connections between onstage and offstage tragedy, see Williams (1979).

23. I am using the term *state* in the broad sense, encompassing all branches of government and the Communist party, including officially sponsored institutions of art and scholarship.

24. Similar research is being carried on regarding another category of revived ritual drama, *nuoxi*.

25. I do not know the outcome for certain but, while the performance was an artistic success, the financial deficit of the event and the difficult economic circumstances in China since that time make it very unlikely that the troupe was established.

26. Staff of the local art center were the senior people in charge, but they did not themselves perform and did not have the expertise to stage Mulian opera on their own. The modern term for director (*daoyan*) was used for their leading figure, while the leading folk artist was described as the *zhangtaishi*.

27. The invited audience primarily consisted of scholars in the field of drama research in China. (Three Japanese scholars, a French cinematographer, and I were also invited attendees.) A few professionals in the Chinese drama world were also present by invitation. As the performance proceeded, an uninvited audience of elderly opera lovers and the (apparently) well-connected grew in numbers.

28. A supplement is distinct from a wage. Those who had retired or lost their positions in the late 1980s without having become state employees would have had no other income during this time, but those who had become state employees would have had a wage or pension in addition. Even troupes that were inactive were generally still paying salaries.

29. The range of clown scenes in Mulian opera is wide, and a full examination is beyond the scope of this paper. Only selected instances directly relevant to the argument of this chapter are presented here.

30. Good persons may also practice deception, as in the case of Guanyin's tempting Mulian to forsake his vows of chastity and vegetarianism, as a test.

31. This is one of many points where the resonances with Mikhail Bakhtin's (1984) study of Rabelais are especially provocative. A comparable study of Mulian opera and its historical context remains to be done. I would here only underline the suggestive parallels regarding laughter, excess, and ambiguity.

32. At least some of the drama scholars attending the performance appeared quite estranged from folk drama. They observed that the performance was crudely done and reflected only a peasant perspective on the world. The dominant concern of the scholarly conference that followed the performance was the light cast on the history of Chinese drama and its regional diversity by the study of contemporary variants of this early drama cycle. The interest of Chinese intellectuals and scholars of drama in local and folk opera forms does not imply that the gulf between intellectual and folk artist has been obliterated (see Judd 1990).

33. Controversy surrounding an influential television epic on the Chinese past, *Heshang*, was still raging and was a subject of comment outside the theater in Huaihua in the autumn of 1989.

7

Memories of Revolution and Collectivization in China

The Unauthorized Reminiscences of a
Rural Intellectual

PAUL G. PICKOWICZ

SCHOLARS INTERESTED IN unofficial and counterhegemonic accounts of the tumultuous events that have unfolded in rural China in the last half-century confront many frustrations. In sharp contrast to the present political situation in Eastern Europe and the former Soviet republics, the Communist party is still very much in power in China. In the wake of the Tiananmen Square crisis of June 1989 and the sudden collapse of communist regimes throughout the world, rural dwellers in China know that the state is highly sensitive to acts of remembering that subvert what remains of its moral and political legitimacy among peasants. Indeed, in the summer of 1991 a socialist education campaign was waged throughout rural North China, in part to resuscitate master narratives that emphasize the theme of intimate relations between the socialist state and the peasantry.

Another problem that faces scholars of unofficial histories is that research access to the vast countryside, where nearly 80 percent of the people live, is still severely limited. Peasants in North China know of the demise of communist regimes in foreign lands and share many of the views about socialism held by their counterparts in the former Soviet Union and elsewhere, but the few foreign scholars who gain research access to village life are usually monitored very closely, and villagers, naturally, are afraid to speak in detail about the socialist past.

Finally, it must be acknowledged that efforts to discover unofficial writings that discuss rural China are hindered by the simple fact that peasant culture is not very literate (Link, Madsen, and Pickowicz 1989:72–87). That is, peasants are not inclined to write private reflections about the past that are both systematic and lengthy. This is why Western scholarly interest in unofficial texts focuses almost exclusively on the highly accessible writings of sophisticated urban intellectuals (Barme and Minford 1989). It is true that some of these urban works describe personal experiences in rural China in the 1950s and 1960s, but such writings, however fascinating and insightful they may be, are not the same as peasant writings. The fact is that unofficial histories written by rural villagers are extremely rare.

Between 1978 and 1987 I traveled five times to Raoyang county, Hebei province, to work on the research project that resulted in the publication of *Chinese Village, Socialist State* (Friedman, Pickowicz, and Selden 1991).[1] Only once during that time did I see a lengthy unofficial text. Late in the evening of September 19, 1985, as I was finishing an interview with a 72-year-old peasant named Geng Xiufeng (pronounced Gung Sho-fung), I noticed a stack of papers on the windowsill by his brick bed and asked what it was. He said it was a handwritten draft of his "memoir." Without pausing, he handed me the manuscript. Unfortunately, county-level party and security operatives, unaware of the existence of this work, were obviously unhappy with Geng's willingness to share the manuscript and forced him to retrieve it from me the next morning. I assumed that was the last I would ever see of the controversial text.

I learned later, however, that Geng completed a revision of the memoir in March 1988. I wrote to say I would be pleased to comment on the work. To my great surprise, the revised work, still in handwritten form and bearing the highly moralistic, almost Confucian, title "Renjian zheng dao" (loosely translated as "The True Path") arrived after considerable delay at my office in a brown paper packet plastered with no less than 33 Chinese postage stamps. In a characteristically bold cover letter, Geng explained that he had sent out three copies: one to the central government, one to the provincial government, and one to me. The center and the province had not responded. Geng proclaimed that his personal story revealed nothing less than the solution to the problem of world hunger, and he wanted to get his message to the United Nations. His assertion that he knew the "correct" way to bring prosperity to the rural poor implied that the Chinese Communist party had long ago veered from the true path.

I never asked Geng why he called "Renjian zheng dao" a *huiyi lu* (a term that means recollection, memoir, reminiscence, or record of memories), but the reasons are fairly obvious. By the mid-1980s, significant numbers of well-known, elderly public figures, inside and outside the party, were publishing *huiyi lu*. It was a fad that allowed such people (many of whom were discredited during the Cultural Revolution) to earn royalties by "setting the record straight" before their death. Geng was not, however, a well-known public figure like the other writers of mainstream *huiyi lu;* always immodest, he simply regards himself as an important person whose story has been submerged for far too long. The *huiyi lu* genre is perfectly appropriate for such a writer.

Geng's *huiyi lu* cannot be regarded as formal "history" (*lishi*), "treatise" (*lunwen*), or "essay" (*wenzhang*) because it confines itself exclusively to Geng's memories of his own activities and of events that he witnessed personally. It is not a work of scholarship (*xuewen*) because it provides no documentation, and it cannot be viewed as autobiography (*zizhuan*) because it excludes discussions of all aspects of Geng's life that do not bear directly on rural collectivization, a process that began in communist base areas in North China in the prerevolutionary era and was completed in the early 1960s. But Geng's peasant's-eye version of cooperative and collective formation (and the massive famine that followed) is different from the *huiyi lu* printed by official publishing houses because it conflicts with virtually all state narratives and mythologies that discuss the transition to socialism in the rural sector, where the revolution was supposed to be among friends.

Geng Xiufeng's memoir deserves attention because it allows us to hear the voice of a "village intellectual" (*nongcun zhishifenzi*), a voice rarely heard by foreign scholars.[2] These local "educated elements," whose numbers rarely exceeded 30 or 40 per hinterland village in the prerevolutionary Republican era (1911–49), were respected by the community for their seemingly vast knowledge of the world beyond the sorghum fields. Literate individuals like Geng were often members of better-off households simply because only such families could afford to pay primary-school tuition fees (Averill 1990:292–97; McCord 1990:174–79). Writings like *Renjian zheng dao* are rare, however. If such documents do exist, they rarely reach a public audience. In China it was the self-imposed responsibility of the literati (usually urban) and, later, intellectuals and party policy makers (also usually urban) "to speak for the peasants," including Geng (see Siu 1990; Siu and Stern 1983).

The early experiences of local intellectuals like Geng are rarely highlighted in official narratives because they are inconsistent with the official view that the party and the poor peasantry (*ping nong*, or what Soviet ideologists called *bednyaks* in the late 1920s) deserve almost all the credit for resisting Japan and introducing a genuinely socialist cooperative movement.

Born in 1913 in Wugong village, Raoyang county, Hebei province, Geng Xiufeng came from a family better off than most, with 50 *mu* (8.3 acres) in 1928 (Friedman, Pickowicz, and Selden 1991:52–58, 61–63, 65–74). The average family holding in his village was approximately 2.7 acres. Immediately after World War II, Geng's household was classified as "middle peasant" (*zhong nong*, or what the Soviet party called *serednyaks*). In late 1947, however, in a brief extremist phase of the communist-led land-reform process, outside party investigators placed Geng's household in the dreaded "rich peasant" category (*fu nong*, or what the Soviets called *kulaks*) reserved for class enemies of the revolution. Several months later the household (along with more than 60 others unfairly classified as "rich peasant") were reclassified as "middle peasant."

Geng received a total of seven years of primary education, an extraordinary amount by local standards. More importantly, like so many others in his category throughout North China, he attended a "new style" (i.e., postimperial) primary school from 1923 to 1928, when even hinterland youths were exposed to the militantly nationalistic currents associated with the Nationalist party (*Guomindang*) and the revolutionary Northern Expedition. Scholars of the Republican era have done very little research on the impact of the May Fourth Movement (1919) on rural society, but it is clear that in addition to becoming ardent patriots in the mid-1920s, Geng and many other rural elites were also exposed, far more extensively than official sources acknowledge, to the collectivistic, utopian socialist and anarchist currents normally associated with the urban May Fourth Movement (Dirlik 1989:57–145). These particular currents, which made their impact on rural intellectuals like Geng long before they learned anything about the Communist party, taught self-help, mutual aid, local governance, and, most significantly, distrust of state power. Urban anarchists like Wei Huilin, who wrote for journals that were accessible to teachers in hinterland county seats, preached that peasants could govern themselves (Ge, Jiang, and Li 1984:669–70).

Young people like Geng got their modern ideas not from the Communist party but from their idealistic teachers. Even now Geng credits his primary-school teacher (a man named Liu Zisheng, whom he idolized) and his elder brother, Geng Manliang (a graduate of a county-level teacher training school), with providing a fundamental political education that continues to serve Geng today. And the most basic political lesson learned by Geng and other educated village elites in their teenage years was that China, once a great and respected civilization, was now a humiliated (*chi*) and insulted (*wuru*) nation. China endured insult after insult, they learned, because it was weak. The nation was weak and defenseless because it was disorganized, poor, and backward. In short, the people were not acting in concert.

Although their enormous contribution is virtually ignored in official sources, Geng and hundreds of thousands of other scions of noncommunist rural elites were intensely patriotic and devoted themselves to the communist-led resistance movement once the war with Japan broke out in 1937. Geng was 24 at the time. During the war years his family continued to farm, but Geng held a number of village and county-level jobs that dealt with education and publishing. Without the enthusiastic help of local elites and educated people, the Communist party would have had significantly more difficulty mobilizing ordinary folk, who were always wary of strangers who spoke with an unfamiliar accent.

Even before the war ended Geng Xiufeng began to shift his attention to the subject that really fascinated him: agrarian socialism. Even though, according to his own account, Geng was not a Communist party member and did not get his ideas about cooperative formation from party sources, he organized a number of small, semisocialist agricultural cooperatives during and after the devastating famine of 1943. As a cadre in the employ of the new communist provincial government in Baoding, Geng continued to promote co-op formation in the early 1950s, before such work became a state priority. In 1953 Geng was heavily involved in his home village of Wugong in the formation of one of the first large co-ops that involved nearly all the households (401) of a single village. In 1958 Geng was an official in the gigantic people's commune that was set up in his home district during the disastrous Great Leap Forward. In brief, during the period from 1943 to 1964 (when a bout with tuberculosis forced him to retire from his state job at the age of 53), Geng worked tirelessly both inside and outside state organizations at the village, district, county, prefectural, and provincial levels to promote co-op formation, earning the nickname "collectomaniac" (*hezuomi*, literally "cooperation devotee") in the process. After his "retirement" he continued to give unofficial (and sometimes unwelcome) advice to village and county leaders, many of whom, Geng makes clear, regarded him as a nuisance. "Take a rest," the county party committee said!

"RENJIAN ZHENG DAO" AS A REJECTION OF MARXIST-LENINIST CATEGORIES

In the mid-1940s, Geng Xiufeng accepted help from and eventually joined the Communist party, but he takes great pains in his memoir to demonstrate that his conception of agrarian socialism was rooted in a knowledge of local peasant life and was strikingly different from the view that dominated state thinking in the mid-1950s. His agenda, which he ardently believed would win the support of typical peasants, stressed local governance and the primary objective of bringing economic prosperity, not mere subsistence, to all the rural social classes. By contrast, the Communist party, like the party of Stalin before it, was primarily interested in state building and industrialization (Lewin 1975: 214–66). The party was drawn to agricultural cooperation and, eventually, collectivization as the best way to gain total control over the rural economy, to get direct access to all harvests, and to use the labor of peasants to fund rapid urban industrial development. These fundamentally different orientations would bring Geng, and peasants in general, into constant, painful conflict with state authorities.

Geng begins his memoir by making it clear that his interest in agrarian socialism was not inspired by the policies of the Communist party or the writings of Chairman Mao. His point of departure was the profound sense of humiliation and shame he internalized as a schoolboy in the 1920s. "When I was in primary school," he recalls, "my teacher was always talking about national shame." The problem was that rural China was desperately poor and no one seemed to know what to do about it. Writing in 1988, Geng continued to think of rural dwellers in the 1940s as "a loose sheet of sand" (*yi pan sansha*), disorganized and going nowhere.

In sharp contrast to romantic Maoist mythology, Geng's hard-boiled and highly paternalistic image of ordinary peasants is not very flattering. According to Geng, their "cultural level" was low, they clung stubbornly to a way of life that barely permitted survival, and they did not seem to feel the same sense of shame he and other local intellectuals felt about the plight of their civilization. Ordinary peasants, some of whom were lazy (*lan*) and incompetent (*bu neng gan*), needed to be led by people who had intimate knowledge of local problems and possessed a vision of a new and better society. Ordinary peasants, Geng implies, were not capable of coming up with new ideas themselves, but, deeply suspicious of strangers and outsiders, they were willing, on occasion, to trust educated rural elites who spoke their language. Indeed, local educated people had a sacred moral responsibility to lead the peasants out of their poverty. "How was I able to adopt this moral position?" Geng asks. "It was something entirely passed on to me by my teacher." The ultimate moral responsibility of every rural intellectual, he insists, was to find a way for "the poor to throw off the shackles of poverty once and for all." Geng gives no credit whatsoever to the Communist party for his political awakening, nor does he refer even once in his memoir to the state's need for sources of revenue during the resistance war or after the revolution.

In "Renjian zheng dao" Geng asserts that in 1943 he reached the momentous conclusion that the only way out for the rural poor, which in his essentially non-Marxist view embraced virtually everyone (including most of the so-called landlords and rich peasants), was to engage in cooperative agriculture, or what he called "land partnership groups" (tudi hezuo zu). Participants were to retain private ownership of the land they contributed, and distribution of income was to be based, in part, on the amount and quality of land invested. "If everyone understood this logic," he recalls in his memoir, "overcame selfish habits (zisi xiguan), and pooled their land, the difficulties of every family could be resolved." By the early 1950s these types of organizations were officially labeled by the state as semisocialist "agricultural producer's cooperatives" (nongye shengchan hezuoshe). Beginning in the spring of 1944, well before Geng joined the Communist party and well before the Japanese surrendered, he started organizing groups of four to ten households, first in his native village of Wugong and then in surrounding villages. In the early 1950s he continued to promote cooperation as a minor official in the new Hebei provincial bureau of agriculture and forestry.

Initially, party functionaries were annoyed with Geng's lack of Leninist-type discipline. But his own sense of what he was doing in 1943, when he suddenly and without permission abandoned his cultural work for the county resistance and returned to his poverty stricken village, is that he was behaving like heroic and self-sacrificing traditional Chinese intellectuals who put down their pens to save the poor during times of crisis. One day, Geng recalls, he just dropped his pen and walked out. One of his colleagues in the print shop, mindful that the party was intolerant of unexcused absences, pleaded, "Don't do it! Magistrate He personally asked for you to work here; you can't leave without checking it out with him first!"

For Geng, an exceedingly self-righteous man, the superiority of cooperative farming was self-evident. The land itself, he insisted, was not that bad. The problem was that many poor families were unskilled and short of farm tools, draft animals, labor power, and capital for investment in all-important agricultural and household sidelines. Some families had adequate labor and skills, but owing to shortages of land and capital, their labor and skill could not be utilized effectively within the family economy.

If groups of five to ten families pooled their resources, he argued, it would be possible to accumulate bits of capital not available to ordinary farmers. The capital could be used in the winter to run small sideline industries that produced for the market. By wisely reinvesting sideline profits to expand sideline activities, co-ops would eventually be able to purchase collectively owned farm tools and draft animals to boost crop yields. "The reason that people are so poor," Geng reasoned, "is that their base (*jichu*) of production is too small. . . . Furthermore, the larger the number of people involved, the more likely that people of talent will surface; those who can farm should farm and those who can do sidelines should do side-lines. There will be work to do year round and, naturally, incomes will increase."

Opposition to Geng's ideas in the mid-1940s was deeply rooted. Ordinary peasants, in spite of their poverty, were extremely reluctant to experiment with the little they had or to depart from time-honored ways of doing things. According to Geng, some peasants said, "You must be looking for trouble; if you put sev-eral families together to farm, you'll never be able to settle the disputes." Others said, "In the last ten thousand generations who has seen several families farming together? You'll only see it when the sun rises in the west!" Many local communists wondered aloud whether Geng was wasting his time. A prominent county-level communist said, "You really are the oldest ancestor of the subjectivists! Everyone knows peasants are extremely selfish (*zisi*) and backward (*lohou*), like a dish of loose sand. Their land is the root of their life. They will argue for the sake of a chicken and squabble about the boundaries of their land. If you ask them to pool their land, they will view it as nonsense, an absolute daydream!"

Geng realized at the time that many Communist party members would be indifferent to or even oppose his ideas about land pooling because, as he was abundantly aware, his views were quite different from "the idea of collectivization in the Soviet Union." He was afraid that the party would accuse him of the ideo-logical crime of "reformism" (*gailiangzhuyi*), that is, the attempt to reform, rather than utterly destroy, the traditional household economy. Thus, in these and many other portions of his memoir, Geng rejects the suggestion that the party was be-hind the first efforts to introduce agrarian socialism in his region. When Geng speaks of the party's attitude toward cooperation in the 1940s and early 1950s, he invariably mentions it in connection with the activities of meddling outsiders whose agendas reflected external state priorities rather than local peasant pre-occupation with household prosperity.

In two crucial respects, of course, Geng's approach to cooperation was in-deed "subjectivist." First, he never wavered from the basic proposition that "if the method is rational (*heli*), people will unite around it." Like late–nineteenth-century Russian populists, Geng believed that education was the key to building a successful agrarian socialist community (see Meisner 1982:28–75). Under no circumstances should peasants be forced to participate; they had to be convinced that cooperation was superior, and it was the job of rural elites to persuade them. To this day Geng has never seriously considered the possibility that voluntary co-operative farming is basically flawed. If peasants were unreceptive to the idea, it was because local elites failed to explain its advantages. If fledgling cooperatives failed, it was only because they had not been run properly. As Geng put it, "If the lock won't open, don't blame the lock (*suo bu kai, bu neng yuan suo*), you can only blame the person who wants to open the lock for not using the right key. If the key fits, the lock will open. It's very easy." One of the things that distinguishes Geng's colorful discussion of rural society from stiff official accounts is his frequent use of local colloquial expressions and folk analogies of this sort. "If you don't tell people," he asserted, "they won't know (*ren bu shuo, bu zhi*); if you never begin the drilling process, you'll never make it through a piece of wood" (*mu bu zuan, bu tou*).

Geng's approach to agrarian socialism departed from the method adopted in the Soviet Union in the 1920s and in China in the mid-1950s in another respect. He agreed that the traditional system, even with its large middle-peasant majority, involved the exploitation of hired hands and tenants and, thus, elements of class conflict. But like other rural elites influenced by non-Marxist May Fourth currents in the 1920s, he did not believe that encouraging violent class struggle was the way to carry out the revolution or transform the rural economy along cooperative lines. Geng regarded virtually all the inhabitants of hinterland Hebei, including those later regarded as class enemies by the Communist party, as victims of the wrenching poverty and hopelessness that stalked the land. Geng wanted to find a way out for everyone, not just those who happened to be at the bottom at a particular point in time. The issue was not one of class but one of consciousness. Only those who truly believed in the superiority of cooperation would make good co-op members.

When the first co-op of four households organized by Geng began to do well in the summer of 1944, a public security officer in the county seat jokingly referred to Geng's home village as "little Moscow." Although it was meant as a compliment, the remark made Geng a bit uncomfortable. First, Geng claimed he already knew in 1943 that "great losses were suffered" in the brutal drive for collectivization in the Soviet Union, in part because there was no sense of "voluntary participation and mutual benefit" (*zi yuan liang li*). The Soviet model, he insisted, was not what he had in mind and would not be welcomed by peasants. Second, what he proposed would unite the various rural classes rather than rip them asunder; it was a proposal that could be "supported by all the classes in the village." Echoing the sentiments of urban utopian socialists who were active in China before much was known about Marxism-Leninism (Dirlik 1991; Zarrow 1990), Geng insists in his memoir that his method was a "more civilized (*wenming*) way than the method of class struggle, because it put the idea of humanity in the forefront of things."

Geng declared that even small landlords were capable of supporting the sort of revolution he had in mind. "I myself had a relative who was a landlord," he recalled. "He was very interested in land partnership and wanted to try it. Among the rest of my well-off relatives there was not a person who doubted or opposed the method. They all said that in the future everyone should take this road. Why? Because everyone had run out of patience with the old road. They all believed that this was an unselfish (*dagong wusi*), mutually beneficial (*huxiang*) way that united people on the correct road." Geng's remark is extraordinarily interesting, not because it is literally true that all landlords eagerly supported agrarian socialism but because his perspective on class relations on the North China plain is so radically different from the caricatures one routinely finds in official sources.

Geng's vision, then, was that poor people (a multiclass category that included almost everyone), through hard work and self-reliance, could make agrarian socialism work. This strategy, he repeats time and again, involved "relying on the strengths of the group to resolve everyone's difficulties." In times of bounty, all would share in the bounty; in times of disaster, the burden would be divided evenly.[3] Expressing a rural version of some fundamental assumptions associated with the May Fourth Movement, Geng was convinced that the transition to co-operative farming would result in the replacement of the autocratic "patriarchal system" (*jiazhang zhi*) of production with a more rational "democratic system" (*minzhu zhi*). If people believed in cooperation, "magical" (*qi gong*) results were possible. Geng explains, "Nothing is more important to the people than their production. Even if they have to sacrifice in the short run, they will do it willingly if their production problems can be solved. Anyone can see that it is worth losing a sesame seed to gain a watermelon (*diao le zhima, shi ge xigua*)."

Geng and like-minded people achieved considerable success in promoting rural cooperatives in Hebei in the late 1940s and early 1950s. In 1945 he finally joined the Communist party, but like other rural elites who accepted party leadership during the war against Japan, his relations with the new state builders were always somewhat tense (Friedman, Pickowicz, and Selden 1991:63–74). After Geng joined the party, his work continued to be guided by the non-Marxist ideas about local autonomy and mutual aid that he had embraced as a youth. Geng saw himself not as a disciplined Leninist unquestioningly representing the interests of the state and party center, but rather as a traditional-style savior and defender of the common people.

Geng's huge ego and his profound dissatisfaction with official versions of local history published before and during the Cultural Revolution (1966–76) forced him repeatedly to object in public whenever the agents of the state, on behalf of Chairman Mao and the party, took full credit for the work he and others had done to promote agrarian socialism (Nankai daxue lishi xi and Wugong dadui cun shi zu 1978). Time and again he irritated petty state authorities by insisting that the official party view of the history of cooperative formation in Hebei was incorrect. Official publications said that all cooperative formation was inspired by the thought of Chairman Mao; Geng consistently argued that he had developed his ideas on his own. In his 1988 memoir he boldly repeats this position: "When I read [Mao's] 'Get organized' I was quite pleased; I could see that Chairman Mao's ideas were the same as my own. Chairman Mao supported our desire to form land partnerships."

Geng's deeply rooted suspicion of the motives of the state are captured beautifully in the following anecdote. In the spring of 1963, he recalls, the Tianjin Writers' Association and the Hebei Arts Association sent a team of writers to Wugong to collect information for a book that was supposed to sing the praises of socialism and the party. One writer, Zhang Qingtian, drafted a chapter titled

"Comrade Geng Xiufeng," in which he mentioned Geng's pioneering effort to form a four-household co-op in the fall of 1943. But higher-level party officials objected to the draft, saying, "This chapter has a fundamental problem. We don't want it! It says that before Chairman Mao wrote 'Get Organized' Geng was already organizing a group. Is that to say he was wiser than Chairman Mao?" The authorities sent a delegation to Tianjin to pressure the publisher to omit the sacrilegious chapter. The section on Geng was finally included in the book, perhaps because Mao's political standing had declined after the Great Leap (*Huakai di yi zhi* 1963:32–41). But the chapter was cut by almost 60 percent when a more orthodox edition of the book appeared in 1973 (*Huakai di yi zhi* 1973:79–83).

One gets the strong impression from "Renjian zheng dao" that Geng Xiufeng's support of the Communist party has always been conditional. He and other rural elites worked with the party in the early years because they believed the party had agreed to play the leading role in coordinating the efforts of people like them. The first two lines of the introduction to Geng's memoir read "Poor peasants have only one demand of the party: lead us in a permanent transition from poverty to prosperity. If the party wants to satisfy this demand, it must recognize that there is nothing more effective than the method of agricultural cooperation and peasant cooperation." Geng's point, of course, is that when the party is unwilling to take the lead, others should do so. In 1943, according to Geng, friends tried to discourage him by saying, "If your method really works, the party would have recommended it long ago, instead of waiting for you to think of it!" Geng countered by saying that he did not accept the idea that it was always necessary to wait for orders from the party before taking the initiative. "The party is emphasizing resistance to Japan; it has no time to work on this issue right now," he chided. "There is no reason why we can't go ahead first (*xian zuo dian*)."

In a similar vein, Geng argued that peasants should not blindly accept misguided orders issued by the state, nor should the state try to force its will on rural people. To make this point, Geng tells a story about the damage done to cooperative work in his village in early 1945 when outside party functionaries, ignorant of local conditions in communist-controlled base areas, forced the co-op to function in a more "egalitarian way" by reducing the amount of grain distributed according to individual land investments. In this case, party heavy-handedness almost destroyed the co-op when nearly half its members suddenly dropped out.

Stressing once again the notion that peasants must be allowed to run their own affairs and must be protected from the grasp of the state, Geng adds, "From what I could tell, the use of the method of administrative commands (*xingzheng mingling*) was not at all appropriate for the self-governing economic organizations (*zizhi xingzhi*) of peasants." His suspicion of the state partly explains why Geng does not celebrate the land-reform movement initiated by the party in 1946–48. Geng personally witnessed the land reform, but he mentions this watershed event only once in his memoir: "It would be wonderful if all cadres [in the 1950s] understood that the mass line insists upon voluntary participation [in cooperatives] on the basis of mutual benefit. When the methods adopted during land reform and the Three-anti campaign [of 1951] are used, we are not able to get good results. No matter what views we hold, we cannot resort to force."

"RENJIAN ZHENG DAO" AS A RURAL CRITIQUE OF STATE POWER

The homespun critique of state power contained in "Renjian zheng dao" is credible, in part, because Geng Xiufeng's perspective is not in the least inspired by an antisocialist or anticommunist political agenda. In theory, Geng and the party-state shared the view that the peasant household economy should be replaced by cooperative forms of social and economic organization. But Geng's conception of cooperation focused almost exclusively on the issue of peasant prosperity. Rural abundance was not a means to some other end, but a legitimate end in its own right. That is why Geng became so incensed in late 1947 when a highly successful co-op he had founded, made up entirely of poor and middle peasants, was labeled a "rich peasant" organization during a violent class-struggle movement initiated by party outsiders. He constantly repeated the view that rural co-ops were "self-governing economic organizations." The peasants themselves should decide on all issues related to consumption and investment without outside interference. There was nothing wrong with prosperity; evidence of prosperity is what would convince uncommitted peasants to try cooperation. Neither was there anything wrong with cooperative sideline production, marketing, and commerce.

Geng also opposed artificial economic leveling within co-op organizations. Individual incomes should be based partly on the amount and quality of labor done by an individual and partly on dividends on land and capital invested by an individual in the group. Such groups were semisocialist in the sense that they respected both private and collective economic interests. Absent from Geng's memoir is any discussion of how the formation of voluntary co-ops would benefit the emerging state, although, of course, co-op members, like all individual farming households in the late 1940s and early 1950s, paid taxes to the state that were based on household incomes.

The tone of Geng's memoir shifts dramatically when the topic turns to the catastrophic consequences of the forced collectivization and communization of agriculture that unfolded so suddenly between 1955 and 1960. Speaking on behalf of fellow villagers, he does not look upon the disasters of those years as unfortunate errors in party work, a perspective one finds in all self-serving official criticisms of collectivization (see, e.g., Central Committee of the Communist Party of China 1981:15–16), but rather as the logical outcome of policies designed to expand state power by mercilessly squeezing the peasantry. At this point Geng's memoir is reminiscent of eyewitness accounts of the forced collectivization of Soviet peasants in the late 1920s and early 1930s (Conquest 1986:144–63, 225–59). Rural socialism no longer had anything to do with peasant prosperity, self-governance, respect for private property, individual initiative, voluntary participation of people from all classes, or production for a regulated, but free, market. The transition to socialism in the countryside now meant forced collectivization and communization, the confiscation of private property, the death of household sideline production, high prices for consumer goods, high taxes, high quotas for compulsory grain deliveries to the state at low state prices, and absolute state control of markets and commerce. In short, cooperation was not a means of achieving peasant prosperity; it was viewed by the party as a means of building state power, financing urban industry, and subsidizing a high standard of living for city dwellers.

Geng's memoir is strangely silent on the first phase of the state's war on the peasantry—the sudden and forced collectivization of agriculture in early 1956. His failure to comment on this period can be explained, in part, by Geng's absence from his home village during this time. It is also likely that Geng now feels pangs of guilt about his own naive support for the collectivization drive. Geng, like many others, undoubtedly accepted for a time the party's argument that collectivization was in the long-term economic interest of the peasantry.

His testimony regarding the crimes of the state focuses instead on the Great Leap Forward, an event he did experience in his home district. An eyewitness to the devastation brought to central Hebei by the Japanese in the early 1940s, Geng nevertheless insists that during the Great Leap "more people died than at any other time." In the famine that followed the Great Leap, he writes, "there was incredible inflation in the price of privately owned grain: three yuan for a catty [1.1 pounds] of corn, five yuan for a catty of wheat, and one yuan for four catties of radishes." Geng recalls that one old-timer told him, "I wanted to see the abundance of socialism by the time I got old; who could imagine that things would be worse than before [the revolution]."

In the spring of 1958, just before the Great Leap exploded across the Chinese countryside, Geng was transferred from his job in the provincial capital to a work team that was operating out of his native village of Wugong. When the Great Leap began, Geng served as a commune official in his home district. For the sake of convenience, his comments on the Great Leap can be grouped into three categories, each of which focuses on a key aspect of the state's war on the peasantry: the frenzy to launch production "sputniks," the deadly consequences of excessive state grain confiscation, and the criminal illogic of the state's absolute refusal to allow collectively produced crops to be transported and sold beyond county borders during a time of famine.

On the matter of production sputniks, that is, the announcing of astounding output records, Geng explains that because his native village was already famous as a model collective unit, tremendous pressure was brought to bear on its leadership in 1958 to lie about productivity. Hebei provincial governor Liu Zihou demanded that Wugong "send aloft five production sputniks." Local officials, caught between the conflicting demands of the state and the people but fully aware of

the consequences of failing to be responsive to the dictates of powerful party outsiders, urged Geng and others who were trusted by local people to cooperate:

> After the 1958 fall harvest a commune party secretary named Yin
> wanted me to send up a cabbage sputnik, that is, output of 100,000
> catties per *mu* [one-sixth acre]. I said, "We can't produce that much!"
> He said, "Why can't you just take cabbage from some other fields and
> put it in these fields, then you'll have more?" I responded, "We can't
> do something that stupid. It will do harm and cost money too. If you
> want to write fake numbers, write whatever you want." Yin said, "If I'm
> a fake, then who's real? They say that in Anguo county a *mu* of wheat
> produces more than 3,000 catties. Is that real? Xinli village near Tian-
> jin gets 100,000 catties of rice per *mu*. Is that real? They're all fake. The
> Soviet sputnik has already taken off. Wugong has already been awarded
> lots of red flags for merit in the past, but now we can't even seem to
> send up one sputnik. It's driving me crazy. At times like this it is im-
> possible to be a decent person."

The falsification of crop estimates was much more than a propaganda game.
As in the Soviet Union in the early 1930s, the state's annual requisitions of grain
were based on such ridiculously high estimates. Before the Great Leap, Geng recalls, the local county party secretary, Xu Jianzhong, had worked out a demanding
grain requisition contract with Wugong, based on past performance and opti-
mistic crop estimates. During the Great Leap, however, even Xu was criticized by
higher-ups who wanted more, and the contract system was scrapped.

Before the fall harvest of 1959, Geng writes, a "certain [provincial] bureau
chief," whose name he still would not mention, brought a news reporter to the
commune. Local people estimated that, at best, the commune would get 270 catties of grain per *mu*. The reporter suggested to the state official that the figure
would be much higher if grain equivalents for melons, pears, peaches, radishes,
and sweet potatoes were added to the grain production figures. Geng recalls bit-
terly and self-critically, echoing the experiences of some local leaders in the Soviet
Union in the early 1930s, "The commune party committee didn't agree to the falsification, but we members decided not to speak out after grumbling a bit among
ourselves. This guy was a high official. What could we do? As a party official I
was even more helpless. I didn't dare to make a sound. All I could do was put my
head down and ask myself, Why is it that the higher the level of the cadre, the
less likely they are to have their heart in doing something for the country? . . .
Why is it that the higher the cadre, the more likely the cadre will cheat the party
and the people?" As a result of the report written by the urban outsiders, the state
confiscated 10,800,000 catties of grain from the commune, rather than 4,000,000
catties. "We heard that every commune had high requisition increases as well,"
Geng says. "But we had the largest increase because we were so famous. It was a
case of whipping an ox that was already moving rather quickly!"

Starving, angry peasants vented their fury on local leaders like Geng, whom they now looked upon as collaborators. According to Geng, one old-timer cornered him: "The grain we produce in this village comes from sweat that falls from our brows and splashes in eight directions, it doesn't grow out of the pens held by intellectuals. Who are you kidding? During the war we helped you guys make it through. We took care of your food and clothing, but you haven't paid us back (zhi en bu hao). On the contrary, we've been cheated. Don't you have the heart of a human?" Using fascinating analogies drawn from traditional stories to characterize the situation, Geng replied that he had no way of knowing what was going on in the Heavenly Palace (tian gong), a local way of referring to the inner sanctums of the state center.

In his memoir Geng describes how Wugong Commune budget director Zhang Fengshan protested strenuously at a county-level meeting. "How will anyone have anything to eat?" he screamed. The county's response was to fire Zhang. The state, of course, got its grain. In 34 surrounding villages, Geng recalls, hungry people went on strike, as they had in the Soviet Union three decades earlier. "People were in an extremely bad mood. No one would come to meetings, the cotton plants were left unattended, there was no fall plowing, some draft animals died of hunger, and newborn piglets were thrown away at birth. It seemed like the end of the world." Geng remembers: "Commune members placed all their hopes for having enough food on the summer 1960 wheat harvest. Who could have known that the state would requisition even more grain in summer 1960 than it had in summer 1959." Local people moaned, "The higher-ups have become traitors."

The third Great Leap–related incident discussed by Geng happened in the summer of 1962. By the preceding fall, crop outputs in his commune were relatively good, explains Geng, because a piecework contract system had been implemented to give hungry peasants a reason to labor. The vegetable harvest during the summer of 1962 was especially bountiful. Elsewhere, however—including in the urban sector—the post–Great Leap famine was taking a devastating toll. "The living standards of urban people were very low in this period. There were very few vegetables available in the cities. The members of the brigades wanted very badly to be able to sell vegetables to get money to invest in the various things needed for production. But the county party committee said that the people were prohibited from transporting and selling vegetables across county lines. People were tense because they had vegetables to sell, but couldn't sell them."

Geng and others protested to no avail at the county level. In desperation Geng wrote a letter of appeal to the budget director of the provincial party committee, complaining that the senseless policy was causing "suffering for urban and rural folk alike." But the collective, having surrendered all its rights to the state, was unable to win approval for its plan. Consequently there was a huge loss of vegetables throughout the commune. In Dongliman village, 20,000 catties of cabbage rotted. More than 20,000 catties of radishes belonging to Yangquan village rotted in the storage bins of the Xiaoti supply and marketing cooperative. As in Ukraine

30 years earlier, mountains of food rotted while people starved to death. One way or another, the economy was going to be centrally controlled.

To make matters worse, the Shijiazhuang prefectural party committee tried to cover up the incident. A certain secretary Li from Huotong county was sent by the prefecture to investigate the allegations made by Geng on behalf of the local people. According to Geng, in his report Li charged that "it is not true that half the vegetables were lost because they couldn't be shipped out. The problem is the attitude of Geng Xiufeng." Those loyal to the state builders regarded Geng then, as they regard him now, as an undisciplined troublemaker, but Geng steadfastly clings to the view that the incident was another case of "party people protecting party people."

Geng's sense of frustration with the multiple disasters brought by the Great Leap debacle and antagonistic village-state relations is captured best, however, in his comments on a defiant letter of protest he wrote in December 1960 to the party center in Beijing. By late 1960 severe food shortages had taken a heavy toll on older people, including local party elites. Geng Xiufeng and his kinsman Geng Changsuo, a well-known local leader who had been collaborating closely with the state since the early 1950s, were hospitalized in the same room of a bare-bones commune clinic along with a commune official named Xu. All three were diagnosed as having dropsy, also common in the Soviet famine of the 1930s. All three were fed a home remedy called *kangtangmian*, which consisted of fine chaff, noodles, and a bit of sugar. "This was special treatment available only to cadres," Geng recalls; "ordinary people couldn't get access to it."

While hospitalized, Geng talked to his two roommates about the crisis. For some time, inarticulate local people had been "begging" Geng Xiufeng, widely perceived as a worldly man who knew the strange ways of those in high office, to write a letter of appeal. The three agreed that perhaps the people at the top were being lied to by grass-roots leaders and thus did not know the extent of the hunger and privation. The letter, drafted by Geng and approved by the other two, made the following major points. First, local people should have a contract with the state that required requisition quotas to be based on reasonable estimates of crop outputs. Estimates should not be made by outsiders who simply glance at the fields. Second, it is necessary to recruit cadres who understand the science of agriculture. Here Geng means that the state has no right to demand that villagers plant crops that are needed by central planners but are unsuited to local soil conditions (for a discussion of these problems see, e.g., MacFarquhar 1983). Third, it is necessary to abandon the fundamentalist idea that crops cannot be transported and sold across county lines. The letter, reproduced in toto in the memoir, was dated December 30, 1960.

All hell broke loose when Geng tried to get official commune approval to send the letter to Tan Zhenlin, the Politburo member responsible for agricultural affairs during the Great Leap. One wide-eyed commune party secretary said: "To write a letter to the center is no joke! The advantages are few, the disadvantages many (*you li bu da, you hai bu xiao*). . . . If you insist on going ahead, just sign your own name!" In the end, the letter, signed by Geng Xiufeng, Geng Changsuo, and the man named Xu, was sent to Tan Zhenlin, the provincial party committee, and the Tianjin municipal party committee. A second commune party secretary exploded when he heard the news. Without denying that the three had spoken the truth, the enraged official said, "You sent a letter to the center? Are you crazy! It wasn't enough that you signed it yourself, you had to drag Changsuo along. He's a red flag in this province. If you make a mistake, it doesn't matter, but if you cause Changsuo to make a mistake, that will be the end of our red flag!" Suffer in silence, he implied, or the commune would surely be singled out for punishment by the all-powerful state and lose its "red flag," or model, status.

THE POLITICS OF MEMORY

Geng Xiufeng's moralistic "Renjian zheng dao" reveals that peasants (a category which most certainly includes educated middle peasants like Geng) have by no means forgotten the past, even if the form and content of their remembrances are strikingly different from what one normally finds in the writings of articulate urban intellectuals. It is true that Geng's memoir is a "modern" text in that its narrative is framed in categories such as nationalism, socialism, and democracy that are alien to traditional village life. In this sense Geng's work lies in the mainstream of twentieth-century Chinese political discourse, from Liang Qichao to Fang Lizhi. But Geng's memoir is also very old-fashioned.

For one thing, Geng unflinchingly assumes the paternalistic posture of late imperial village elites, whose status in the community was defined, in part, by their unusual knowledge of the ways of the world outside the village. Although Geng regards himself as a modern, democratic thinker, he has never accepted the orthodox Maoist view that the mass of poor and uneducated peasants is in any way superior to him. Unlike traditional Confucian elites, however (or Leninist elites for that matter), Geng never really saw himself as a leader who was doing the work of the state. He was willing to use the state (and, in turn, he was certainly used by the state), but he viewed himself as someone who was exclusively concerned with the economic welfare of the peasantry. Geng could be described as a nationalist in that he felt the pain of national humiliation and was aware of the glaring symptoms of national weakness, but, influenced in school by early-twentieth-century anarchist and mutual-aid currents, he did not believe that national problems could only be solved by the machinations of a strong and coercive state. As a "natural" local elite, he took pride in taking the side of the peasantry when the economic interests of rural people clashed with the interests of insensitive centralizers.[4]

Geng's memoir is also old-fashioned in a stylistic sense. Its rural and local flavor becomes especially apparent when Geng reconstructs, line by line, earthy and humorous conversations he had with peasants years ago. One gets the impression that Geng has been taking notes all these years. Told in the local language, these dialogues are filled with colloquial expressions, colorful local sayings (chengyu), and references to the rich legacy of traditional stories passed on for centuries in outdoor plays (see chapter 6, this volume). "Why did all the ancient kingdoms collapse?" he asked. "Isn't it because people destroyed one another for private gain? I was deeply influenced by the old-style operas that called for upright officials who speak out for justice, officials who think of the people instead of themselves, officials who despise flatterers and the type of leaders who gain for themselves by doing harm to others."

After reading this unusual document, one is left with many questions. Precisely why did Geng take time in the mid-1980s to write an account of events that most villagers are too young to remember? Since Geng appears to be among the very few in rural China who continue to cling to a socialist vision, why is his testimony worthy of our attention? Are his views nothing more than the grumblings of a bitter and isolated old man, or do they, in some way, throw light on the experiences of peasants in general in the immediate pre- and postrevolutionary years? What, if anything, is the present-day political significance of his disturbing account of the past?

One begins to answer these questions by underscoring the fact that both Geng and the memoir are taken seriously by state authorities—that is, conservative county and prefectural officials. "Renjian zheng dao," written in the relative openness of the post–Cultural Revolution and post-Mao 1980s, is somewhat akin to the pioneering testimonies about forced collectivization and famine that surfaced in the Soviet Union after the death of Stalin. In both cases, written remembrances prepared during a brief interlude of openness were attacked when the harsh winds of orthodoxy again began to blow. That is why Geng's memoir, completed just prior to the Tiananmen massacre of June 1989, stands no chance whatever of being published in China in the near future. In the summer of 1991, a visitor to Wugong was told that the 78-year-old Geng is now regarded by some authorities as a "Soviet-style dissident." It is difficult to know exactly what this means, but it is apparent that in the environment of ideological crackdown of the early 1990s, the party-state is extremely defensive and undoubtedly regards the kind of text prepared by Geng to be subversive at three different levels.

First, Geng's discussion of rural social relations in communist-controlled base areas prior to the party's seizure of state power nationwide seriously discredits the standard Marxist-Leninist perspective on class struggle that is still taught in schools throughout China. Geng's memoir specifically challenges the view that village society on the North China plain was made up of wealthy landlords and rich peasants pitted against a ruthlessly exploited mass of decent poor and lower-middle peasants. He argues, in a way that resonates with the memories of most peasants I have interviewed, that it was common poverty, not exploitative class relations and class polarization, that characterized village life. The class-struggle campaigns imposed by party outsiders were always counterproductive, in Geng's view, because they divided rather than united the community and consistently brought out the worst in local people. The rigid class labels upon which the party insisted were never carefully defined and, therefore, seemed alien to local people accustomed to thinking of their communities in terms of neighborhood, lineage, household, generation, and gender configurations.

Geng's "politically incorrect" account of the class dynamics of the resistance war and revolutionary periods emphasizes the key roles played by the sons of traditional village elites, most of whom were highly educated by local standards and most of whom fell into the "landlord," "rich peasant," and "prosperous middle peasant" categories carved out later by the party. Their nationalist consciousness, he implies, was far more developed than that of most peasants, and the party relied upon such youthful elites to do the grass-roots work of mobilizing the rank and file during the war. Many of these young elites joined the party, led village party branches for a time, and even accepted the idea that rural people needed a social revolution. Many were also betrayed, victimized, and silenced in the vindictive and often violent class-struggle campaigns that followed.[5]

All of this is important today in the eyes of frightened party elders because, whatever they might be doing to "reform" China's economy, the party's monopolistic domination of politics and society rests, more than ever, on the increasingly shaky assumption that Marxism-Leninism is a valid doctrine. According to the latest version of the Chinese constitution, it is illegal for citizens to oppose the "four cardinal principles," one of which asserts the ideological hegemony of Marxism-Leninism. Yet this is precisely what Geng Xiufeng has done by criticizing the party's attempts to manufacture class struggle in the countryside in the 1940s and 1950s.

Second, Geng's elaborate account of the origins and purposes of cooperative formation in the 1940s and 1950s confronts the idea that the Communist party was always acting in the best interests of its peasant supporters in the first decade of the postrevolutionary era. Geng and the party shared the view that the traditional household economy was doomed. But his vision of self-governing cooperatives eventually collided with the views of state builders in Beijing who saw collectives, communes, and state farms as the best way to control and systematically bleed, in Geng's view, the rural economy.

Not only did Geng routinely oppose state and party manipulation of village economic and political life, he made it clear that in the early days of voluntary co-op formation, it was often households of former village elites, labeled landlord, rich peasant, and prosperous middle peasant by outside party functionaries, who showed the keenest interest in cooperative agriculture. The most destitute villagers were often the last ones inclined to experiment. Thus, Geng questions the view expressed by Mao Zedong in 1955 (and Stalin in the late 1920s) that former landlords and rich peasants were the rural class enemy hopelessly committed to the traditional household economy. In brief, Geng's anti-Leninist critique of constant state and party interference in village life amounts to a rejection of another of the "four cardinal principles," namely, the notion that all citizens must unquestioningly accept the leadership of the Communist party.

But what about Geng's faith in socialism? Is it not true that in this area he has always been atypical? Considering that rural people were generally pleased with the state's decision to decollectivize agriculture in the early 1980s, are not Geng's views about the superiority of cooperative agriculture pitifully out of touch with mainstream peasant concerns?

It is true that only a tiny percentage of Chinese peasants entered the type of voluntary, semisocialist co-op advocated by Geng in the 1943–1954 period. From 1955 to 1960, the state was required to use various means of coercion to gather the rest of the peasantry into poorly organized and highly unpopular co-ops, collectives, and communes (Friedman, Pickowicz, and Selden 1991:185–245; MacFarquhar 1983; Riskin 1987:81–147). It is also the case that since decollectivization in the early 1980s, the peasants in Geng's region of China have shown little or no interest in collective economic activity. But, as this essay has tried to show, it is not Geng's personal brand of socialism that links him to the experiences of other peasants, but rather his hostility toward the ever-growing power of the state. Geng's memoir is of great interest not because he is an agrarian socialist but because he provides evidence that documents the incredible damage done to peasant livelihood by the state and party in the 1950s and 1960s. He explains, in effect, why peasants are so hostile to what they have experienced as socialism, and why they remain highly suspicious of the state in the decollectivized present.

The implications of Geng's argument are very interesting. Throughout what was once known as the socialist world, and especially in such industrially under-developed societies as Russia and China, it was usually assumed by revolutionary elites that the process of socialist revolution, by definition, involved national unification and state building. The state sought to fund its ambitious industrial initiatives by squeezing the rural economy. The existence of collective farms and central control of markets, commerce, and prices made it easier for the state to exploit the peasants. It is hardly surprising, therefore, that peasant hostility toward the Communist party and socialism in such places as the Soviet Union before 1989 and China today takes the form of extreme resentment of state power (Conquest 1986; Lewin 1975; Link 1992:27–28). Indeed, one gets the impression that one of the most important dynamics of the anticommunist revolutions that have swept the world is the demand for more local control and autonomy and less state power. Where the revolutions of the early and middle twentieth century involved various attempts to build strong states, the revolutions of the late twentiethth century, especially those that have shaken the socialist world, seem to involve attempts to break down strong states. It is this sense of animosity toward the Chinese state, shared by many peasants who have been victimized by party power, that is captured so nicely in Geng Xiufeng's memoir.

Third, Geng's views are regarded as subversive by the authorities because he so obviously opposes the privatization of the rural economy that has taken place, with the blessing of the party, since the early 1980s. He does not deal with this issue in an explicit way in "Renjian zheng dao," but it is an unmistakable subtext of the memoir. Everyone in the village knows that Geng is an ardent opponent of private economic activity and private gain. Geng believes that the private economy is incapable of bringing prosperity to the mass of ordinary peasants. Thus, when he writes about the weaknesses of the private economy in the 1940s, everyone realizes he is also commenting on the limitations of the private economy that surfaced after 1978.

The word "selfish" (zisi) appears frequently in Geng's moralistic text. The problem with the system of "families going it alone" (dan gan hu) is not only that it offers no long-term hope for the majority of smallholders, but also that it engenders unhealthy competition that pits one Chinese against another. Like class-struggle politics, it divides people rather than unites them. "If you make money and acquire land," Geng asserts, "then you will buy animals and farm tools; if the size of your farm grows, you will have to exploit hired labor, thereby putting yourself into the category of rich peasant or landlord."

Geng, like William Hinton (1990), appears not to appreciate that peasants who were exploited by state-controlled collectives for nearly 30 years pay no attention to his critique of the pursuit of private interest or his advocacy of voluntary co-ops. He has no difficulty making the fine distinction between his life-enhancing "free association" socialism and the life-negating socialism of the parasitic state. But few peasants care to make such distinctions.

More important, however, is the fact that the Communist party is angered by Geng's stubborn fidelity to what he regards as socialist principles. In effect, in conversations with neighbors and friends and in his memoir, Geng is suggesting that the central government is leading the peasants away from the path of common prosperity and security, just as it did in the late 1950s. In Geng's view, the state has simply discovered what it believes is a better way of exacting tribute from the countryside. The state is no less interested than it was in the heyday of collective farming in requiring peasants to sell grain to the state at low, state-fixed prices and in collecting as much tax revenue as possible (Friedman 1990). Geng is well aware that many of the most exploitative features of village-state relations during the collective era continue to characterize village-state relations in the privatized present. It is hardly surprising, therefore, that travelers in rural North China in the summer of 1991 saw considerable evidence that the state regards "tax evasion" (tou shui) and overt "refusal to pay taxes" (kang shui) as major problems.[6] Peasants, for their part, deeply resent being preyed upon by corrupt and money-hungry state officials.

From the late Qing dynasty onward, many urban elites believed that China was weak because the state was weak. Consequently, late imperial reformers, the Nationalist party, and the Communist party each tried to strengthen the state. State building, especially under the communists since the late 1930s, took a terrible toll on the peasantry. Geng's profound suspicion of an exploitative state resonates with deeply rooted views held by significant numbers of peasants in places like China and the former Soviet republics, where rural people endured decades of forced collectivization. In this sense, Geng, a highly paternalistic rural intellectual, is proud to regard himself as one of the peasants.

"Renjian zheng dao" is brave and defiant, but it is also quite sad because, among other things, it tells a complex story of betrayal. Geng Xiufeng and other rural elites supported the Communist party and urged their neighbors to do so because they chose to believe that the party was leading a revolution that would bring prosperity and power to all rural dwellers. When the revolution turned out to be a cruel hoax, Geng (and others like him) felt betrayed. But he willingly confesses that he, in turn, betrayed his neighbors by collaborating with the faceless outsiders who brought so much misery to the community. The hostility that characterizes present-day village-state relations is, perhaps, the main legacy of the long collective era.[7] Why is this state of affairs important? It is difficult to say. But at the very least it means that, contrary to the views expressed by frustrated observers in the aftermath of the Tiananmen crisis, the Chinese peasantry should not be regarded as a social group that can be relied upon to rush to the rescue of the beleaguered socialist state.

––––––––– Notes –––––––––

1. I want to thank Edward Friedman and Mark Selden for sharing with me so many of their ideas about life on the North China plain.

2. For a portrait of rural intellectuals in late imperial and Republican times, see, for example, Fei (1968); M. Yang (1968); and Yeh (1978).

3. Geng's communal vision has much in common with writings on moral economy (see, e.g., Scott 1976). There are important differences, however. For instance, Geng does not celebrate an earlier, pre-capitalist rural economy, nor does he express any aversion for market activity.

4. Very little research has been done on the protests of rural elites during the early phases of socialist construction. For a provocative discussion of similar issues in late imperial and Republican times, see Duara (1988a).

5. For a discussion of related events in South China, see Siu (1989a).

6. I want to thank Joseph W. Esherick for bringing this information to my attention.

7. For discussions of village-state relations, see, for example, Chan, Madsen, and Unger (1992) and Zweig (1989a).

8

Old Ghosts and New Chains

Ethnicity and Memory in the Georgian Republic

STEPHEN F. JONES

Time is but the stream I go fishing in.
—Henry David Thoreau

T HE ORGANIZING MYTHS of the Soviet Union and the structures that have propagated those myths are disintegrating. The loss of legitimacy by the center has demolished the most important myth—that of a voluntary and lawful union based on interethnic cooperation, Soviet patriotism, and a syncretic "Soviet" culture. The rapidity with which the union unraveled revealed its fragile legitimacy. Mikhail Gorbachev's policies publicly exploded the facade of Soviet unity, an idea that had long since lost resonance among non-Russians in the union. Previous policies of urbanization and mass education and the creation of republican state structures with their symbolic paraphernalia of national constitutions, emblems, and hymns had already promoted, at least among the larger, territorially based, non-Slavic nations, a strong sense of separateness.[1] Since the 1960s, the end of terror and of ideological monolithism, along with the deconcentration of power and the influence of transnational movements for human rights and self-determination, has encouraged the public articulation of this separateness in the form of nationalism.

An important part of this growth in national identity among non-Russians was the embellishment of their own national histories, which existed alongside of, but sometimes overlapped, the official narrative. National identity both draws upon and feeds into national history; it is the framework for all counterhistories among non-Russians. Soviet policies, among non-Slavs in particular, were only partially successful in limiting or shaping the dominant myths and memories of non-Russians. The society described in Russian writer Andrei Platonov's macabre novel, *The Pit and the Pendulum* (1978)—a society where people could only "imagine recollections," where traditional objects were "unknown ancient things," and where even words had lost their cultural resonance to become "sounds to fill up the empty ache" in people's heads—remained the totalitarian's dream. The Soviet state, in its attempt to smash national histories, only fragmented them. The disordered pieces of the past, treasured as fragments of a more "real" time, were reconstructed by private citizens into new counterhistories. Ironically, the state strengthened those counterhistories by providing the vehicles for their propagation, such as "national" literatures, folklore societies, and museums.

The modern "homo sovieticus," particularly in non-Slavic republics, has become increasingly attached to traditional customs and values. The initial attraction of Soviet ideology—that it would bring greater social mobility and a better standard of living—faded as the state proved unable to keep its promises. Paradoxically, most Western scholars see this growing attachment to the past as a result of "modernization," which, despite the Soviet drive to undermine national consolidation, promoted growth in national consciousness and thereby a greater interest in national roots (Rakowska-Harmstone 1974; Suny 1980:200–226, 1989). Gorbachev, in his book *Perestroika: New Thinking for Our Country and the World,* concedes: "The growth of educational and cultural standards, alongside modernization of the economy, leads to the emergence of an intelligentsia in every nation; the growth of national self-consciousness and the growth of a nation's natural interests in its historical roots" (1987:119).

Most Soviet area specialists, myself included, rely on recorded materials and statistics to buttress this argument. We have, with the exception of Christel Lane (1981) and a few others in the West, failed to explore the more concrete methods of national cultural preservation: public imagery, commemorative days, songs, and customs. Many Sovietologists in the past overrated, even in the darkest days of Stalinism, the number of "blank pages" created by the Soviet authorities in non-Russian national histories and the power of totalitarian states to eliminate societies' own versions of their history.[2] Vladimir Dedijer, who, as one of Josip Broz Tito's right-hand men, experienced the difficulties of creating a new "communist man," remarked: "Memory, as transmitted through folk songs, epic poems, and oral traditions, has the power to destroy empires, as water has the strength to crack stones" (cited in Butler 1989:4).

The absence of research on the informal channels of resistance to official Soviet myths, due in part to the emphasis in Soviet studies on history and political science, has left us with an overblown perception of the power of totalitarian states. Interest-group theories, when applied to the USSR, did not explore the more everyday spheres of privacy and resistance such as memory and family.

SOME QUESTIONS OF DEFINITION

History is used by official propagandists to legitimize authority and create value consensus in the state, and by nationalists to promote a desired self-image and national cohesion. History has been, as Eric Hobsbawm wrote, "selected, written, pictured, popularized and institutionalized by those whose function it is to do so" (Hobsbawm and Ranger 1983:13). In recent decades, deconstructionists and poststructuralists have shown the hidden ideological biases even of allegedly "objective" historical narratives by Western scholars.

History is part of a society's collective memory about itself. Maurice Halbwachs, in *The Collective Memory* (1980), suggests that history begins where collective memory leaves off—that it records, condenses, dramatizes, and orders its own material in a way that collective memory does not. Despite this proper conceptual difference (see chapter 5, this volume), both history and collective memory are interwoven into the complex fabric of national and cultural consciousness. They both contribute to a "national history" that is commonly accepted by the majority of an ethnic group or nation. Multiethnic societies may sustain a number of "national histories."

Unofficial national history in state socialist societies is a heterogeneous and unstable phenomenon. It is multivocal and pluralistic, created by anonymous storytellers, academics, and even officials. The spoken word, books, television, newspapers, artistic images, rituals, and education can all be conduits of unofficial national history. Official cultural and political elites have greater opportunities for creating what Antonio Gramsci calls "civil hegemony" in the spheres of culture and history, but their message is always influenced and modified by popular ideas as it filters down. The most successful ruling classes, Gramsci argues, have been those that have adapted to popular beliefs and sentiments (cited in Joll 1977:chapter 9).

The Soviet experience in Georgia and other republics suggests that ruling circles in the USSR, in their attempt to propagate an official history, have conceded to and been influenced by demands from below. But at the same time, as propagators of an iconoclastic and universalist ideology, they have come into conflict with national traditions and memories. Since the 1960s, this conflict has contributed to the breakdown of the Soviet civil hegemony in the USSR, especially among non-Russians. The attempt by native communist leaders to forestall this breakdown by incorporating national traditions and customs into official history provided the propagators of the nationalist discourse with legitimate mechanisms for the promotion of a popular national history. Although not always overtly oppositional, this popular history slowly reduced the official story to an increasingly irrelevant superstructure.

SOVIET POLICIES: HANDMAIDEN OF UNOFFICIAL
NATIONAL HISTORY

The August 1991 putsch in the USSR demonstrated yet again that a policy may produce the opposite of its intended result. National history and identity among non-Russians was strengthened within a Soviet system that used its monopoly of information to promote internationalism. Soviet leaders may well ask where they went wrong.

In the USSR, as a utopian state, past and future are constructed to serve the present. In Soviet literature, as Katerina Clark points out, "the future goal and past glories invest the present with their significance" (1981:175). Soviet citizens are brought up to view past events and figures teleologically, judging them by their contribution to the present. This concept of the past resembles the nationalist view. Admittedly, nationalists have no concept of a break in historical time, which for communists is signaled by the arrival of socialism, but in the USSR, particularly after the cooptation of Russian history by Stalin, continuous time ousted the early Soviet vision of their society as posthistorical.

For nationalists, and this includes moderate patriots in Western industrial societies, the nation is concrete, omnipresent, and fundamentally unchanged since the time of its "birth." Like Soviet propagandists, nationalists see the past as bound by and as part of the present. The nineteenth-century Georgian writer Ilia C'avc'avadze, known by his compatriots as the father of the Georgian nation, exemplifies this view. In an article titled "The Nation and History," he declared that the past, present, and future of a nation "are so bound to one another, that one without the other is unimaginable, incomprehensible, and unknown" (1977:346). For C'avc'avadze and the contemporary Georgian historians who frequently cite this article, the Georgian past is a series of lessons about the present. Georgians, like many other non-Russian groups in the USSR, were encouraged to accept this teleological relationship of the past to the present not only by a global consensus on the naturalness of nation-states, but also by the Soviet system's own approach to history. In short, Georgians' view of past oppression as part of their present existence and of ancient heroes as timeless fighters for national honor was encouraged by the national-communist vision that had dominated Soviet history since Stalin.

But this nationalist message would have been less successful without the impressive educational and cultural structures erected in the USSR. Inspired by the communist ideology of modernization, mass education, and social egalitarianism, and by the practical considerations of running a huge, multilingual empire, Soviet policies led to a vast array of state-subsidized structures, from film studios and theaters to newspapers, publishing houses, and universities. Native leaders were provided with these structures to promote the Soviet message, but native intelligentsias used them to project what Caroline Humphrey (chapter 2, this volume) calls their "evocative transcripts" of national continuity and continuing struggle against domination.

The large native intelligentsias were themselves part of these state structures. The creative intelligentsia was given a particularly high profile. From the beginning of Soviet power, writers and artists were seen as "producers of culture" whose role was to bring art into life and legitimize Soviet rule.[3] But Western scholars of Soviet literature have demonstrated how values contrary to the Soviet ideological canon have pervaded cultural production in the USSR since the 1930s.[4] Especially in the republics, despite the loyalty of many writers to the Soviet system, the producers of culture have helped undermine the Soviet version of the past. Authorized to "nationalize" communism to help counter popular disillusionment with Marxism-Leninism and to forestall the emergence of a dissident nationalism, they promoted a discourse that centered on the nation rather than the multinational state. Katherine Verdery, in her recent work on Romania, suggests that command economies characterized by a shortage of resources, along with the "indigenization" of Marxism, forced groups within creative intelligentsias to compete for the state's attention by promoting projects that enhanced the state's national-cultural legitimacy (Verdery 1991a:72–134).

Mutatis mutandis, this Romanian pattern was true in the majority of the union republics in the USSR, with the exception of the Slavic republics of Ukraine and Belorussia, where assimilation into the central Russian culture was more successful. Writers, of whom there was a state-subsidized surfeit in the republics, were permitted to preserve their own cultural authority and the republican government's legitimacy by borrowing from the past. But the symbiotic relationship between republican leaders and native cultural elites led to a message ultimately subversive of Soviet values.

Both the receivers and the transmitters of culture were transformed by Soviet policies aimed at raising educational levels. By the 1960s, there was a large and sophisticated audience in the USSR, unreceptive to official propaganda but open to the counternarratives circulated by republican cultural elites. Increasingly, Soviet audiences subverted or transformed the official language, symbolism, and rituals of the authorities. This subversion is best illustrated by Soviet jokes, which ridicule or invert Soviet symbolism, but it extends to sculpture, film, and literature, which transform the past into challenges to contemporary Soviet domination.[5] A typical example is the popular Georgian film *Tsarsulis mogoneba* (Memories of the Past), which depicts a Georgian landlord resisting collectivization. For Georgians, the landlord became the tragic hero, and the collectivizers, the misled.

Soviet propaganda creates a chasm between official and popular reality. Under these conditions, official history, as part of official reality, becomes suspect, and personal memory becomes the "truth." In Western pluralist systems, history, as conveyed by historians and the media, is seen, on the whole, as more trustworthy than personal memories. In Soviet-type states, where citizens have routinely experienced the contradiction between official history and memory, it is the other way around (see Nora 1989).

Propaganda and the absence of information encourage rumor. Rumor, according to Jan Vansina (1985:6), if it is not contradicted, can quickly become "commonly accepted" and in time add to a people's collective historical consciousness. In March 1956, a demonstration in Georgia was brutally suppressed. Close to twenty-five people were killed. The rumor that dozens more were killed and secretly buried by the authorities became part of accepted fact until Georgian newspapers, benefiting from glasnost, confirmed the lower figure. At an extreme, Soviet propaganda created a mentality of total disbelief, thereby undermining its own story even when it approximated the truth (see Sinyavsky 1990:210).

A further paradox of Soviet policies, despite the massive social transformation of the 1930s onward, is a curious retardation of social change in rural areas. Restrictions on internal mobility from village to town and the absence of rural and urban markets slowed the breakup of traditional rural structures. The Soviet emphasis on welfare and on the family as a means of control encouraged families to exploit a well-developed patronage system to solve everyday economic, social, or career problems. Tamara Dragadze (1988) argues that the Georgian family encourages children to depend on kin and fellow Georgians, not only for reasons of "tradition" but also because it is essential for "getting ahead" in a system where permissions and petitions are required at every level. For rural youths without family influence, she argues, "rarely could accommodation be found and paid for, residence permits granted, or jobs found" (Dragadze 1988:39). Similarly, the second, or underground, economy in Georgia could not function effectively without extensive family and kinship networks. The continuing existence of such traditional patterns obstructs the inculcation of new values and new memories.[6]

In many republics, then, the official Soviet canon, despite its adaptation to national cultures, was by the 1960s alien to influential opinion makers, the educated urban populace, and even rural communities. From inside the official ideological framework emerged an evocative transcript, a coded public discourse with a subversive message that was perfectly understood by the vast majority of native officials, who could do little about it. The more oppositional national history—areas that the official cultural nationalism could not absorb—was "privatized," or forced into informal channels of social communication. In Georgia, where kinship and peer networks are important, the Soviet system's crude propaganda, shortage economy, and obstructive bureaucracy strengthened the private sphere of ethnic and familial interdependence and enhanced Georgians' sense of solidarity against alien rule. This process produced the space for a rich counterculture. A major element in this counterculture, alongside the second economy and contemporary literature, was unofficial national history.

THE WARRING PASTS

Who are the Georgians? Indigenous to Caucasia, Georgians have a long history of statehood. By the fifth century AD, most Georgian tribes shared a common religion (Orthodoxy), and although they still spoke a variety of languages, they employed a common alphabet. As the Mohammedan faith spread among their Persian and Turkish neighbors to the south, Christianity, art, and the eastern dialect of Kartvelian began to form the basis of a distinct and unified Georgian culture. By the eleventh and twelfth centuries, Georgians were enjoying their Golden Age, and a Georgian-dominated imperium straddled the Caucasian isthmus from the Caspian to the Black Sea.

But subject to marauding peoples such as the Mongols and Osmanli Turks, and later the Persian Safavids and Ottomans, a united Georgian state was lost in the thirteenth century, and Georgian regions remained disunited until they were collected again under the Russian empire in the nineteenth century.[7] In the nineteenth century, following the schema of national development for small European nations posed by the Czech historian Miroslav Hroch (1985), the Georgians had reached phase "A" (a concern for native language and tradition by a small group of intellectuals) by the 1830s, phase "B" (the diffusion of national ideas by a significant group of patriotic agitators) by the 1860s, and phase "C" (a full national revival with involvement of the broad masses) by 1918, the year of their independence (Hroch:1985).

In the 1920s, Georgians, like other non-Russians in the USSR, benefited from a policy of affirmative action. They were encouraged to develop their national cultural identity and to decolonize their history. The image of a Georgian liberation struggle against the Tsarist behemoth became part of the official canon. Soviet actions that could be interpreted as imperialist, such as the invasion of Georgia by the Red Army in 1921, were quietly forgotten.[8] This tolerance ended during the Stalinist period. Moscow, in its attempt to integrate non-Russian national history into a new Soviet myth of working-class internationalism and Russian historical superiority, used censorship, Russification, and historical invention. Traditional festivals and customs were attacked, as were national churches.

In Georgia, the new Stalinist myth emphasized the historical "tradition" of Russo-Georgian friendship and imposed a class model on Georgian national development. Georgian history after 1921 became part of Soviet history, lacking any nationally specific qualities. Using its control over libraries, museums, education, and the media, the Soviet regime successfully created a haziness about certain periods in Georgian history that contradicted the story of Russo-Georgian harmony, such as the Georgian anti-Soviet revolt of 1924.[9] Most Georgian historians were not allowed to consult *Spetskhran,* the special archival reserves that covered the "unacceptable" periods in Georgian history. But these attempts to rework the Georgian past had little affect on Georgians' perceptions of themselves in relation to Russia and the USSR. A vast majority of Georgians continued to see themselves as victims of a culturally inferior colonial state. The existence of a large, unskilled, Russian service class in Georgia confirmed this popular view.

Neither has the Marxist notion that nations are modern inventions ever been accepted. Georgians, including most native historians, conceive of an unchanging Georgian ethnos that can be traced to the Golden Age of Queen Tamara or beyond. The official Soviet view of solidarity among oppressed peoples directly contradicts Georgians' own conception of themselves as frontier Christians who fought Muslim empires and Caucasian mountaineers for national survival. The official story of the Soviet "liberation" of Georgia in 1921 is interpreted by Georgians quite simply as annexation.

Georgians' own version of their history tells a different story. The native aristocracy's Muslim apostasy and its trade in Georgian slaves with the Turks, primarily in west Georgia, are forgotten.[10] The Golden Age is perceived in terms similar to those of a modern nation-state driven by ethnic rather than dynastic interests, and the notion that subnational or regional loyalties undermined national solidarity during the medieval period is rejected.[11] In common with other peoples, Georgians support a series of myths about their "Great Past" and its uniqueness in the world. But interesting as this is, the question that concerns us here is not the substance of Georgian myths, but how Georgians maintained a national history that so successfully challenged the official Soviet story.

Oral Communication

In a society that controls written information, oral communication—through songs, proverbs, folktales, reminiscences, and artistic performances—is a vital means of preserving the past. In the twentieth century, radios, television, and print media, despite government controls, have extended the range and impact of this form of memory transmission. Technology has increased rather than inhibited the range of oral communication. In Georgia, multigenerational families, extensive social networks, the importance of interpersonal relationships, and a strong tradition of poetic memorization make oral communication particularly significant in sustaining national history. An emphasis on memorization in the Soviet educational system reinforced Georgian schoolchildren's familiarity with their native poets and writers. The memorization of whole stanzas of Shota Rustaveli's twelfth-century Georgian epic, *The Knight in the Panther's Skin,* which embodies Georgians' self-ascribed characteristics of heroism and loyalty to kin and friends, and which recalls the Golden Age of the Georgian renaissance, is still valued among Georgians today. Georgian women, one is constantly told, were required to learn this epic by heart as part of their dowry.

One of the most important institutions for the oral transmission of national history in Georgia is the *keipi,* or feast.[12] The keipi is convened for important family events such as birthdays and rites of passage, for "namedays" and saints' days, or for no particular reason at all. It plays a central part in Georgian social life;

families and friends are brought together, gossip is exchanged, and networks are reaffirmed. The occasion is absorbed into a heady celebration of Georgian history and tradition. The keipi illustrates Donald Horowitz's point that strong kinship ties and a perceived threat of assimilation—in the Georgian case the threat comes from Russians—lead to a situation in which myths of ancestry and the past take on great importance (Horowitz 1985).[13] Toasting, which dominates the keipi, is suffused with themes of genealogy and the glories of Georgian history.

The keipi is a conduit for unofficial history and Georgian national mythology. It is a symbol of the extravagant Georgian personality, which contradicts the Soviet ideal of sobriety and self-discipline. It touches on every aspect of Georgian culture, from song and poetry to ancestor worship and the country's natural beauty. Song, which is an especially rich source of Georgian memory, is central, as it is in Lithuania, to both informal and formal occasions. Polyphonic and a cappella, the songs require participation by a group, but no instruments, so they can be sung wherever and whenever Georgians gather. Despite a male choral tradition, the pervasive popular musical culture in Georgia encourages both sexes to memorize the songs. The songs are rarely about specific events but are infused with a patriotic lyricism and symbolism recalling heroes and places and with allusions that remind Georgians of their uniqueness. Often, songs are settings for poems by nationalistic writers. Invariably, the keipi is interspersed with songs familiar to all at the table.

Georgian Soviet history was, until glasnost shattered the official sensitivity surrounding its bloody errors, rarely mentioned at the keipi (except for the Second World War and, more occasionally, Stalin). This "taboo" encouraged Georgians to cultivate their myths of antiquity and forced them into a heroic past where their superiority and distinctiveness could be illuminated. The Georgians' version of the Soviet past was expressed in less public forums than the keipi. It did not always contain detailed pages, but neither was it blank. For listeners and narrators, the "secret" nature of this past and its frequently tragic intertwining of familial and political history made it emotionally charged and all the more important to remember. Today, Georgian newspapers are full of the memories of children whose parents suffered or disappeared in the 1930s.

There is not space here to discuss the role of rumor, anecdotes, and reminiscences in the preservation of Georgian national history, but these, too, are nurtured by a state whose message is perceived by the population as inaccurate and false. The state's use of national songs, its patronage of a folklore "industry" in the institutes of higher education, and its stress on family tradition and respect for elders help create a strong resonance for orally transmitted national history.

HISTORY AND LITERATURE

A peripheral people victimized and threatened with assimilation, Georgians use their ancient history to validate their claims to cultural and political superiority

over their Russian colonizers and to distinguish themselves from the large numbers of non-Georgians in their community. Georgian history deals overwhelm-
ingly with the glories of the medieval period and with the Georgian literary and
political renaissance of the 1860s. For Georgians, as for the Irish, history is an
"ethical reality" that embodies the moral struggle of the Georgian nation against
domination.[14]

In Georgian historians' hands, the Georgian writers of the second half of the
nineteenth century become official symbols of opposition to tsarism, but more importantly, they become unofficial symbols of the native intelligentsia's resistance,
then and now, to Russification. The most important of them, Ilia C'avc'avadze,
who is routinely referred to in scholarly and newspaper articles as "the Great Ilia,"
was canonized by the Georgian church in 1987 for his "service to the nation"
(Kiziria 1990:26). C'avc'avadze's own writings are an indication of the centrality
of the past to Georgian identity among intelligentsia circles in the late nineteenth
century. In 1888, he wrote: "A nation which begins to forget its history becomes
diluted, degenerates, and loses its face. . . . The erasure of its past and former life
from memory is an indication of a nation's complete disintegration" (1977:346).

Georgians' preoccupation with the past, an obsession shared by many cultural elites in Central and Eastern Europe, was accentuated by a Soviet system
that politicized history and used it as a prop for its own legitimacy. The Soviet
historiographical tradition of partisanship, its canonization of "progressive" figures, and its teleological purpose reinforced Georgian historians' own tendencies
to idealize the national past.

In the nineteenth century, writers in Georgia (and Central Europe) were the
voices of conscience, social thought, and the nation. This tradition was reinforced
by a Soviet system that continued to accord writers high status and support.
Although widely different in their responses to the demands of this system, by the
1960s most Georgian writers conformed to what Czeslaw Milosz has called the
"aesthetic Ketman," who is characterized as burrowing "into ancient texts," reedit-
ing ancient authors, or choosing "university careers because research into literary
history offers a safe pretext for plunging into the past and for converse with works
of great aesthetic value" (Milosz 1990:68–69).

In Georgia, the dominant fictional genre became the historical novel, which,
in the tradition of Sir Walter Scott, dealt with national heroes and ancient myths.
The best-known work is Konstantin Gamsaxurdia's *The Right Hand of the Great
Master,* the story of a medieval church architect and stonemason who, after constructing the most beautiful cathedral, was disfigured by his king and patron so
that he could never build its like again. The novel, written in the 1950s, elaborates
a myth known to every Georgian, which surrounds the building of Svetisxoveli,
Georgia's most famous cathedral. Its story, true to the model of many Georgian
novels, perpetuates a popular image of Georgia's heroic past. Other writers responded to Socialist Realism by retreating into lyricism and folk wisdom. Anna
Kalandadze, the doyenne of Georgian poetry, is a good example. Her poems de-

scribe the pain of a lost past and contain endless references to ancient places, churches, and kings. The example below, written in 1962 and describing a famous fresco in the monastery of Betania, is typical.

> There are many springs and valleys
> Before you reach Betania,
> Where the candle of eternity
> burns for ever,
> Where the great king of kings stands
> Arms uplifted,
> So that high ideals may spread among
> Georgians once more
> For his homeland, the supplicant is
> Holy
> There are many springs and valleys
> Before you reach Betania
> (Kalandadze 1981:130)

The burning candles (a way of remembering the dead), the king's supplication for a lost faith, and the symbolic use of words like "springs" and "eternity" convey a nostalgic and nationalistic message that contradicts the dominant Soviet constructions of Georgia's past. Other poets and writers idealize village life and peasant values as an implicit critique of the Marxist-Leninist ethos of dynamism and industrial progress.[15]

Such messages were not simply circulated among the elite. The politicization of literature by the Soviet regime and policies of popular education ensured that every Georgian schoolchild could not only read Gamsaxurdia and Kalandadze but understand the evocative transcript as well. The Georgian language, with its unique script and its linguistic and phonetic difficulty, provided the ideal vehicle for this evocative transcript. The language of Soviet bureaucracy accentuated the private and oppositional nature of Georgian language at all levels, from "high culture" to business communication and slang.[16] The language's non-Indo-European origin made it less vulnerable than Ukrainian or Belorussian to Russification. The language is itself an everyday symbolic reminder of Georgian antiquity, and its ubiquitous use of "kin" or "ancestor" word roots makes it a highly potent symbol of Georgians' link with their past.[17] Soviet sensitivity to language politics encouraged Georgians to preserve their belief that language is the embodiment of a nation's "inner being" and that without it, a nation ceases to exist.[18]

NATIONAL IMAGERY

Georgians share an intense sensitivity to objects and images from the past. They are surrounded by medieval churches and ruins that are repeatedly contextualized in the media as symbols of resistance to alien tyranny. Students, unburdened by memories of the enthusiastic destruction of these monuments in the past, lovingly restore them during their summer breaks. Mass production ensures that such ancient images adorn the walls of ordinary Georgians' homes. Georgians are also surrounded by empty memory spaces—places where the Soviet state has refused to commemorate Georgian history—such as the spot where Georgian demonstrators were killed in 1956. In a recent article, James Young suggested that the absence of a monument and the "perpetual irresolution" of memory are memory's "surest engagement" (1992:270).

The attempt to replace Georgian with Soviet symbols had feeble results. A campaign against what Eduard Shevardnadze, in a speech as Georgian party leader in 1981, called "manifestations of nationalism or chauvinism" led to the creation of new "socialist traditions." A Center of Festivities and a Commission on Propaganda and the Introduction of New Traditions and Rituals were set up to promote newly formulated civil marriage ceremonies and "baptisms." Lavish funerals, which resonated with uncontrollable memories, religious and otherwise, were a particular Soviet target (see Jones 1988). But local and national traditions incorporated into the new Soviet rituals to encourage popular support became, instead, new avenues for the further celebration of "Georgianness." Tbilisoba, a festival created in the 1970s to honor the capital and counter attendance at religious events, became a celebration of the city's 1,500-year history and had the unintended effect of engaging Georgians more intensely in their own national history.[19]

In similar fashion, the vast majority of Georgian films made in the 1970s and 1980s were based on Georgian village life and childhood memories, with the Soviet context presented as the vaguest of frameworks. Soviet monumental art, designed to express what Christel Lane called "the timeless solidity of the new system" (1981:222), was adapted to celebrate Georgian writers and kings as well as revolutionaries and Soviet leaders. Artworks were erected in memory places such as ancient battlefields or next to medieval churches. The official pantheon of Georgian heroes and public figures is located at the Church of the Holy Mount in Tbilisi. Even when the model is Soviet, as in the case of war memorials, the portrayal of the Georgian ethnic type and the display of Georgian names conveys a Georgian, rather than a Soviet, memory. The most familiar monument in Georgia, *Deda Kartlisa,* exemplifies this paradox. A highly stylized portrait of a Georgian mother sculpted in the Soviet monumental style, she towers above the capital of Tbilisi with a bowl of wine in one hand and a sword in the other, symbolizing Georgians' own self-image as hospitable but fierce defenders of their homeland. Dressed in national costume, she reinforces the image of belonging to a Georgian "national family."

In sum, the Soviet state, in its attempt to refashion Georgian memory and myth, only deepened their hold. The Soviet system's neotraditionalist stress on patriotism, its sacred view of ritual objects, its emphasis on state-supported mass culture (socialist in content, national in form), and its imposition of state controls in many areas of social life that forced Georgians back onto kinship and ethnic resources—all provided mechanisms for the propagation of Georgians' own collective myths and memories. By the 1970s, the counterhistory of Georgian society had made tremendous public inroads into official myth.

THE NEW PAST

Bernard Lewis writes that a new future always requires a different past (1975:11). Georgia's future, as outlined by the new nationalist government, relies heavily on a reactivated and reconstructed past.[20] The old ideas and structures have been replaced. In August 1991, a Center for the Study of National Political History and Theory was set up in Georgia to lead in the task of legitimizing the new order.[21]

Concurrently, the Georgian past is undergoing destruction, rediscovery, and reinvention.[22] This development is comparable to the decolonization of memory experienced by other colonial peoples. Party history has been demolished, as is vividly symbolized by the removal of all monuments and street names associated with the revolution. The old symbols have been restored and public spaces reclaimed. Plekhanov Street, named after the "father of Russian Marxism," has been renamed David the Builder Street after one of the most successful Georgian kings. The ambiguous memory of Stalin among Georgians, as both powerful local boy and Russianized tyrant, is being transformed by Georgian glasnost into that of a universal dictator who betrayed his homeland.[23]

Soviet festivals and public holidays have been replaced with Georgian Independence Day and St. George's Day (for the patron saint of Georgia). The national emblem, flag, and hymn of the independent republic of 1918–21 have been restored. The remains of Georgian kings have been returned, and new parties and organizations have adopted the names of their pre-Soviet equivalents. Writers and exiles have been rehabilitated. Even the election of a new president, Zviad Gamsaxurdia, the son of the novelist Konstantin Gamsaxurdia who stoically resisted the Socialist Realist canon, represents renewed continuity with the Georgian past. A writer and historian, Zviad Gamsaxurdia rapidly reshaped the Georgian past to reflect his country's projected future, and one can already detect a creeping amnesia about the Soviet period as people attempt to create a more national, rather than Soviet, identity for themselves.

In addition, there are new (rather than restored) "memory symbols," such as the memorial commemorating the spot where 20 demonstrators were killed by Soviet troops in April 1989 (see Jones 1990). The declaration of Georgian independence took place on the second anniversary of the killings (April 9, 1991), and the presidential elections occurred on May 26, the day when Georgian independence was declared in 1918. The old myths of class solidarity and internationalism, the supreme value of industrial progress, and the continuity of Russo-Georgian friendship have all fallen before an active and powerful history that stresses antiquity, struggle, territoriality, Christianity, and rural tradition.[24]

In the social and political context of Georgia, the institutionalization of the new Georgian history has significant repercussions for the non-Georgian minorities. Georgians make up 70 percent of the total population of the republic, but are in a minority in most border areas.[25] This ethnic makeup, combined with continuing intraregional differences between Georgians and with economic crisis, has led to a sense of national insecurity. As the Soviet center collapsed, this insecurity gave Georgia's territorial boundaries new significance and increased the salience of group boundaries within the republic. The historical rediscoveries and the new opportunities for promulgating Georgian popular history are central to the new assertiveness of Georgian nationalists. Memories of conflict with Muslims throughout their history, with Russians and Armenians in the nineteenth and twentieth centuries, and with Ossetians and Abkhaz in the independence period of 1918–21 have been resurrected. The emphasis on Christianity—Georgians were converted in the fourth century—as a mark of antiquity and civilization has become a source of conflict with non-Christian minority groups. Zviad Gamsaxurdia, alluding to Georgians' participation in the Crusades, has described Georgian Christianity as having a special "militant" or "military" quality (*Samshoblo*, no. 22, November 1990:5).

Claims to territory based on the legitimacy of prior settlement have produced a battle of competing histories among the different national groups in the republic. Bernard Lewis points out that memory is vital in determining immemorial rights and privileges (1975:66). A number of Georgian parties have begun to distinguish between "native" and "non-native" groups within the republic. Those such as the Armenians, Ossetians, Russians, and Azerbaijanis are seen as recent arrivals with little or no "authentic" past in the country. From the perspective of Georgian nationalists, these groups have no inalienable right to territory or citizenship. They are essentially "guests," and as such cannot be expected to join the Georgian group, whose membership is now defined by genealogy.

Thus the Mesxetians, an ethnically mixed population including Islamicized Georgians who were expelled from their southern Georgian homeland in 1944, are today rejected as "Georgians." "Native" Georgians, who campaigned for their return in the 1970s, now refuse them resettlement in Georgia. Likewise, the South Ossetians, many of whom were until recently being slowly "Georgianized," find Georgian group barriers no longer porous. In December 1990, their autonomous province was abolished by the Supreme Soviet of the Georgian Republic and renamed Samachablo, the Georgian historical name for the region.[26] An indication of the importance of history in current conflicts was the criminal charge brought against the Ossetian leader T. G. Kulumbekov for the spreading of "distorted historical facts."[27]

An important element in Georgians' self-demarcation is their claim to "Europeanness." The Georgian intelligentsia has always countered Persian and Ottoman influence in Georgia by strongly identifying with European ideas. The elaborate theory of Georgian-Basque ethnic affinity and the stress on Georgia's past cultural and economic links with countries in the Mediterranean basin are part of this emphasis. In a pamphlet by Zviad Gamsaxurdia, titled "Georgia's Spiritual Mission" and published when he was president of the Georgian Republic, the European myth was subject to some reinvention. Gamsaxurdia places Georgia firmly in the European mainstream by tracing Georgian descent to the ancient Mediterranean Pelasgian culture. Manipulating Greek and Roman sources in a highly dubious manner, he portrays Georgia as a source of spirituality in the Greek world. He invokes the theory of ancient Georgian chroniclers who traced Georgian ethnogenesis to the biblical Japhet, who, he suggests, is identical to Jupiter, the planet of the white race. This strange concoction ends with the assertion that Georgia's special mission is to serve as a bridge between East and West. The pamphlet seems to be the theoretical basis for a new myth concerning Georgians' place and identity in the world. It has already been eulogized in the government newspaper *New Georgia* as representing "a new stage in Georgian culture and science."[28]

The Georgians' new official history, with its emphasis on genealogy, national resistance, victimization, and the Golden Age of Georgian hegemony, is designed to rally Georgians behind a nationalist program of opposition to imperial power and to a leadership that identifies the state with Georgian sovereignty. It has serious implications for non-Georgians by placing them outside the dominant state-controlling group. This is in part a legacy of the Soviet system of union republics that gave constitutional and political privileges to the titular group and identified the republic as the group's historic homeland. Titular groups are now rapidly constructing histories to prove their case. Minority groups are forced to do the same. The new warring of the pasts reflects political struggles in the present, and Vladimir Dedijer's assertion that men are prepared to die for "memory" is becoming only too apparent in Georgia as the old ghosts of enmity and conflict impose new chains of national exclusiveness on the Georgians and their minorities.

CONCLUSION

George Will, in a recent review, declared that nations are naturally forgetful and that democracy makes them more so (1991:7). Will is probably thinking of his own American nation or perhaps that of the English, both of which have a history of dominance and national security, and in neither of which does the past play a major role in competitive politics. Memory politics in multiethnic democracies, however, such as Spain, Canada, and India, keep the past very much on the political agenda—yet Will's point is nevertheless intriguing. Could it be said that in Soviet-type states people are less likely to forget their past than in democracies?

The historical and cultural variables that determine the extent to which the past features in a people's national identity are complex. In most of the Central and Eastern European countries where communism came to power (including the Russian empire), the politics of history had already demonstrated the past's vital importance in the nineteenth century. Nevertheless, the intensity of memory politics in almost every Soviet-type state suggests a strong relationship between communist power and a resistance to forgetfulness among large segments of the population.[29] Although every memory cannot be interpreted as oppositional, the need to remember is inextricably linked with the assertion of personal identity against an impersonal state.

Václav Havel declared in a recent interview that "life under totalitarianism had certain advantages." These included the awakening of "certain potentials in people that would not be expressed to the same extent in a normally function-ing democracy."[30] One wonders whether he had in mind the intense reverence for the national past evident among people in most communist systems. And is this phenomenon due in part, as Adam Zagajewski suggests, to systems that lack the West's "subtle and skeptical machinery of analysis [that] works incessantly, keep-ing a malicious eye on everything: language, love, courage"? In short, does the closed nature of Soviet-type societies contribute to society's continuing reverence for its mythological past?[31]

The thesis of this paper is that in the Soviet Union, the system itself, in its inter-action with traditional structures in Georgian society, *did* reinforce the channels, both informal and formal, that created and preserved Georgian national history. To paraphrase Marx, the peddlers of the official Soviet past produced their own grave diggers. These grave diggers are now busily burying what is left of the old past.

--------- Notes ---------

I would like to thank the following people for their comments on a previous draft of this paper: Edwina Cruise of Mount Holyoke College, Gia Nodia of the Kennan Institute, George Hewitt of the School of Oriental and African Studies, Ron Suny of the University of Michigan, and members of the School of American Research Advanced Seminar "Secret Histories: the Politics of Memory Under Socialism."

1. I distinguish the non-Slavic, territorially based republics because in the Soviet period they proved more resistant to Russianization than did the Ukrainians, Belorussians, and non-Slavic peoples without a recognized territory.

2. This statement applies especially to totalitarian theorists. See, for example, C. J. Friedrich and Z. K. Brzezinski (1966).

3. I have borrowed the term "producers of culture" from Katherine Verdery (1991a).

4. See Vera Dunham (1976), especially her chapter "The Big Deal"; and Katerina Clark (1985).

5. A good example of symbolic inversion in a Soviet joke is the following: Under capitalism, there is exploitation of man by man. Under communism, it is the other way around.

6. Kay Ann Johnson noted a similar effect on Chinese rural families due to state policies (Johnson 1983, especially chapter 1).

7. The best works in English on Georgian history include Allen (1932); Suny (1989); and Lang (1957).

8. This coincided with the decline of the "Pokrovsky school," named for M. N. Pokrovsky (1868–1932), in Soviet historiography. Pokrovsky and his followers, though Marxists, resisted the crude manipulation of history that characterized the 1930s.

9. Georgians whom I spoke to in the 1970s and 1980s, although they knew of the 1924 revolt, had little idea who participated, who planned it, and why it failed. Their knowledge of the independence period of 1918–21 was similarly vague.

10. Bernard Lewis (1975:chapter 3) notes that twentieth-century Arab nationalists do not like to be reminded of their part in this trade either.

11. See, for example, "The Problem of National Diversity Within Georgia," BBC *Summary of World Broadcasts,* Feb. 11, 1989, SU/0382 B/3.

12. For research on the *keipi* in English, see Mars and Altman (1987) and Holisky (1989).

13. Prys Morgan, in her discussion of the Welsh, notes that romanticism of the distant past also compensates for the absence of a more immediate history, something the Georgians and Welsh have in common. See Morgan in Hobsbawm and Ranger (1983:43–100).

14. Oliver MacDonagh, in the first chapter of his brilliant study of Anglo-Irish conflict (1989), discusses the Irish people's view of their history. The parallels with Georgian attitudes are illuminating.

15. See, for example, the works of the popular Guram Rcheulashvili (1977).

16. For a discussion of changes in the Russian language under the impact of Soviet policies, see Sinyavsky (1990:190–225).

17. The Georgian language plays a most vital role in Georgian identity. In 1978, attempts to reduce its status within the Soviet Union led to massive demonstrations in protest (see Jones 1989).

18. The 1980 Christmas message of Ilia II, the Georgian patriarch, in which he declared, "Where language declines, so the nation falls," is a typical example of this view. In 1986, the Georgian church celebrated Georgian Language Day by publishing a pamphlet titled *Glory to the Georgian Language* (see Jones 1988, 1989).

19. Ironically, the first postcommunist Georgian nationalist government abolished the festival because of its "communist" origins.

20. The new government, led by President Gamsaxurdia and his Round Table–Free Georgia Bloc, was voted into power in October 1990. Overthrown by a military coup in January 1992, it was replaced with a provisional government led by Eduard Shevardnadze.

21. *Foreign Broadcast Information Services,* FBIS Sov 91–158 (1991).

22. Most of the information in this section comes from Georgian newspaper reports, primarily from *Samshoblo* (Homeland), *Sakartvelos Respublik'a* (The Georgian Republic), *Axali Sakartvelo* (New Georgia) and *Shvidi Dghe* (Seven Days).

23. How successful the press campaign has been in changing Georgian attitudes toward Stalin is another question. Many intellectuals are anxious to separate Stalin from Georgia altogether, suggesting he was Ossetian in origin or a Russified communist with few links to his homeland. Tengiz Abuladze, in the film *Repentance,* internationalizes Stalin, making him a global phenomenon. Stalin will always remain a problematic memory for Georgians. Should he be confronted as a significant historical figure, remembered for his evil deeds, or blotted out altogether? The Germans have wrestled with a similar dilemma since the fall of the Third Reich.

24. This is partly reflected by changing newspaper titles. *K'omunist'i* (Communist) became *Sakartvelos Respublik'a* (The Georgian Republic), *Saxalxo ganatleba* (People's Education) became *Eri* (Nation), and *Axalgazrda K'omunist'i* (Young Communist) became *Axalgazrda Iverieli* (Young Iverian), a reference to the ancient name of east Georgia.

25. The largest minorities are the Armenians (8.1 percent), Russians (6.3 percent), Azerbaijanis (5.7 percent), Ossetians (3 percent), and Abkhaz (1.8 percent). These are 1989 census figures. See Jones (1990:129) for a fuller statistical table.

26. For a discussion of interethnic relations in contemporary Georgia, see Jones (1992).

27. FBIS Sov 91 154 (1991).

28. This text is only in Georgian (*Samshoblo,* no. 22, November 1990). *New Georgia's* review of the pamphlet is in its November 14 issue (no. 1), 1990.

29. Soviet states have had their successes in manipulating history, but at best their record is one of only partial success. The nature of communist structures designed to enforce forgetfulness is, of course, related to the communist ideology itself. Perhaps the ideology's neophilia is also related to peoples' refusal to forget, although the experience of the Bretons and the Catalans suggests that minorities in democracies place a similarly high value on their history. Perhaps it is alienation from the system, rather than the system itself, that encourages solace in the past.

30. "Uncertain Strength: An Interview with Václav Havel," *The New York Review of Books,* vol. 38, no. 14, August 15, 1991.

31. For an excellent review of Zagajewski's book, see Neal Ascherson, "How to Leave a House of Slavery," in *The New York Review of Books,* vol. 38, no. 14, August 15, 1991. The quotation comes from Ascherson's review.

9

Recounting the Dead

The Rediscovery and Redefinition of
Wartime Massacres in Late- and
Post-Communist Yugoslavia

ROBERT M. HAYDEN

T HE PECULIAR IMPORTANCE of history to the regimes of Eastern Europe is well known. In what has been described as an ethnic shatter zone, the myths of nation that have been used to justify the creation of nation-*states* produced nationalist(ic) ideologies that played on the alleged superiority of a particular group and its long, mystical connection with a particular countryside—usually more of the countryside than members of that nation currently controlled (see, e.g., Jelavich 1990; A. Djilas 1991).[1] The various Yugoslav nations fell easily into this pattern, developing in the nineteenth century separate nationalist ideologies that contested with the simultaneous development of the idea of Yugoslavism—of one state incorporating all of the South Slavic nations.

The tension between these individual national ideologies and that of Yugoslavism left the first Yugoslavia (1920–41) a tenuous, unstable state almost from the moment of its birth (Banac 1984; A. Djilas 1991), and ensured that the Second World War in Yugoslavia was a brutal, multifaceted blend of resistance to occupation, civil war, and communist revolution.[2] While individual nationalisms were largely suppressed during most of the period of communist rule (1945–90), they came roaring back in the late 1980s, leading first to the disintegration of the League of Communists of Yugoslavia (LCY) into separate, republican-based national(ist) communist parties in 1989–90, and then to the election of openly nationalist(ic) noncommunist parties in the elections of 1990.[3]

The resurgence of nationalism in Yugoslavia is a particularly fascinating subject for the examination of secret or hidden histories, for several reasons. First,

the initial development of nationalist political strategies in the late 1980s was a
product of intellectuals and politicians who operated *within* the still-hegemonic
communist parties of the various republics, particularly Slovenia and Serbia.[4]
While these actors made use of secret histories, their doing so was part of an effort
to establish or maintain control of the ruling League(s) of Communists—it was
subversion rather than resistance. Once this effort had succeeded in breaking the
League of Communists of Yugoslavia into separate national communist parties
in each republic, this same nationalism was used to discredit, first, the communists in most of the republics and, second, the unified Yugoslav state itself. Thus,
in Yugoslavia in the 1980s and early 1990s, we can see the invocation and manipulation of hidden and oppositional histories from within and without the state
socialist power structure. In both cases, "private knowledge" that had been long
suppressed was used to challenge the versions of events that had been carefully
constructed and officially approved during the communist period.

Late- and post-communist Yugoslavia also provides an interesting case study
in the use of secret histories because, while the demise of state socialism in Eastern Europe is clearly the end of one kind of totalizing state, the creation of "civil
society" is not automatic (see, e.g., Kligman 1990). Instead, in at least some of the
national(ist[ic]) political milieus of Eastern Europe, the totalizing socialist state is
in danger of being replaced by a totalizing nationalist one. As one Slovenian writer
has put it, with an eye towards Yugoslavia, "Nationalism . . . only exchanges the
ideology of the universal liberation of 'the working class' for the ideology of 'total
national sovereignty.' This is not in any sense a matter of rational categories, but
rather of sovereignty as a value in itself, as the highest value, the cost of which is
irrelevant" (Šetinc 1990:17).

This replacement of one totalizing ideology with its structural opposite ne-
cessitates a supplanting of official history.[5] Because that official history had some
basis in experiences still within living memory, this replacement of communism
with nationalism must itself create a new secret history of the communist movement and period of rule. Indeed, to succeed, the new official history must convert
the "social memory" (see Connerton 1989) underlying the old official history into
a secret archive, officially both denied and suppressed. Thus, in considering late-
and post-communist Yugoslavia, we may examine a dialectic between the competing official histories necessitated by competing totalizing ideologies, each of
which will produce a corollary secret history.

In the space of a chapter it is not possible to cover in detail both the use of
secret histories by political actors within the communist regimes in the several republics and the later use of accounts of long-suppressed massacres to undermine
the old history of the communist revolution and to justify the new nationalisms
within each republic. These efforts to revise the hegemonic history approved by
the LCY were quite different, since the first attempts to do so were aimed at
undermining the totalizing communist state in an attempt to create a pluralistic,
democratic Yugoslavia, while the later revisionists were trying to use hidden his-

tories to justify the dismemberment of Yugoslavia into separate nation-states (see also Hayden 1991a). Nevertheless, since the second process was dependent on the earlier occurrence of the first revisions of official history, a brief account of the first use of hidden histories to challenge LCY historical orthodoxy is necessary.

Undermining the Myth of the Infallible Party: 1982–1987

The first point to be made about the use of secret histories by political actors within the one-party system is that it arose only as the LCY's control over society was weakening. In the 1980s, more or less coincidentally after the death of Marshall Tito, Yugoslavia entered a period of "permanent crisis," with a stagnating economy, inflation that reached extreme levels by 1989, and rising unemployment (see Rusinow 1988). What began as an economic crisis gradually became a political one as writers began increasingly to link the troubles of the Yugoslav economy with the cumbersome nature of the "self-management socialism" system that Yugoslavia had institutionalized in the constitution of 1974 (see, e.g., Mirić 1984) and that was one of the country's primary sources of international and intellectual prestige. This was the "socialism with a human face" that had been prohibited to the rest of Eastern Europe by the Brezhnev doctrine.[6]

At the same time that the "permanent crisis" was weakening the image of self-management, there began a number of journalistic and literary forays into occurrences during the war and the period of the break with Stalin in 1948, which had not been permitted in Yugoslav public debates until that time. The major Serbian weekly NIN began a long series of articles in 1982 on the prison camp on Goli Otok, set up by Tito's government in 1948 to house those who sided with Stalin in the great quarrel between the two leaders. These articles were based on accounts of and by survivors of the camp, including interviews with some of these people. While the existence of this camp had never been denied, the nature of the cruelties practiced there, and the sheer numbers of people sent there on the basis of little or no evidence, came as a shock to the Yugoslav public.

The newspaper revelations about Goli Otok were followed by a number of more artistic, literary treatments of taboo topics. The Yugoslav nominee for the 1986 Academy Award for best foreign film, one of the five finalists that year and winner of the Golden Palm at Cannes, was a frank account of the injustices of the period following the break with Stalin.[7] The country's nominee the following year, though not as successful internationally, was a story about the same period that cast thinly veiled aspersions on the actions of the Communist party and the government. The plot of the film showed the communists acting without scruples or principles in their efforts to remain in power, while an allegorical strain showed the communists to be fools in their efforts to establish the "new socialist man."[8] In 1988, another film became the first to treat sympathetically the urban bourgeoisie, who had been among the most victimized by the communists through expropriation, ruinous taxation, and class-based discrimination.[9] On a more current topic, a young writer published a novel on the ethical and moral problems faced by an honest judge in a politically charged judicial system (Drašković 1981).

A different attack on the system was mounted by journalists in 1988, when they "discovered" the curious case of Andrija Gams, formerly professor of law at Belgrade University, who had been forced into retirement in 1971. The cause of Gams's fall was a withering attack on the concept of "social property," the conceptual key to the theory of socialist self-management (see Hayden 1990b:33–37), that he had made at the time of the drafting of the 1974 constitution. Gams had finished a treatise on property at that time but was not permitted to publish it. In 1986, Gams's book was finally published—and in 1987, it won a major prize for writing on social criticism. The story of Gams's travails was highly publicized in connection with this award, thus transferring his own history from the hidden realm of the purely personal to that of public knowledge.

These various works are only examples of the kinds of criticisms—scholarly, journalistic, and literary—that challenged the LCY's version of the past in the 1980s. Most of these criticisms, which were directed at a pan-Yugoslav audience and sometimes an international one as well, were aimed only at undermining communism and not at building nationalist sentiment. Clearly, there were aspects of the works in these various genres that made them mutually reinforcing. In the initial stages of the development of this critical corpus, literature could perhaps be most evocative and bold. Literary works that criticize official history both activate and depend on secret histories for their effectiveness. That is, the stories of the fictional characters are most moving when they most resonate with the audience's unexpressed social memory, or with what everyone knows but no one can state. Because of its visual impact, film may be among the most effective media for the evocation of secret histories, when the structure of the film itself may become a "commemorative ceremony" for social memory that cannot be directly expressed (cf. Connerton 1989).[10] At the same time, the power of the film will be enhanced as public accounts of past history begin to recognize the elements previously suppressed. In Yugoslavia in the early 1980s, there seems to have been a kind of feedback effect at work between scholarly and journalistic reexamination of what had until then been settled history and artistic exploration that went past these initial, often cautious, reexaminations.[11]

Nationalism in the Late 1980s: The Case of Serbia

With the weakening of the established paradigm of self-management socialism, the turn to nationalism by Yugoslavia's political elites is not surprising. One of the first major political moves in that direction was made by communist politicians in Serbia in 1987.[12] Serbia may have been the republic most disadvantaged by the constitution of 1974, which had otherwise decentralized the country to the point of confederation. Where the other republics received almost complete powers, including the exclusive power to execute *federal* powers in their respective territories, Serbia was handicapped by the strengthening of the two "autonomous provinces" within its borders. These provinces, Kosovo and Vojvodina, were virtually independent of Serbia and could pass legislation without review by the Serbian parliament. Serbia, on the other hand, could pass its own legislation only with the consent of both provinces. Furthermore, the provinces each had their own independent representations in federal executive and legislative bodies—representations that, combined, were greater than that of Serbia.

Within Serbia in the 1980s, there was increasing awareness and resentment of the positions of the provinces of Kosovo and Vojvodina and the loss of Serbian control over territories that were, in theory, still part of the republic. The resentments were particularly acute in regard to Kosovo, once the heart of the medieval Serbian kingdom and site of the great defeat of Serbian forces in 1389 that led to the 500 years of Ottoman domination. Kosovo, long inhabited by Albanians as well as Serbs and Montenegrins and contested by all of them, was becoming increasingly Albanian as members of the other groups emigrated and the Albanian birthrate became the highest in Europe. Regardless of the actual cause of the non-Albanian flight from Kosovo, many Serbs blamed it on the actions of the provincial government, which was dominated by Albanians and was said to be abetting a campaign to drive non-Albanians out of the province.[13] In 1981, the Kosovo Albanians began a campaign of resistance to Serbian domination, which Serbia met by increasing its police and paramilitary activities in the province. In this climate, the populist leader Slobodan Milošević, then president of the League of Communists of Serbia, was able to use the issue of Kosovo to come to power in a virtual nationalist coup within the Serbian league in October 1987 (see Čavoški 1991; Djukić 1992). Milošević thus accomplished a Ceausescou-like transformation of a nominally communist party into an openly nationalist one (cf. Verdery 1991a).

By 1988, Serbian resentment was taking public form as a questioning of the very basis of the Yugoslav union, the "brotherhood and unity" of the Yugoslav peoples. A celebrated dissident philosopher published an article claiming to document an anti-Serbian program in the Communist party of Yugoslavia before the war, with the implication that the same program was carried on by the LCY after the war (Tadić 1988). Along the same lines, another historian claimed to have found documents proving that right after the war, the communists had planned to give Kosovo to Albania. In the following year, intellectuals' support of nationalism was manifested in a memorandum by the Serbian Academy of Sciences and Arts that argued that Serbia was at a disadvantage within Yugoslavia and proposed a program for Serbian national development. This memorandum ignited a political battle between the leaderships of the various republics that was described by the Zagreb weekly news magazine *Danas* as a "verbal civil war."

Milošević, now president of Serbia (rather than of the party), used the Kosovo issue as his primary weapon, capitalizing particularly on the six-hundredth anniversary of the Battle of Kosovo in June 1989. In that year he extended his approach

to criticize the political acts that had put Serbia into such an unfavorable constitutional position in 1974. It was at this stage that other hidden histories came into
play, with the rehabilitation of those who had criticized the 1974 constitution at
the time it was being drafted, and who had been made to suffer for their criticisms.

The major scandal had been the purge of the Belgrade University law faculty
in 1971 that had removed Andrija Gams and other professors, following a faculty
symposium that had been highly critical of the proposed new constitution. The
issue of the law faculty's journal that contained the papers from the symposium
had been banned, and several of the most critical faculty members had been removed from the faculty, some into retirement, some simply into unemployment,
some to jail.[14] One of these last figures was suddenly discovered in the summer
of 1989, when interviews with him and stories about his trials appeared in major
Serbian newspapers. By having these stories publicized, Milošević was able to de-
pict Serbia as having been the victim of a conspiracy.

A second use of hitherto hidden histories came into play with the "discovery"
that a number of factories and other economically important institutions had been
removed from Serbia in the years immediately following the war, and set up in
Slovenia and in other republics.[15] This assertion was backed up with both documents and personal accounts, which improved its credibility.

By the end of the 1980s, then, secret histories were being used in Serbia to
bring into question the basic elements of Yugoslav communist ideology, but from
within the League of Communists of Serbia. The point of the exercise was to hold
on to power when the appeal of communism itself as an ideology was fast disappearing due to the economic chaos caused by the "permanent crisis." By turning
to nationalism, Milošević was able to stage a coup within the one-party system,
replacing a traditional, internationally oriented communist government with a
nationalistic one and taking over the form of communist rule while scrapping
much of communist ideology. The decentralized nature of Yugoslav politics, which
placed virtually all power in the hands of the elites within republics that were defined on a national basis, made this nationalization of Yugoslav politics not only
possible but perhaps likely (see Woodward 1989; cf. Roeder 1991). While Milošević carried this process out first, he was merely a forerunner for the total collapse
of Yugoslav politics into nationalistic antagonisms, which took place in 1990–91.

COUNTING THE BODIES, 1990–1991

One of the most potent weapons for building nationalism seems to be the uncovering of (semi-)hidden massacres. The transfiguration of the dead into martyrs is
perhaps the most powerful mechanism of symbolic politics, and funerals provide
a supreme moment for transforming ritual into political theater (see Esherick and
Wasserstrom 1990). The discovery and celebration of martyrdom have thus taken
prominence in nationalist politics in Yugoslavia in 1990–91. At the same time, and

perhaps by necessity, the old martyrs to the wartime nationalism of communist historiography (Serbs killed by the Croatian regime, or Muslims killed by Serbian royalists) have been marginalized, and in at least some cases their martyrdom and perhaps even the fact of their deaths have been denied (see Denich 1991). The result of this new accounting of death and transfiguration of the dead has been to produce a propaganda war of competing nationalist histories of violence and injustice.

The most ferocious fronts in this war have been centered on the victims of the civil war of 1941–45, particularly the massacres of Serbs by Croats and of Croats by communists. Both fronts are focused on events in and surrounding the fascist "Independent State of Croatia" (Nezavisna Drzava Hrvatske, or NDH) and are centered on two revisions of the history established during the communist period. The first challenge has been to the moral superiority of Tito's communist-led Partisans over the forces of the NDH. For this front, the major focus has been on newly acknowledged massacres of NDH troops and personnel by the communists in 1945. The second challenge has been to the moral inferiority of the NDH regime itself, particularly insofar as that regime has been depicted as having been based on a uniquely vicious and virulent Croatian nationalism, incarnate in the Ustaša, the Croatian fascists who ran the NDH. In the political milieu of Yugoslavia in 1990, the first revision was actually not controversial in itself, but the second has incited a vehement response from Serbs, who have rediscovered Ustaša atrocities that had been hidden, at least officially, for 50 years.[16] Thus, the propaganda war has seen three campaigns, each based on the resurfacing of a different secret history.

Communists as Mass Murderers in 1945

In socialist Yugoslavia, one of the founding myths of the state was the moral superiority of the communists and their Partisan army to the Croatian fascists, or Ustaša, and to the Serbian royalists, or Četniks, during World War II. The Ustaša particularly were reviled because of their genocide against Jews, Serbs, and Gypsies, and were seen as having been worse even than the Nazis in their cruelty.[17] While the communists admitted to having fought a tough, vicious war and to having executed many traitors and war criminals, they did not admit to having themselves committed massacres.

This element of the Partisan myth held up within Yugoslavia, at least publicly, until 1989–90. There had always been stories within Yugoslavia, however, of Partisan massacres of Ustašas and Četniks at the end of the war. These stories were, in fact, published in Yugoslav émigré circles after the war, but such publications could not be brought into Yugoslavia or openly mentioned, much less discussed, within the country. Furthermore, the émigré sources were themselves suspect because of their fanatical hatred of communist Yugoslavia. The various stories received substantiation from a more reputable source, however, when Milovan Djilas

published his war memoirs in English in 1977 (M. Djilas 1980)—even though at
that time the book could not be published, discussed, or even mentioned in Yugoslavia. Djilas, who was in a position to know, said that many Ustašas, Četniks,
and other opponents of the communists surrendered to the British in Austria in
1945.[18] After they were repatriated by the British to Yugoslavia, all were killed.
Djilas left no doubt of the scope of the massacres:

> According to what I heard in passing from a few officials involved in
> that settling of scores, the number [of dead] exceeds twenty thousand—
> though it certainly must be under thirty thousand. . . . A year or two
> later, there was grumbling in the Slovenian Central Committee that they
> had trouble with the peasants from those areas, because underground
> rivers were casting up bodies. They also said that piles of corpses were
> heaving up as they rotted in shallow mass graves, so that the very earth
> seemed to breathe. (M. Djilas 1980:447)

These descriptions of underground rivers and heaving piles of corpses seem almost
the stuff of epic poetry, and they would certainly seem to indicate that there were
indeed witnesses to the atrocities who could not speak openly.

Djilas's depiction of Partisan guilt went largely unnoticed (it was, after all, only
one brief passage at the end of a book of 450 pages) until the story was repeated,
this time with extensive reports from witnesses and the few survivors, in Nikolai
Tolstoy's *The Minister and the Massacres* (1986). That book, primarily an extended
accusation against Sir Harold Macmillan for having made the decision to repatriate
the Yugoslavs, carried extraordinary details of the massacres (Tolstoy 1986:130–
207). Tolstoy published accounts by survivors of the massacres, some of whom
had been pushed into caves after having been shot but not seriously wounded.
Some of these accounts had been published in émigré journals and newspapers
but had not received the wide international publicity and credibility that Tolstoy's
book afforded. While in 1986 a public discussion of the matter was still not possible within Yugoslavia, the book received extensive coverage in Western Europe,
and its contents became widely known in Yugoslavia.

In 1990, what was widely known but officially unacknowledged within Yugoslavia became central to a new image of Yugoslav communism and of the Ustaša.
The transformation of the communist massacres from secret history to public knowledge was dependent on political changes within Yugoslavia. In January
1990, Tito's communist party, the League of Communists of Yugoslavia, self-
destructed in bickering between the leagues of communists of Serbia, Croatia, and
Slovenia at the party's last (and aptly named "extraordinary") congress; nationalism was replacing class struggle within each of these parties (see Rusinow 1991:5–
6). By that stage, Slovenia was already undergoing a transformation away from
the one-party state, with the formation of new political parties and demands for
free elections. These demands were met: elections were held in Slovenia in April
1990 and in Croatia in May–June 1990. In both cases, nationalist noncommunists

won the elections (but see note 3), although the former communist parties, now renamed the "Party of Democratic Change" in Croatia and the "Party of Democratic Renewal" in Slovenia, were the largest opposition parties in terms of votes obtained.

Perhaps in part to discredit these large opposition parties and in part to inflame nationalist passions within their republics, both the Croatian and the Slovenian governments undertook to publicize the massacres committed by the communists in 1945. Their efforts included widely publicized church ceremonies and excavations of ossuaries in caverns (see, e.g., *Danas*, July 17, 1990 [cover story]), and the publication of commemorative volumes on the newly discovered massacre sites (e.g., Žanko and Šolić 1990).[19] The disruptive potential of the material was recognized in a political cartoon in the Zagreb newsweekly *Danas* (July 17, 1990:2), showing two figures huddling in a cavern full of bones, with one saying, "Do you really think this is an inspirational place for discussions on constitutional changes?"

From the published accounts of the massacres, it is clear that knowledge of them was widespread but repressed so long as the communists remained in power. Indeed, one of the commemorative volumes had a section titled "The eruption of suppressed memories" (Žanko and Šolić 1990:24–32). These accounts also show that knowledge of the massacres was kept alive by transmission of the stories from the actual eyewitnesses to their children. It is likely, however, that public acknowledgment of the massacres would not have come had the communists remained in power. In Croatia and Slovenia in 1990, the republican leagues of communists had already seen a transition in leadership from the Partisans, who had held power for 40 years, to men born in the 1940s. These younger men, though not themselves guilty of participating in the massacres, could not admit that they had occurred. This reticence was regretted after the fact: a week after the widespread publicity of the massacres began, the League of Communists of Croatia–Party of Democratic Change issued an "appeal for reconciliation" of all parties in Croatia:

> We are aware of the fact that our call for investigations of the entire truth, for forgiveness and civil reconciliation should have come earlier, but we believe that even now it is not too late. Our call would have had greater moral legitimacy if the Party had issued it while it was in power. That doesn't reduce the sincerity of our intentions today. (Žanko and Šolić 1990:94–95)

In the distinctive circumstances of Croatia, the call for "civil reconciliation" could not be uncomplicated. The key here is the qualification: civil, as opposed to national. The difference is between a reconciliation of citizens or political parties, on the one hand, and of nations—the Croats and the Serbs of Croatia—on the other. It is at this point that the second front of historical revisions in Croatia becomes relevant.

DIMINISHING THE GENOCIDAL PRACTICES OF THE
CROATIAN STATE, 1941–1945.

The fascist NDH had both a policy and a well-developed practice of genocide against Serbs, Jews, and Gypsies, complete with concentration camps and village massacres. Official Yugoslav historians after the war declared that over 700,000 Serbs had been killed by the Ustaša. Beginning in the 1960s, however, the extent of the slaughter of Serbs by the wartime Croatian state was contested by some unorthodox, nationalist Croatian historians, who were condemned for nationalism and whose works were suppressed (see Tudjman 1990). Indeed, the actual number of victims of the Ustaša may have been inflated (see discussion in A. Djilas 1991:125–27). Even so, the view that the NDH practiced genocide did not receive serious public challenge within Yugoslavia until 1990.[20]

The numbers of Serbian dead and their importance as indicators of a distinctly Croatian genocide have now become matters of great controversy in Yugoslavia. The central figure in the argument is Dr. Franjo Tudjman, one of Tito's Partisans during the war and later a general in the Yugoslav People's Army, turned historian, Croatian nationalist, dissident and political prisoner in the 1970s, politician in 1990, and finally president of Croatia in the first free elections after the war, in May–June 1990. Just before the elections, Tudjman published a book (1990) that attempted in two ways to diminish the genocidal acts of the NDH. First, Tudjman argued that the number of Serbs murdered had not, in fact, been so great as indicated by official statistics (Tudjman 1990:79–101).[21] Thus, empirically, the alleged genocide of the NDH was said to be overstated. Second, Tudjman argued against the absolute criminality of genocide itself, by equating it with the massacres and other crimes with which history is rife. In his words:

> Throughout history there have always been attempts at a "final solution" for foreign and undesirable racial-ethnic or religious groups through expulsion, extermination, and conversion to the "true religion." . . . It is a vain task to attempt to ascertain the rise of all or some forms of genocidal activity in only some historical periods. Since time immemorial, they [genocidal practices] have always existed in one or another form, with similar consequences in regard to their own place and time, regardless of their differences in proportion or origin. . . . Reasoning that would assign genocidal inclinations, reasoning or goals to only some nations or racial-ethnic communities, to only some cultural-civilizational spheres and social-revolutionary movements, or to only some individual religions and ideologies is completely mistaken and beyond any sense of historical reality. (Tudjman 1990:166)

By this reasoning, the NDH was simply another of history's brutal actors, and there was nothing particularly noteworthy or blameworthy about the Croatian genocide of 1941–45.

The issue crystallized around the numbers of dead in the concentration camp of Jasenovac, which in orthodox postwar historiography was accepted as the Serbian Golgotha, where hundreds of thousands of Serbs were murdered. In the new Croatian historiography, the actual number of Serbs killed in Jasenovac was only in the tens of thousands, and the Ustaša also killed all those who opposed their regime, including Croats (see Boban 1990). By this reading, the alleged genocide of Serbs by the NDH was a gross exaggeration on the part of communists and Serbian historians, who sought to discredit the anticommunist NDH. The implications of the new Croatian position were presented succinctly by a professor of history at Zagreb University:

> There is a tendency in the works of [Serbian historians] to cite the Ustaša policy as uniquely genocidal, with Serbs as the sole victims. The issue is far more extensive and complicated. Genocidal policy was represented not only by the Ustašas, and the Serbs were not the only victims. On the territory of wartime Yugoslavia, genocide was the policy of other military-political forces, too, notably the occupationists and the Serbian Chetniks. Hence, other South Slavic peoples (Croats, Muslims and others), were also victims of genocide. . . .
>
> The Serb—or any other—people, alone, was not the sole victim of Ustaša policy. Croats who offered widespread resistance to the Ustaša regime were victims too. Any assessment of the Ustaša regime and its policies is incomplete without an account of the circumstances in Yugoslavia and internationally that allowed them and their policies to get and exercise power. In other words, Ustasism, with all its characteristics and consequences, was not genetically Croat, but was the product of specific historical circumstances. (Boban 1990:588–89)

But this position is at least as tendentious and as open to challenge on factual grounds as orthodox postwar historiography (see Hayden 1992a). In regard to numbers, it is indeed likely that the figures for Serbian dead in Jasenovac itself have been inflated or exaggerated. Arguments like Tudjman's, however, do not take into account the massacres of Serbs that took place outside of the concentration camps, in Ustaša raids on Serbian villages; most Serbian victims probably died in those raids (A. Djilas 1991:121–24; 125–26). Moreover, for Serbs, Jasenovac has become a metonym for the entire Ustaša campaign to eliminate the Serbs from Croatia. Arguments that attempt to minimize the number of victims at Jasenovac and to deny the ultimate evilness of the Ustaša campaign against Serbs ignore this metonomy and are thus both offensive and ominous to Serbs, especially those living in Croatia.

The symbolic importance to Serbs of the NDH genocide was expressed by Dr. Jovan Rašković following the armed clash between Croatian police and Serbs in the village of Borovo Selo in May 1991, which was at that time the worst case of

Serb-Croat conflict since the 1940s. Rašković, a relatively moderate leader of Croatia's Serbs in a political milieu in which there are no true moderates, analyzed
the politics of Dr. Tudjman's government in the following terms:

> [The Croatian leadership] underestimated the importance of the geno-
> cide of the Croatian Ustaša in Serb-Croat relations. Thinking that would
> attempt to minimize and hide genocide, and thereby to establish an
> image that genocide is unimportant and pass over it, is immoral. That
> type of politics, which both scientists and the leadership have carried
> out for purely political reasons, has shown itself to be completely
> counterproductive, because the Serbian nation in Croatia has under-
> stood it as a call for recidivism. . . . Instead of explicitly and wisely
> establishing its view of genocide and doing what had to be done at
> the moment of assuming power, recognizing certain collective national
> rights for the Serbs precisely because of the genocide, the new gov-
> ernment went exactly the other way and established an atmosphere in
> which it was alleged that Croats had been victimized by Serbs. As if
> Serbs had constructed Jasenovac and as if there should now be estab-
> lished some balance for this imaginary imbalance! (*Vreme*, May 6,
> 1991:5)

The new Croatian history, then, was aimed at replacing the established orthodoxy of Croatian genocide against Serbs. By denying the quality of the evil and
minimizing the numbers of those killed, the new Croatian history seems designed
to suppress the experience of Croatia's Serbs, who remember very well the massacres of their people in 1941–45. Thus, the new Croatian history may force those
experiences into hiding, transforming them into secret histories.

RESTATING CROATIAN GENOCIDE: UNCOVERING MORE
USTAŠA MASSACRES

In reaction to the rapid development of the new Croatian history, Milošević's
regime in Serbia began its own propaganda effort to ensure that the crimes of the
NDH against Serbs would not be forgotten. Throughout the summer of 1990, as
Croatian and Slovenian newspapers carried stories about the communist massacres at the end of the war, the major Serbian paper, Belgrade's *Politika*, ran a long
series of stories on atrocities committed by the Ustaša and the NDH, largely stick-
ing with materials from official sources and orthodox postwar historiography. By
1991, however, the Serbian counter to the new Croatian history took the form of
uncovering secret histories of Ustaša massacres that had not entered into official
histories.

   In April 1991, Belgrade television ran a documentary film recording the 1991
entry of investigators into a cave in Bosnia and Herzegovina where scores of
Serbs, including many children, had been massacred by the Ustaša.[22] The exis-

tence of this cave and its ossuary, like that of those in Slovenia and Croatia, had been known to local people but never acknowledged formally by the government. The film showed exhumations, long lines of coffins, and mourners finally able to bury their dead. The political effect of the film was twofold. First, it continued the discrediting of the old (pre-Milošević) communist regime, which had kept knowledge of the massacre hidden and was therefore "anti-Serb." Second, and more important, the film reinforced orthodox history of the brutality of the Ustaša and the reality of their genocidal campaign.

The discovery of Ustaša victims in Bosnia and Herzegovina continued into the summer of 1991. In August, a huge public funeral was held for what Radio Belgrade described as "three thousand victims of the Ustaša genocide, whose bones were recently removed from ten caves in Herzegovina" (BECT 80 [July 31, 1991]).[23] Radio Belgrade's report of the funeral indicated a massive political event, the result of great effort: after "nine months of recovering bones from Herzegovinian caves," the "victims of the Ustaša" were buried in a mass grave. The line of coffins stretched for one and a half kilometers; the liturgy was sung by the patriarch of the Serbian Orthodox Church, and speakers included Serbian politicians from Bosnia and Herzegovina, politicians from Serbia, and leading Serbian nationalist intellectuals (BECT 85 [August 5, 1991]).

The Serbian campaign to rediscover and reinforce memory of the Ustaša massacres of Serbs was continued in August 1991 with the opening of an exhibition of films about the genocide (*Vreme,* August 19, 1991:18). Material accompanying the films explained that the "Ustaša crimes do not fade with time," and that "no people, except Serbs, has experienced such a Golgotha." At a moment in which Serbs in Croatia were pressing an armed uprising against the secessionist government of Croatia, it seems clear that the film exhibit was designed both to demonize Croats as a "genocidal people" and to stir the passions of Serbs as having been among the great victims of the twentieth century.

"VERBAL CIVIL WAR" AND THE NEW OFFICIAL HISTORIES

As the Yugoslav federation collapsed into civil war between Serbs and Croats in Croatia during the summer of 1991, the propaganda warfare of the two regimes intensified. Belgrade's leading papers, *Politika* and the others of its publishing house, which had been taken over by Milošević in 1987 (see Hayden 1991b), ran jingoistic accounts in which Croatian forces were "Ustaša" and the Croatian government "Ustaša" or "fascist." The major Croatian paper, *Vjesnik,* referred to Serbian fighters as "Četniks" or "terrorists" and to the Serbian government as "Bolshevik" or "communist."

In both republics, the major television and radio networks had already been brought under strict government control and served only as propaganda organs for nationalistic jingoism. In Croatia, the republican government banned the central government's YUTEL network, which had been the only reliable source of

television news in all of Yugoslavia, as being "anti-Croat," and drove the leading
quasi-independent news weekly, *Danas*, into a forced (and fraudulent) bankruptcy
proceeding (*Vreme*, August 19, 1991:16–17). In Serbia, the remaining independent news sources (Student Radio B-92 FM, Independent Television "Studio B,"
the daily *Borba*, and the weekly magazine *Vreme*, all located in Belgrade) also came
under strong government pressure, while YUTEL was restricted to broadcasting
only very late at night.

Under these circumstances of "verbal civil war," the newly minted nationalist
official histories are likely to remain in place and unchallengeable within each of
the two republics, Serbia and Croatia. Their mutual inconsistency, far from providing opportunity for questioning the new history in either republic, is instead
much more likely to provide justifications for suppressing dissenting views, since
anyone who might challenge the official view will be seen as ipso facto supporting
the other perspective, and thus to be a traitor.

THE MORAL AUTHORITY OF MURDEROUS REGIMES

These competing new histories may reveal some truths about the regimes that
propound them, as well as about the phenomenon of secret histories. The Croatian discovery of massacres by communists and the Serbian concentration on the
crimes of the Ustaša in the last "Independent State of Croatia" are meant to discredit the moral authority of the communists in the first case and Croatian nationalists in the second, and to disqualify them from politics. The Croatian minimizing
of the genocidal actions of the NDH is simply the reverse of this message—an attempt to fend off the implications of communist postwar historiography—while
the Serbian rediscovery of Ustaša victims is an effort to restate, and thus repro-
duce, the image of Croatian political immorality.

These histories are categorical and totalizing. If one accepts them, then the
stigmatized groups are indeed disqualified from politics. This totalizing effect,
however, makes the promoters of the new histories vulnerable as well. If the claim
to political legitimacy is based on the immorality of the opposition, then any revelation of immorality on the part of those promulgating the histories may inflict
serious political damage on the accusers themselves. In the Yugoslav case, this
vulnerability of the promulgators of a totalizing history can be seen in the failure
of the League of Communists of Croatia to deal with the communist massacres
of repatriated prisoners until they were forced to do so when the massacres were
revealed, celebrated, and transformed into mass martyrdoms by the new noncommunist governments of Slovenia and Croatia. Despite their own personal lack
of guilt and their genuine desire for reform, the new generation of communists
could not themselves uncover the crimes committed by their predecessors, because those crimes destroyed the moral superiority of the communists over their
nationalist opponents.

This vulnerability of the promulgators of totalizing history, in turn, may account for their efforts to suppress previous historical accounts and other sources of data. The means for such suppression may be found in changing rituals of commemoration. Thus, the new Croatian government changed the anniversary of the first uprising in Croatia against the fascist occupation forces in 1941 from the date of an attack by communists to the date of an attack by noncommunist resistance. Other changes in commemoration can be seen in the actions of Tudjman's government in changing the names of streets in Zagreb, removing names that commemorated communists, communist Yugoslavia, and even the internationalism of nonalignment.[24]

Perhaps most revealing in this regard, the government changed the name of the Square of the Martyrs of Fascism to the Square of the Croatian Leaders. The name "Martyrs of Fascism" could be too closely tied to the Ustaša genocide, which the new historiography was aimed at minimizing. Similarly, the new government has largely ignored the concentration camp at Jasenovac. The communists had built a massive monument and a museum there and had bused school children to the site, but the new government's view of Jasenovac has been to ignore its existence. Again, this action of the government in ceasing old forms of commemoration fits with the new historiography, which views the evils of Jasenovac as having been overstated.

Of course, new books of the revised history have been written, and more will come. These books have and will further ignore or reject the previously established history, removing it from intellectual and popular political discourse, at least for a while. This process of revision must in turn create new secret histories, based either on firsthand knowledge of events now officially to be unacknowledged, or on knowledge of the superseded books. And in this context, the excesses of the government may come back to haunt it. For example, a nonparty movement has been under way in Zagreb to restore the name of the Square of the Martyrs of Fascism, even as the civil war with Serbs has intensified.

But the tragedy of the new histories in Yugoslavia is not just an intellectual one, and its victims are not only those whose knowledge must remain unacknowledged and repressed. In Yugoslavia in 1991, the new totalizing histories have been used to justify civil war. In this atmosphere of increasing polarization, the cost of suppressing alternative histories has been measured in blood.

August and December, 1991

POSTSCRIPT

With the spread of the civil war into Bosnia and Herzegovina since March–April 1992 (see Bogosavljević et al. 1992), the impact of earlier hidden histories has been reduced, while comparisons of current atrocities with the official histories of World War Two have increased. The most important elements of this latter process have been the comparisons of "ethnic cleansing" and Serbian-run death camps in Bosnia-Herzegovina with the Nazi practices of genocide.[25] In fact, the more apt comparison would be with the genocidal campaigns of the Ustaša during World

War Two; and while the recent Serb atrocities may have been most widespread, Croat and Muslim forces have also engaged in ethnic cleansing through terror and the creation of camps for civilians. By comparing the latest atrocities only with those of the Germans in the 1940s and by focusing only on the Serbs, the international media and political leaders have created an easy new history that will absolve them of their own responsibility for helping to provoke the Yugoslav disaster by their premature recognition of Croatia and Bosnia (see Hayden 1992a): everything can be blamed on the Serbs.[26] Yet this easy new history has consequences that must cause intellectual unease.

First, if similar ideologies and processes of ethnic cleansing were espoused and practiced by Germans and Croats in the 1940s and Serbs in the 1990s, there may be identifiable strains of Central European political and social thought that induce such activities. Looking at each set of practices in isolation obscures the possible generality of the processes in question. Second, the equation of Serbian atrocities in 1992 with German genocide in the 1940s facilitates forgetting the Serbian victims of the Croatian genocide of 1941–45. In this sense, the new history obscures what had been the official and accepted memories of World War Two, thus making the dead of that time—both those who had been memorialized after the war and those just "discovered" in 1991—victims once again: their deaths were now, indeed, in vain.

This second consequence must be bitter for Serbs, who will some day be forced to confront a painful truth: the hidden histories that the Serbian government revealed and propagated in 1991–92 were used to incite Serbs into committing atrocities rivaling those of their earlier German, Croatian, and Muslim tormentors. Because of these atrocities, the legitimacy of the Serbian cause has been lost, and the Serb victims of the 1940s, once honored dead, will be forgotten.

September 1992

CODA

The redefinition of the massacres of World War II was made manifest by the U.S. government's invitation to Croatian president Tudjman to attend the opening of the Holocaust Museum in Washington, D.C., in April 1993. While Tudjman's presence was protested by some at the opening ceremonies and was also subject to some criticism in the press, all of the criticisms centered on Tudjman's revisionist minimizing of the Holocaust itself (see, e.g., *New York Times*, April 22, 1993). His dismissal of the Ustaša's genocidal campaigns against the Serbs of Croatia and Bosnia was not even mentioned. Thus the Serb victims of the 1940s have now been officially forgotten.

September 1993

------- *Notes* -------

1. Since I take this general point to be so well known as not to need substantiation, I will limit the references in this paper to recent works dealing with Yugoslavia.

2. The history of the period 1941–45 in Yugoslavia is now being addressed by revisionist historians of all nationalist persuasions. A readable account by a highly placed communist participant is Milovan Djilas's *Wartime* (1980), a book that has the cachet of having been banned, along with Djilas's other works, by the communist regimes in Yugoslavia until 1989.

3. This last generalization requires the usual Yugoslav qualifications about regional variation. Slovenia elected a communist but nationalist president along with an anticommunist nationalist parliament; Serbia elected a new Socialist party formed by the leadership of the old communist party and inheriting all of that party's substantial tangible assets; and Montenegro elected the old League of Communists. The common thread was not the ideology of political economy so much as it was that of nation; even the communists had abandoned the ideology of class struggle for that of each nation.

4. One of the most confusing elements of Yugoslav politics in the late 1980s was the relationship between the League of Communists of Yugoslavia, which operated at the level of the federation, and the separate leagues of communists of each of the republics or autonomous provinces. The relationship was originally based on the principles of "democratic centralism" and was thus hierarchical; a person had membership primarily in the federal LCY (to which dues were paid), and only through it, membership in the republican/provincial leagues. In 1989–90, however, the republican leagues of Slovenia and Croatia demanded a "confederalization" of the LCY into a "League of Leagues," in which no binding authority issued from the central LCY, which would have been eliminated as a party. When this demand was rejected at the "Fourteenth Extraordinary Congress" of the LCY in late January 1990, the Slovenes and Croats walked out, thus destroying the LCY (see Rusinow 1991:5–6). The Slovenian-Croatian ultimatum—"confederation" or secession—was repeated at the constitutional level by the republican governments in 1990–91 (see Hayden 1990a; Rusinow 1991). Because "confederation" meant the end of Yugoslavia as a state, it was resisted by other republics, notably Serbia, in reaction to which Slovenia and Croatia seceded, thus sparking the civil war of 1991.

5. While the subject cannot be addressed here, it is becoming clear that communism and nationalism, as totalizing ideologies meant to deal with the problems of industrialization and modernization, were structural opposites—consciously so in the minds of some of the major designers of each. Thus Marx may have consciously tried to refute theories that had the nation, rather than the class, as the driving force of history (see Szporluk 1988), while Hitler copied elements of Marxism but replaced the class struggle with a race struggle (see Dumont 1986).

6. The sources on Yugoslav self-management are truly vast. The single best introduction to the subject is Rusinow's *The Yugoslav Experiment* (1978).

7. The film was called *Otac je na Službenom Putu* (When Father Was Away on Business).

8. The title of this film was *Srečna Nova Godina,* 1949 (Happy New Year, 1949).

9. This film, *Bal na Vodi,* was released in the United States as *Hey Babu Riba.*

10. The Soviet Georgian film *Repentance* may stand as emblematic of this use of film as commemorative ceremony. While regarded internationally as an allegory of Stalin's terror, the film also works for Georgians as an allegory of their larger historical and cultural struggles and of the basic moral issues that underlie them (see Christensen 1991).

11. Of course, pointing out the feedback does not account for the initial opening of the door to these dissident accounts. Perhaps the best explanation for the collapse of the censorship that had previously kept these particular histories secret was the exhaustion of both the ideology of communism and a corresponding failure of the will of the ruling class (see Ash 1990); but this failure would have been accelerated by the new, revised (and revived) history.

12. In analyzing Serbia, I do not want to imply that that republic exhibited a unique revival of nationalism. Slovenia in particular was developing its own variety of right-wing nationalist movement (see, e.g, the "Slovenian National Program" in *Nova Revija,* no. 57, and Hribar 1989). An account of the development of the Slovenian nationalist movement, by one of its major participants, can be found in Rupel (1990). A more critical view of some of the rhetorical structures of Slovenian nationalism is contained in Bakić-Hayden and Hayden (1992).

13. Srdjan Karanović's *Film With No Name* (Film za sada bez naziva), a dramatic film treatment of the hostility and lack of understanding between Serbs and Albanians in Kosovo, was released in 1988 but was criticized by Serbian officials for being too even-handed.

14. The ban on *Anali Pravnog Fakultete u Beogradu*, no. 3, May–June 1971, was lifted in 1990, and the issue was reprinted.

15. See *Intervju* (Beograd), *Potapanje Srbije*, special issue, August 11, 1989.

16. One of the disputed points in current Yugoslav history, both Serbian and Croatian, is whether there was a deliberate suppression of knowledge of many of the Ustaša's crimes, in the name of promoting the communist goal of "brotherhood and unity." Serbs assert a coverup, Croats deny it.

17. A concise discussion of the Ustaša, their ideology, and their genocidal practices can be found in A. Djilas (1991:103–28).

18. Milovan Djilas was one of the leaders of the Yugoslav Communist party during the war, and a major general in the Partisan army. At the end of the war, he was one of the four leaders (including Tito) who ran the country. In 1954, he shocked his comrades and the world by renouncing communism, and began a career as a dissident that had him in and out of prison for years. A prolific writer of political essays, fiction, a biography of the Montenegrin poet-prince Njegoš, and several volumes of his autobiography, he could not be published in his own country until 1989. Since Djilas himself is Montenegrin and hence a Serb, his confirmation of massacres of Ustaša members could not be written off as Croatian nationalist propaganda.

19. *Danas* was in 1990 the most important newsweekly in Croatia, with a format similar to that of *Time* in the United States. The volume by Žanko and Šolić was published by the publishing house of the largest daily newspaper in Croatia, *Vjesnik*, and was sold in that paper's kiosks throughout Yugoslavia.

20. On the other hand, many such challenges were made outside of Yugoslavia among Croatian émigré groups. Unfortunately, the role of these external groups in keeping alive outside of Yugoslavia memories that were suppressed and denied within the country cannot be explored here, but the phenomenon of "long-distance nationalism" (Anderson 1992) is important.

21. Tudjman makes similar claims in regard to the number of Jews killed in the Holocaust, saying that the total numbers of victims were exaggerated (Tudjman 1990:147–58).

22. I watched this documentary when it was first broadcast, but do not have details of the broadcast or of the documentary.

23. BECT is an "electronic magazine" produced by the Electrotechnical Faculty of Belgrade University and distributed by electronic mail throughout the world. As an electronic medium, it is more than ephemeral for scholarly purposes. "Hard copy" of BECT materials cited in this paper are in the author's files.

24. Similar street-name changes were also made in other Yugoslav cities, including Belgrade.

25. These comparisons were made by many newspapers and magazines in August and September 1992. A particularly tendentious form of reporting on these developments can be found in a staff report to the Committee on Foreign Relations of the United States Senate, written in August 1992 (Galbraith and Maynard 1992). The so-called death camps might better be compared with the American Civil War camps such as Andersonville than with Auschwitz. In this regard, it is worth noting that the commandant of Andersonville was the only person executed for war crimes after the Civil War—and in 1909, the Daughters of the Confederacy erected a monument to the memory of this "hero-martyr" (McPherson 1988:802).

26. Compare the statement delivered by the acting secretary of state of the United States, Lawrence Eagleburger, at the London Conference on Yugoslavia, August 26, 1992: "It is Serbs, alas, who are most guilty today of crimes which mimic those of their former tormentors, and which violate the sacred memory of ancestors who suffered at their hands." It is interesting that Secretary Eagleburger, himself a former U.S. ambassador to Yugoslavia, fluent in Serbo-Croatian and well aware of the events of 1941–45, does not name the Serbs' "tormentors" of that period. This act of forgetting presumably was prompted by current politics: Croats and Muslims are now victims of the Serbs, and the Germans are now allies.

References

Abu-Lughod, Lila
    1990   "The Romance of Resistance: Tracing Transformations of Power through Bedouin Women."
        American Ethnologist 17(1):41–55.

Academy of Sciences of the Mongolian People's Republic
    1969   *Bugd Nairamdakh Mongol Ard Ulsyn Tuukh* (History of the Mongolian People's Republic),
        3 vols. Ulaan-baatar: State Publishing House.

Ah Cheng
    1990   "Father." In *Furrows: Peasants, Intellectuals, and the State: Stories and Histories from Modern
        China*, H. Siu, ed., pp. 311–18. Stanford, CA: Stanford University Press.

Ahern, Emily Martin
    1973   *The Cult of the Dead in a Chinese Village*. Stanford, CA: Stanford University Press.
    1981a   *Chinese Ritual and Politics*. Cambridge: Cambridge University Press.
    1981b   "The Thai Ti Kong Festival." In *The Anthropology of Taiwanese Society*, E. M. Ahern and
        H. Gates, eds., pp. 397–425. Stanford, CA: Stanford University Press.

Allen, W. E. D.
    1932   *A History of the Georgian People*. London: Routledge and Kegan Paul.

Amnesty International
    1989   *People's Republic of China: Preliminary Findings on Killings of Unarmed Civilians, Arbitrary
        Arrests and Summary Executions since June 3, 1989*. August. New York.

Anagnost, Ann
    1989   "Prosperity and Counterprosperity: The Moral Discourse on Wealth in Post-Mao China."
        In *Marxism and the Chinese Experience*, A. Dirlik and M. Meisner, eds. Armonk, NY: M. E.
        Sharpe.

Anderson, Benedict
    1983   *Imagined Communities*. London: Verso Press.
    1992   "Long-Distance Nationalism: World Capitalism and the Rise of Identity Politics." Paper
        presented at the conference "Identity, Nation, and Nationalism" at the University of Cali-
        fornia, Berkeley, September 10, 1992.

Anderson, Eugene
    1975   "Songs of the Hong Kong Boat People." *Chinoperl News* 5:13–14.

Arendt, Hannah
    1951   *Totalitarianism*, part 3, *The Origins of Totalitarianism*. New York: Harcourt, Brace and
        World.

Ash, Timothy
    1990   "The Year of the Truth." In *The Magic Lantern*, Timothy Ash, ed. New York: Random House.

Averill, Stephen C.
    1990   "Local Elites and Communist Revolution in the Jiangxi Hill Country." In *Chinese Local
        Elites and Patterns of Dominance*, J. W. Esherick and M. Rankin, eds. Berkeley: University
        of California Press.

Babcock, Barbara A.
    1984   "Arrange Me into Disorder: Fragments and Reflections on Ritual Clowning." In *Rite,
        Drama, Festival, Spectacle*, J. J. MacAloon, ed., pp. 102–28. Philadelphia: Institute for the
        Study of Human Issues.

Bahro, Rudolf
    1978   *The Alternative in Eastern Europe*. London: Verso.

Ba Jin
    1989   "A Cultural Revolution Museum." In *Seeds of Fire*, G. Barme and J. Minford, eds., pp.
            381–82. New York: Noonday Press.
Bakhtin, Mikhail
    1984   *Rabelais and His World*. Helene Iswolsky, trans. First published 1965. Bloomington: Indi-
            ana University Press.
Bakić-Hayden, Milica, and Robert Hayden
    1992   "Orientalist Variations on the Theme 'Balkans': Symbolic Geography in Yugoslav Politics,
            1987–90." *Slavic Review* 51:1–15.
Banac, Ivo
    1984   *The National Question in Yugoslavia: Origins, History, and Politics*. Ithaca: Cornell Univer-
            sity Press.
Barme, Geremie
    1989   "The Chinese Velvet Prison: Culture in the 'New Age,' 1976–1989." *Issues and Studies*
            25(8):42–62.
Barme, Geremie, and Linda Jaiven, eds.
    1992   *New Ghosts, Old Dreams: Chinese Rebel Voices*. New York: Random House.
Barme, Geremie, and John Minford, eds.
    1989   *Seeds of Fire: Chinese Voices of Conscience*. New York: Noonday Press.
Barthes, Roland
    1986   "The Reality Effect." In *The Rustle of Language*, R. Barthes, ed., pp. 141–48. New York: Hill
            and Wang.
Bawden, Charles R.
    1961   *The Jebtsundamba Khutukhtus of Urga: Text, translation and notes*. Wiesbaden: Harrassowitz.
    1966   "An event in the life of the eighth Jebtsundamba Khutukhtu." In *Collectanea Mongolica*,
            W. Heissig, ed. Asiatische Forschungen, Bank 17. Wiesbaden: Harrassowitz.
    1968   *The Modern History of Mongolia*. London: Weidenfeld and Nicolson.
Bazardorzh, P.
    1973   *Ardyn Aman Zokhiol Dakh'Shashny Esreg Uzel Canaa* (Antireligious views in the people's
            oral literature). Ulaan-baatar: Mongolyn Erdem Delgeruulekh Niigemleg.
Benjamin, Walter
    1969   "Theses on the Philosophy of History." In *Illuminations*, Harry Zohn, trans., Hannah
            Arendt, ed. New York: Schocken.
Bernstein, Thomas
    1984   "Stalinism, Famine, and Chinese Peasants: Grain Procurements during the Great Leap
            Forward." *Theory and Society* 13(3):339–77.
Binns, Christopher
    1979   "The Changing Face of Power: Revolution and Accommodation in the Development of the
            Soviet Ceremonial System, I." *Man* 14(4):585–606.
    1980   "The Changing Face of Power: Revolution and Accommodation in the Development of the
            Soviet Ceremonial System, II." *Man* 15(1):170–87.
Blake, Fred
    1978   "Death and Abuse in Chinese Marriage Laments: The Curse of Chinese Brides." *Asian
            Folklore Studies* 37(1):3–33.
Bloch, Marc
    1925   "Mémoire collective, tradition et coutume." *Revue Synthèse Historique* 40:73–83.
Bloch, Maurice, and Jonathan Parry
    1982   "Introduction: Death and the Regeneration of Life." In *Death and the Regeneration of Life*,
            M. Bloch and J. Parry, eds., pp. 1–44. Cambridge: Cambridge University Press.
Boban, Ljubo
    1990   "Jasenovac and the Manipulation of History." *East European Politics and Societies* 4:580–92.
Bodnar, John
    1991   *Remaking America: Public Memory, Commemoration, and Patriotism in the Twentieth Cen-
            tury*. Princeton: Princeton University Press.

Bogosavljević, Srdjan, Vladimir Goati, Zdravko Grebo, Jasminka Hasanbvegović, Dusăn Janjić, Branislava Jojić, and Paul Shoup
    1992   *Bosna i Hercegovina izmedju Rata i Mira* (Bosnia and Herzegovina between war and peace). Belgrade-Sarajevo: Forum za Etni ke Odnose.
Bourdieu, Pierre
    1968   "Outline of a Sociological Theory of Art Perception." *International Social Science Journal* 20:589–612.
Brown, William A., and Urgunge Onon, trans. and annot.
    1976   *History of the Mongolian People's Republic* (Academy of Sciences of the Mongolian People's Republic, 1969, *B-NMAUlsyn Tuukh*, vol. 3, Ulaan-baatar: State Publishing Committee). Cambridge, MA: Harvard University Press.
Burawoy, Michael, and Janos Lukacs
    1992   *The Radiant Past: Ideology and Reality in Hungary's Road to Capitalism.* Chicago: University of Chicago Press.
Burke, Peter
    1989   "History as Social Memory." In *Memory: History, Culture, and the Mind,* T. Butler, ed., pp. 97–113. Oxford: Basil Blackwell.
Butler, Thomas
    1989   "Memory: A Mixed Blessing." In *Memory: History, Culture and the Mind,* T. Butler, ed. Oxford: Basil Blackwell.
Campeanu, Paul
    1988   *The Genesis of the Stalinist Social Order.* Armonk, NY: M. E. Sharpe.
Casey, Edward S.
    1984   "Commemoration and Perdurance in the *Analects,* Books I and II." *Philosophy East and West* 34:389–99.
    1987   *Remembering: A Phenomenological Study.* Bloomington: Indiana University Press.
C'avc'avadze, Ilia
    1977   *Ilia C'avc'avadze,* vol. 2. Tbilisi: Savc'ota Sakartvelo.
Čavoški, Kosta
    1991   *Slovodan Protiv Sloboda* (Slobodan against freedom). Belgrade: Dosije.
Central Committee of the Communist Party of China
    1981   "Resolution on Certain Questions in the History of Our Party since the Founding of the People's Republic of China." *Beijing Review* 26:10–39.
Chan, Anita, Richard Madsen, and Jonathan Unger
    1992   *Chen Village: The Recent History of a Peasant Community in Mao's China.* 2d ed. Berkeley: University of California Press.
Chang Cheng-p'ing
    1969   *K'u-ko tzu-tz'u* (Collection of crying songs). Hong Kong: Yu Hua Publishing Co.
Cheater, A. P.
    1991   "Death Ritual as Political Trickster in the People's Republic of China." *The Australian Journal of Chinese Affairs* 26:67–97.
Chen Xitong
    1989   Report to NPC on Quelling the Counter-Revolutionary Rebellion. FBIS, trans., pp. 20–36. First appeared in English in *Xinhua,* Beijing, July 6, 1989.
Chevrier, Yves
    1986   "La servante-maitresse: condition de la référence à l'histoire dans l'espace intellectuel Chinois." *Extrême-Orient, Extrême-Occident* 9, pp. 117–44.
    1988   "NEP and Beyond: The Transition to 'Modernization' in China (1978–85). In *Transforming China's Economy in the Eighties, vol. 1: The Rural Sector Welfare and Employment,* S. Feuchtwang, A. Hussain, and T. Pairault, eds., pp. 7–35. Boulder, CO: Westview Press.
Chirot, Daniel
    1991   "What Happened in Eastern Europe in 1989?" In *Popular Protest and Political Culture in Modern China: Learning from 1989,* J. Wasserstrom and E. Perry, eds. Boulder, CO: Westview Press.

Chong Woei Lien
    1990   "Petitioners, Popperians, and Hunger Strikers: The Uncoordinated Efforts of the 1989 Chinese Democratic Movement." In *The Chinese People's Movement: Perspectives on Spring 1989*, T. Saich, ed., pp. 106–25. Armonk, NY: M. E. Sharpe.

Christensen, Julie
    1991   "Tengiz Abuladze's *Repentance* and the Georgian Nationalist Cause." *Slavic Review* 50:163–75.

Ci Jiwei
    1990   "The Death of Utopia: The Socio-Political Psychology of Modern China." Unpublished essay presented at Stanford University.

Clark, Katerina
    1981   *The Soviet Novel: History as Ritual*. Chicago: University of Chicago Press.

Cohen, Abner
    1979   "Political Symbolism." *Annual Review of Anthropology* 8:87–113.

Cohen, Myron
    1991   "Being Chinese: The Peripheralization of Traditional Identity." In *The Living Tree: The Changing Meaning of Being Chinese Today*, special issue of *Daedalus* 120(2): 113–34.

Colburn, Forrest, ed.
    1989a   *Everyday Forms of Peasant Resistance*. Armonk, NY: M. E. Sharpe.
    1989b   "Foot Dragging and Other Peasant Responses to the Nicaraguan Revolution." In *Everyday Forms of Peasant Resistance*, F. Colburn, ed., pp. 175–97. Armonk, NY: M. E. Sharpe.

Connerton, Paul
    1989   *How Societies Remember*. Cambridge: Cambridge University Press.

Conquest, Robert
    1968   *The Great Terror*. New York: Oxford University Press.
    1986   *The Harvest of Sorrow: Soviet Collectivization and the Terror-Famine*. New York: Oxford University Press.

Coplan, David
    1987   "Eloquent Knowledge: Lesotho Migrants' Songs and the Anthropology of Experience." *American Ethnologist* 14(3):413–33.

DeBernardi, Jean
    1987   "The God of War and the Vagabond Buddha." *Modern China* 13:310–32.

de Groot, J. J. M.
    1892   *The Religious Systems of China*. (1972 ed., Taipei: Ch'eng-wen.)

de Man, Paul
    1982   "Sign and Symbol in Hegel's Aesthetics." *Critical Inquiry* 8:761–73.
    1984   "Autobiography as De-Facement." In *The Rhetoric of Romanticism*, by Paul de Man, pp. 67–83. New York: Columbia University Press.

Denich, Bette
    1991   "Unbury the Victims: Rival Exhumations and Nationalist Revivals in Yugoslavia." Paper presented at the annual meeting of the American Anthropological Association, Chicago, IL, November 1991.

Derrida, Jacques
    1986   *Memoires for Paul de Man*. New York: Columbia University Press.

Dirlik, Arif
    1989   *The Origins of Chinese Communism*. New York: Oxford University Press.
    1991   *Anarchism in the Chinese Revolution*. Berkeley: University of California Press.

Dittmer, Lowell
    1981   "Death and Transfiguration: Liu Shaoqi's Rehabilitation and Contemporary Chinese Politics." *Journal of Asian Studies* XL(3):455–79.

Djilas, Alexis
    1991   *The Contested Country*. Cambridge: Harvard University Press.

Djilas, Milovan
    1957   *The New Class: An Analysis of the Communist System*. New York: Praeger.
    1980   *Wartime*. New York: Harcourt, Brace, Jovanovich.

Djukić, Slavoljub
    1992   *Kako se Dogodio Vodja* (How the leader happened). Belgrade: Filip Visnjic.

Dragadze, Tamara
  1988   *Rural Families in Soviet Georgia: A Case Study in Ratcha Province.* London: Routledge.
Drašković, Vuk
  1981   *Sudija* (The judge). Belgrade: Zapis.
Duara, Prasenjit
  1988a   *Culture, Power and the State: Rural North China, 1900–1942.* Stanford, CA: Stanford University Press.
  1988b   "Superscribing Symbols: The Myth of Guandi, Chinese God of War." *Journal of Asian Studies* 47:778–95.
Dumont, Louis
  1986   "The Totalitarian Disease." In L. Dumont, *Essays on Individualism.* Chicago: University of Chicago Press.
Dunham, Vera
  1976   *In Stalin's Time: Middle Class Values in Soviet Fiction.* Cambridge: Cambridge University Press.
Ebrey, Patricia
  1991   *Chu Hsi's Family Rituals: A Twelfth-Century Chinese Manual for the Performance of Cappings, Weddings, Funerals, and Ancestral Rites.* Princeton: Princeton University Press.
Enkh-Amar, S.
  1991   "Bogd khaany tukhai shine barimt (New data on the Bogd Khaan)." *Ardyn Erkh,* June 7.
Esherick, Joseph, and Jeffrey Wasserstrom
  1990   "Acting Out Democracy: Political Theater in Modern China." *Journal of Asian Studies* 49:835–65.
Ezrahi, Sidra Dekoven
  1990   "Dan Pagis—Out of Line: A Politics of Decomposition." *Proof Texts* 10(1):335–63.
Fei Hsiao-tung
  1968   *China's Gentry: Essays on Rural-Urban Relations.* Chicago: University of Chicago Press.
Fernandez, James W.
  1984   "Convivial Attitudes: The Ironic Play of Tropes in an International Kayak Festival in Northern Spain." In *Text, Play, and Story: The Construction and Reconstruction of Self and Society,* S. Plattner and E. M. Bruner, eds., pp. 199–229. Washington, DC: American Ethnological Society.
Forbath, L., and J. Geleta
  1936   *The New Mongolia.* L. Wolfe, trans. London: Heinemann.
Foucault, Michel
  1978   *The History of Sexuality,* vol. 1. New York: Pantheon.
  1982   "Afterword: The Subject and Power." In *Beyond Structuralism and Hermeneutics,* H. Dreyfus and P. Rabinow, eds. Chicago: University of Chicago Press.
Franke, Herbert
  1961   "Some Aspects of Chinese Private Historiography in the Thirteenth and Fourteenth Centuries." In *Historians of China and Japan,* W. G. Beaselly and E. G. Pulleyblank, eds., pp. 115–34. London: School of Oriental and African Studies.
Friedman, Edward
  1990   "Deng versus the Peasantry: Recollectivization in the Chinese Countryside." *Problems of Communism* Sept.–Oct., pp. 30–43.
Friedman, Edward, Paul G. Pickowicz, and Mark Selden
  1991   *Chinese Village, Socialist State.* New Haven, CT: Yale University Press.
Friedrich, Carl J., and Zbigniew K. Brzezinski
  1966   *Totalitarian Dictatorship and Autocracy.* Rev. ed. New York: Praeger.
Fussell, Paul
  1975   *The Great War and Modern Memory.* New York: Oxford University Press.
Gal, Susan
  1991   "Bartok's Funeral: Representations of Europe in Hungarian Political Rhetoric." *American Ethnologist* 18(3):440–58.
Galbraith, Peter, and Michelle Maynard
  1992   "The Ethnic Cleansing of Bosnia-Hercegovina: A Staff Report to the Committee on Foreign Relations, U.S. Senate." Washington, DC: U.S. Government Printing Office.

Gamble, Sidney
    1963   *North China Villages: Social, Political, and Economic Activities before 1933.* Berkeley: Univer-
            sity of California Press.
Gao Yuan
    1987   *Born Red: A Chronicle of the Cultural Revolution.* Stanford, CA: Stanford University Press.
Ge Maochun, Jiang Jun, and Li Xingzhi, eds.
    1984   *Wuzhengfuzhuyi sixiang ziliao xuan* (Anthology of materials on anarchist thought). Beijing:
            Beijing daxue chuban she.
Gellner, Ernest
    1983   *Nations and Nationalism.* London: Basil Blackwell.
    1991   "Civil Society in Historical Context." *International Social Science Journal* 129:495–510.
Giddens, Anthony
    1979   *Central Problems in Social Theory: Action, Structure and Contradiction in Analysis.* Cam-
            bridge: Cambridge University Press.
Gilmartin, Christine
    1990   "Violence against Women in Contemporary China." In *Violence in China: Essays in Cul-
            ture and Counterculture,* J. Lipman and S. Harrell, eds. Albany: State University of New
            York Press.
Goldman, Merle
    1981   *China's Intellectuals: Advise and Dissent.* Cambridge, MA: Harvard University Press.
Goldman, Merle, with Timothy Cheek and Carol Lee Hamrin
    1987   *China's Intellectuals and the State: In Search of a New Relationship.* Harvard Contemporary
            China Series, no. 3. Cambridge, MA: Harvard University Press.
Gorbachev, Mikhail
    1987   *Perestroika: New Thinking for Our Country and the World.* London: Collins.
Gramsci, Antonio
    1971   "State and Civil Society." In *Selections from the Prison Notebooks,* Q. Hoare and G. N. Smith,
            eds. and trans. London: Lawrence and Wisehart.
Grant, Beata
    1989   "The Spiritual Saga of Woman Huang: From Pollution to Purification." In *Ritual Opera,
            Operatic Ritual: 'Mu-lien Rescues His Mother' in Chinese Popular Culture,* D. Johnson, ed.,
            pp. 224–311. Berkeley: Chinese Popular Culture Project.
Graves, Robert
    1929   *Good-bye to All That.* London: Jonathan Cape.
Gross, Jan
    1988   *Revolution from Abroad: The Soviet Conquest of Poland's Western Ukraine and Western Byelo-
            russia.* Princeton: Princeton University Press.
Habermas, Jürgen
    1989   *The Structural Transformation of the Public Sphere: An Inquiry into a Category of Bourgeois
            Society.* Thomas Burger with the assistance of Frederick Lawrence, trans. Cambridge, MA:
            MIT Press.
Halbwachs, Maurice
    1980   *The Collective Memory.* Francis Ditter and Vida Y. Ditter, trans. First published 1950 as *La
            Mémoire Collective.* New York: Harper and Row.
Hamrin, Carol, and Timothy Cheek
    1986   *China's Establishment Intellectuals.* Armonk, NY: M. E. Sharpe.
Hanson, Allan
    1989   "The Making of the Maori: Culture, Invention and its Logic." *American Anthropologist*
            91(4):890–902.
Haraszti, Miklos
    1979   *A Worker in a Workers' State.* Michael Wright, trans. New York: Universe.
    1987   *The Velvet Prison: Artists under State Socialism.* Katalin and Stephen Lardesmann with the
            help of Steve Wasserman, trans. New York: Basic Books.
Harrell, Stevan
    1986   "Men, Women, and Ghosts in Taiwanese Folk Religion." In *Gender and Religion: Com-
            plexity of Symbols.* C. Bynum, S. Harrell, and P. Richman, eds. Boston: Beacon Press.

Havel, Václav
1985   "The Power of the Powerless." In *The Power of the Powerless*, Václav Havel et al., eds. Armonk, NY: M. E. Sharpe.
1991   "Uncertain Strength: An Interview with Václav Havel." Originally published in *Mladý Svět*, reprinted in translation in *The New York Review of Books*, August.
Hayden, Robert
1990a   "A Confederal Model for Yugoslavia?" Paper presented at the annual meeting of the American Association for the Advancement of Slavic Studies, Washington, DC, October 22, 1990.
1990b   *Social Courts in Theory and Practice: Yugoslav Workers' Courts in Comparative Perspective.* Philadelphia: University of Pennsylvania Press.
1991a   "Yugoslavia: From Civil Society to Civil War." Paper presented at the annual meeting of the American Anthropological Association, Chicago, IL, November 21, 1991.
1991b   "Yugoslavia: Politics and the Media." *Report on Eastern Europe*, December 6, 1991:17–26. Munich: RFE/RL Research Institute.
1992a   "Balancing Discussion of Jasenovac and the Manipulation of History. *East European Politics and Societies* 6:207–12.
1992b   "Yugoslavia's Collapse: National Suicide with Foreign Assistance." *Economic and Political Weekly*, July 4, 1992:1377–82.
Heer, Nancy
1971   *Politics and History in the Soviet Union.* Cambridge, MA: MIT Press.
Hill, Jonathan, ed.
1988   *Rethinking History and Myth: Indigenous South American Perspectives on the Past.* Chicago: University of Chicago Press.
Hinton, William
1990   *The Great Reversal: The Privatization of China, 1978–89.* New York: Monthly Review Press.
Hobsbawm, Eric, and Terence Ranger, eds.
1983   *The Invention of Tradition.* Cambridge: Cambridge University Press.
Holisky, Dee Ann
1989   "The Rules of the *Supra*, or How to Drink in Georgian." *The Annual of the Society for the Study of Caucasia* 1:22–40.
Horowitz, Donald
1985   *Ethnic Groups in Conflict.* Berkeley: University of California Press.
Hosking, Geoffrey
1989   "Memory in a Totalitarian Society: The Case of the Soviet Union." In *Memory: History, Culture, and the Mind*, T. Butler, ed. Oxford: Basil Blackwell.
Hribar, Tine
1989   *Slovenska Dr avnost* (Slovenian statehood). Ljubljana: Cankarjeva Zalo ba.
Hroch, Miroslav
1985   *Social Preconditions of National Revival in Europe: A Comparative Analysis of the Social Composition of Patriotic Groups among the Smaller European Nations.* Ben Fowkes, trans. Cambridge: Cambridge University Press.
Huakai di yi zhi (The flower's first blossom)
1963   Tianjin: Tianjin renmin chuban she.
1973   Tianjin: Tianjin renmin chuban she.
Huang Shu-min
1989   *The Spiral Road: Change in a Chinese Village through the Eyes of a Communist Party Leader.* Boulder, CO: Westview Press.
Humphrey, Caroline
1983   *Karl Marx Collective: Economy, Society and Religion in a Siberian Collective Farm.* Cambridge: Cambridge University Press.
Hunan Sheng Xiqu Yanjiusuo (Hunan Opera Research Office), ed.
1984   *Hunan chuantong xiqu juben 56* (Hunan traditional opera plays, vol. 56): *Chenhexi di shier ji* (Chenhe opera, vol. 12)." Changsha: Hunan Opera Research Office.

Hunan Sheng Xiqu Yanjiusuo (Hunan Opera Research Office) and Zhongguo Yishu Yanjiuyuan *Xiqu yanjiu* Bianjibu (Editorial Board of the China Art Research Institute's *Opera Research*), eds.
    c.1985   *Mulianxi xueshu zuotanhui lunwenxuan* (Selected articles from the Scholarly Roundtable on Mulian Opera). Changsha: no publisher listed.

Isaacs, Harold
    1985   *Re-Encounters in China*. Armonk, NY: M. E. Sharpe.

Ishinnorov, S., and G. Tserendorzh
    1990   "Javzundambaagvaanluvsanchoizhinnyamadanzanvanchugbalsambuu (1869–1924)." *Unen*, June 16, p. 3.

Jankowiak, William
    1988   "The Soul of Lao Yu." *Natural History* 12:4–9.

Jelavich, Charles
    1990   *South Slavic Nationalisms: Textbooks and Yugoslav Union before 1914*. Columbus: Ohio State University Press.

Johnson, David, ed.
    1989   *Ritual Opera, Operatic Ritual: 'Mu-lien Rescues His Mother' in Chinese Popular Culture*. Berkeley: Chinese Popular Culture Project.

Johnson, David, Andrew J. Nathan, and Evelyn S. Rawski, eds.
    1985   *Popular Culture in Late Imperial China*. Berkeley: University of California Press.

Johnson, Elizabeth
    1988   "Grieving for the Dead, Grieving for the Living: Funeral Laments of Hakka Women." In *Death Ritual in Late Imperial and Modern China*, J. L. Watson and E. S. Rawski, eds., pp. 135–63. Berkeley: University of California Press.

Johnson, Kay Ann
    1983   *Women, the Family and Peasant Revolution in China*. Chicago: University of Chicago Press.

Joll, James
    1977   *Gramsci*. Glasgow: Fontana/Collins.

Jones, Stephen F. (pseud. C. J. Peters)
    1988   "The Georgian Orthodox Church." In *Eastern Christianity and Politics in the Twentieth Century*, P. Ramet, ed., pp. 286–308. Durham: Duke University Press.

Jones, Stephen F.
    1989   "Religion and Nationalism in Soviet Georgia." In *Religion and Nationalism in the USSR and Eastern Europe*, 2d rev. ed., P. Ramet, ed., pp. 171–95. Durham: Duke University Press.
    1990   "Glasnost, Perestroika and the Georgian Soviet Socialist Republic." *Armenian Review* 43(2–3):127–52.
    1992   "Revolutions in Revolution within Revolution: Minorities in the Georgian Republic." In *The Politics of Nationality and the Erosion of the USSR*, Z. Gitelman, ed., pp. 77–101. New York: St. Martin's.

Judd, Ellen R.
    1990   "Cultural Articulation in the Chinese Countryside, 1937–1947." *Modern China* 16:269–308.

Kalandadze, Anna
    1981   *Leksebi* (Poems). Tbilisi: Sabcota Sakartvelo.

Keane, John
    1985   "Editor's Preface." In *The Power of the Powerless*, Václav Havel et al., eds. Armonk, NY: M. E. Sharpe.
    1988   *Civil Society and the State: New European Perspectives*. London: Verso.

Keller, Bill
    1990   "In Moscow: A Monument to Those It Victimized." *New York Times*, Oct. 31, p. 10.

Kim Seong Nae
    1989   "Lamentations of the Dead: The Historical Imagery of Violence on Cheju Island, South Korea." *Journal of Ritual Studies* 3(2):251–86.

Kiziria, Dodona
    1990   "Two Fathers of the Nation: Reevalution of Spiritual Values in Georgia." *The Annual of the Society for the Study of Caucasia* 2:19–32.

Kleinman, Arthur
1986   *Social Origins of Distress and Disease: Depression, Neurasthenia, and Pain in Modern China.*
        New Haven, CT: Yale University Press.
Kligman, Gail
1988   *The Wedding of the Dead: Ritual, Poetics, and Popular Culture in Transylvania.* Berkeley: University of California Press.
1990   "Reclaiming the Public: A Reflection on Creating Civil Society in Romania." *Eastern European Politics and Societies* 4:393–439.
Konrad, George, and Ivan Szelenyi
1979   *The Intellectuals on the Road to Class Power: A Sociological Study of the Role of the Intelligentsia in Socialism.* New York: Harcourt, Brace, Jovanovich.
Kornhauser, William
1959   *The Politics of Mass Society.* Glencoe, IL: Free Press.
Krell, David
1990   *Of Memory, Reminiscences, and Writing: On the Verge.* Bloomington: Indiana University Press.
Kundera, Milan
1981   *The Book of Laughter and Forgetting.* H. M. Heim, trans. First published 1980. New York: Knopf.
Lane, Christel
1981   *The Rites of Rulers: Ritual in Industrial Society–the Soviet Case.* Cambridge: Cambridge University Press.
Lang, David Marshall
1957   *The Last Years of the Georgian Monarchy, 1658–1832.* New York: Columbia University Press.
Langer, Lawrence
1991   *Holocaust Testimonies.* New Haven, CT: Yale University Press.
Lapidus, Gail
1988   "State and Society: Toward the Emergence of Civil Society in the Soviet Union." In *Gorbachev's Russia: Politics, Society, and Nationality,* S. Bialer, ed. Boulder, CO: Westview Press.
Larson, Frans August
1930   *Larson, Duke of Mongolia.* Boston: Little, Brown.
Lass, Andrew
1987   "Presencing, Historicity and the Shifting Voice of Written Relics in Eighteenth Century Bohemia." In *Bohemia Zeitschrift* 28(1):92–107.
1988   "Romantic Documents and Political Monuments: The Meaning-Fulfillment of History in 19th Century Bohemia." *American Ethnologist* 15(3):456–71.
Lattimore, Owen, and Fujiko Isono
1982   *The Diluv Khutagt: Memoires and Autobiography of a Mongol Buddhist Reincarnation in Religion and Revolution.* Wiesbaden: Harrassowitz.
Lee, Leo Ou-fan
1991   "On the Margins of Chinese Discourse: Some Personal Thoughts on the Cultural Meaning of the Periphery." In *The Living Tree: The Changing Meaning of Being Chinese Today.* Special issue of *Daedalus* 120(2).
Le Goff, Jacques
1992   *History and Memory.* S. Rendall and E. Claman, eds. First published 1977. New York: Columbia University Press.
Levinas, Emmanuel
1969   *Totality and Infinity.* Pittsburgh, PA: Duquesne University Press.
Lewin, Moshe
1975   *Russian Peasants and Soviet Power: A Study of Collectivization.* New York: W. W. Norton.
Lewis, Bernard
1975   *History: Remembered, Recovered, Invented.* Princeton, NJ: Princeton University Press.
Li Canming
1987   "Nujiee Xianxingzhe; Ji Liu Qingyang Tongzhi (A pioneer in women's work: Remembering comrade Liu Qingyang)." In *Beijing nuzhie* (Outstanding women of Beijing). Beijing: Renmin chubenshe.

Li Huaisun, ed.
    1989a   *Mulianxi yanchuben* (Mulian opera performance text). 2 vols. Huaihua: Huaihua Art Center.
    1989b   *Mulianxi lunwenji.* Huaihua: Huaihua Art Center.
Li Qiao et al.
    1990   "Death or Rebirth: Tiananmen, the Soul of China." In *Beijing Spring, 1989: Confrontation and Conflict, the Basic Documents,* M. Oksenberg, L. Sullivan, and M. Lambert, eds. Armonk, NY: M. E. Sharpe.
Lin Yueh-hwa
    1947   *The Golden Wing.* New York: Oxford University Press.
Link, Perry
    1983   *Stubborn Weeds: Popular and Controversial Chinese Literature after the Cultural Revolution.* Bloomington: Indiana University Press.
    1992   *Evening Chats in Beijing: Probing China's Predicament.* New York: W. W. Norton.
Link, Perry, Richard Madsen, and Paul G. Pickowicz, eds.
    1989   *Unofficial China: Popular Culture and Thought in the People's Republic.* Boulder, CO: Westview Press.
Liu Binyan
    1983   *People or Monsters? And Other Stories and Reportage from China after Mao.* P. Link, ed. Bloomington: Indiana University Press.
    1990   *A Higher Kind of Loyalty: A Memoir by China's Foremost Journalist.* Zhu Hong, trans. New York: Pantheon.
Liu Huichun
    1988   "Lun qiju Mulianxi de liubian yu tese (On the transmission and characteristics of *quiju* Mulian opera)." *Xiqu yanjiu* (Art Research) 28:134–55.
Liu Wu-chi and Irving Yucheng Lo
    1976   *K'uei Yeh Chi* (Sunflower splendor). Bloomington: Indiana University Press.
Lo Fulang
    1989   *Morning Breeze: A True Story of China's Cultural Revolution.* San Francisco: China Books.
Lyons, John
    1981   *Language and Linguistics: An Introduction.* Cambridge: Cambridge University Press.
MacCannell, Dean
    1989   *The Tourist.* New York: Schocken.
McCord, Edward A.
    1990   "Local Military Power and Elite Formation: The Liu Family of Xingyi County, Guizhou." In *Chinese Local Elites and Patterns of Dominance,* J. W. Esherick and M. Rankin, eds. Berkeley: University of California Press.
MacDonagh, Oliver
    1989   *States of Mind: A Study of Anglo-Irish Conflict, 1780–1980.* London: George Allen and Unwin.
MacFarquhar, Roderick
    1983   *The Origins of the Cultural Revolution, vol. 2: The Great Leap Forward, 1958–1960.* New York: Columbia University Press.
McPherson, James
    1988   *Battle Cry of Freedom: The Civil War Era.* New York: Oxford University Press.
Madsen, Richard
    1990   "The Politics of Revenge in Rural China during the Cultural Revolution." In *Violence in China: Essays in Culture and Counterculture,* J. Lipman and S. Harrell, eds., pp. 175–202. Albany: State University of New York Press.
Mair, Victor H.
    1983   *Tun-huang Popular Narratives.* Cambridge: Cambridge University Press.
    1986–   "Notes on the Maudgalyayana Legend in East Asia." *Monumenta Serica* 37:83–93.
    87
    1989   *T'ang Transformation Texts.* Cambridge: Harvard University Press.
Mao Tse-tung (Mao Zedong)
    1966   "Where Do Correct Ideas Come From?" In *Four Essays on Philosophy,* pp. 134–36. First published 1963. Beijing: Foreign Languages Press.

Mars, Gerald, and Yochanan Altman
  1987   "The Place of Feasts and Drinking in a Soviet Society." Unpublished manuscript.
Martin, Emily
  1988   "Gender and Ideological Differences in Representations of Life and Death." In *Death Ritual in Late Imperial and Modern China*, J. L. Watson and E. S. Rawski, eds., pp. 164–79. Berkeley: University of California Press.
Mathias, John
  1977   "The Kam Tin Jiao." Ph.D. thesis, Oxford University.
Meisner, Maurice
  1982   *Marxism, Maoism and Utopianism: Eight Essays*. Madison: University of Wisconsin Press.
  1985   "Iconoclasm and Cultural Revolution in China and Russia." In *Bolshevik Culture: Experiment and Order in the Russian Revolution*, A. Gleason, P. Kenez, and R. Stites, eds., pp. 279–94. Bloomington: Indiana University Press.
Milosz, Czeslaw
  1990   *The Captive Mind*. Jane Zielenko, trans. New York: Vintage International Edition.
Mirić, Jovan
  1984   *Sistem i Kriza* (The system and the crisis). Zagreb: Dekade.
Monas, Sidney
  1989   "Censorship as a Way of Life." In *Perspectives on Literature in Eastern and Western Europe*, G. Hosking and G. Cushing, eds. London: Macmillan.
Moore, Sally Falk
  1987   "Explaining the Present: Theoretical Dilemmas in Processual Ethnography." *American Ethnologist* 14(4):727–36.
Nankai daxue lishi xi and Wugong dadui cun shi bianxie zu, eds.
  1978   *Wugong renmin de zhandou licheng* (The course of the battle of Wugong's people). Beijing: Zhonghu shuzhu.
Nathan, Andrew
  1989   "Chinese Democracy in 1989: Continuity and Change." *Problems of Communism*, Sept.–Oct., pp. 16–29.
Niming, Frank
  1990   "Learning How to Protest." In *The Chinese People's Movement*, T. Saich, ed., pp. 83–105. Armonk, NY: M. E. Sharpe.
Nora, Pierre
  1989   "Memory, History." In *50/50: Opyt slovaria novogo myshleniia* (An attempt at a dictionary of new thinking), Y. Afanas'ev and M. Ferro, eds., pp. 439–41. Moscow: Progress Publishers.
Oksenberg, Michael, Lawrence Sullivan, and Marc Lambert, eds.
  1990   *Beijing Spring, 1989: Confrontation and Conflict, the Basic Documents*. Armonk, NY: M. E. Sharpe.
Ong Aihua
  1987   *Factory Women in Malaysia: Spirits of Resistance and Capitalist Discipline*. Albany: State University of New York Press.
Onon, Urgunge, and Derrick Pritchatt
  1989   *Asia's First Modern Revolution: Mongolia Proclaims Its Independence in 1911*. Leiden: Brill.
Ortner, Sherry
  1984   "Theory in Anthropology since the Sixties." *Comparative Studies of Society and History* 26:126–66.
Overmyer, Daniel L.
  1990   "Buddhism in the Trenches: Attitudes toward Popular Religion in Chinese Scriptures Found at Tun-huang." *Harvard Journal of Asiatic Studies* 50:197–220.
Owen, Stephen
  1986   *Remembrances: The Experience of the Past in Classical Chinese Literature*. Cambridge: Harvard University Press.
Platonov, Andrei
  1978   *Collected Works*. T. P. Whitney, C. R. Proffer, A. A. Kiselev, M. Jordan, and F. Snyder, trans. Ann Arbor, MI: Ardis.

Popova, L. P.
    1987   *Obshchestvennaya mysl' Mongolii v epokhu 'probuzhdeniya azii'* (Social thought in Mongolia in the period of the 'Awakening of Asia'). Moscow: Nauka.
Poppe, Nicholas
    1978   *Tsongol Folklore*. Wiesbaden: Harrassowitz.
Pozdneev, A. M.
    1971   *Mongolia and the Mongols*. First published 1896. The Hague: Indiana University Uralic and Altaic Series, vol. 61.
Purevzhav, S., and D. Dashzhamts
    1965   *BNMAU-d Sum Khiid, Lam naryn Asuudlyg Shiidverlesen n': 1921–1940* (Decisions on the lama question in the monasteries of the Mongolian People's Republic, 1921–1940). Ulaan- baatar: State Publishing Committee.
Pusey, James R.
    1969   *Wu Han: Attacking the Present through the Past*. Cambridge: Harvard University Press.
Rakowska-Harmstone, Teresa
    1974   "The Dialectics of Nationalism in the USSR." *Problems of Communism* 22(3):1–22.
Rappaport, Joanne
    1990   *The Politics of Memory: Native Historical Interpretation in the Columbian Andes*. Cambridge: Cambridge University Press.
Rcheulashvili, Guram
    1977   *Motxrobebi* (Stories). Tbilisi: Sabcota Sakartvelo.
Rev, Istan
    1987   "The Advantages of Being Atomized: How Hungarian Peasants Coped with Collectivism." *Dissent* 34(3):335–50.
Riches, David
    1991   "Aggression, War, Violence: Space/Time and Paradigm." *Man* (n.s.) 26:281–98.
Ricoeur, Paul
    1984   *The Reality of the Historical Past*. Milwaukee, WI: Marquette University Press.
Riskin, Carl
    1987   *China's Political Economy: The Quest for Development since 1949*. Oxford: Oxford Univer- sity Press.
Roeder, Philip
    1991   "Soviet Federalism and Ethnic Mobilization." *World Politics* 43:196–232.
Rofel, Lisa
    1989   "Hegemony and Productivity: Workers in Post-Mao China." In *Marxism and the Chinese Experience*, A. Dirlik and M. Meisner, eds. Armonk, NY: M. E. Sharpe.
    1991   "Violence in the Quotidian: Fragments of a Cultural Revolution Memory." Paper presented at the annual meeting of the American Anthropological Association, November 20–24, 1991, Chicago, IL.
Rupel, Dimitrij
    1990   *Od Vojnog do Civilnog Drustva* (From military to civil society). Zagreb: Globus.
Rupen, Robert
    1979   *How Mongolia Is Really Ruled: A Political History of the Mongolian People's Republic, 1900– 1978*. Stanford, CA: Hoover Institution Press.
Rusinow, Dennison, ed.
    1978   *The Yugoslav Experiment, 1948–1974*. Berkeley: University of California Press.
    1988   *Yugoslavia: A Fractured Federalism*. Washington, DC: Wilson Center.
    1991   "To Be or Not to Be: Yugoslavia as Hamlet." Field Staff Report (Europe) 1990–91:no. 18. Indianapolis, IN: University Field Staff International.
Rustaveli, Shota
    1971   *The Knight in the Panther's Skin*. Venera Urushadze, trans. Tbilisi: Sabcota Sakartvelo.
Sabel, Charles, and David Stark
    1982   "Planning, Politics, and Shop-Floor Power: Hidden Forms of Bargaining in Soviet- Imposed State-Socialist Societies." *Politics and Society* 11(4):439–75.

Saich, Tony
  1994   "Writing or Rewriting History? The Construction of the Maoist Resolution on Party History." In *New Perspectives on the Chinese Communist Revolution*, T. Saich and H. v. d. Ven, eds. Cambridge, MA: Harvard University Press.
Saich, Tony, ed.
  1990   *The Chinese People's Movement: Perspectives on Spring 1989*. Armonk, NY: M. E. Sharpe.
Saich, Tony, and Hans v. d. Ven, eds.
  1994   *New Perspectives on the Chinese Communist Revolution*. Cambridge, MA: Harvard University Press.
Sárközi, Alice
  1971   "A Pre-Classical Mongolian Prophetic Book." *Acta Orientalia* (Hung), t. XXIV, fasc. 1, 41–49.
Schechner, Richard
  1985   *Between Theater and Anthropology*. Philadelphia: University of Pennsylvania Press.
Schram, Stuart
  1973   "Introduction: The Cultural Revolution in Historical Perspective." In *Authority, Participation and Cultural Change in China*, S. Schram, ed. Cambridge: Cambridge University Press.
  1989   *The Thought of Mao Tse-tung*. Cambridge: Cambridge University Press.
Schwarcz, Vera
  1986   "Afterword." In *China's Establishment Intellectuals*, C. Hamrin and T. Cheek, eds., pp. 247–56. Armonk, NY: M. E. Sharpe.
  1989   "Memory, Commemoration, and the Plight of China's Intellectuals." *Wilson Quarterly*, autumn, pp. 120–29.
  1991a   "Memory and Commemorations: The Chinese Search for a Liveable Past." In *Popular Protest and Political Culture in Modern China*, J. Wasserstrom and E. Perry, eds., pp. 109–23. Boulder, CO: Westview Press.
  1991b   "Mnemosyne Abroad: Reflections on the Chinese and Jewish Commitment to Remembrance." *Points East* 6(3):1–14.
  1991c   "No Solace from Lethe: History, Memory, and Cultural Identity in Twentieth-Century China." *Daedalus* 120(2):85.
  1992   *Time for Telling Truth Is Running Out: Conversations with Zhang Shenfu*. New Haven, CT: Yale University Press.
Scott, James
  1976   *The Moral Economy of the Peasant*. New Haven, CT: Yale University Press.
  1977   "Protest and Profanation: Agrarian Revolt and the Little Tradition." *Theory and Society* 4(1):1–38 and 4(2):211–46.
  1985   *Weapons of the Weak: Everyday Forms of Peasant Resistance*. New Haven, CT: Yale University Press.
  1989   "Everyday Forms of Resistance." In *Everyday Forms of Peasant Resistance*, F. Colburn, ed. Armonk, NY: M. E. Sharpe.
  1990   *Domination and the Arts of Resistance: Hidden Transcripts*. New Haven, CT: Yale University Press.
Seaman, Gary
  1981   "The Sexual Politics of Karmic Retribution." In *The Anthropology of Taiwanese Society*, E. M. Ahern and H. Gates, eds., pp. 381–96. Stanford, CA: Stanford University Press.
Šetinc, Mile
  1990   "Da li je gradjanski rat u Slaveniji zavrsen? (Is the civil war in Slovenia over?)" *Demokratija Beograd*, Aug. 3, 1990 1(10–11):17.
Shirendev, B.
  1990   *Serel: Tuukhen Nairuulluud* (Awakening: Historical compositions). Ulaan-baatar: Ulsyn Khevleliin Gazar.
Shue, Vivienne
  1988   *The Reach of the State: Sketches of the Chinese Body Politic*. Stanford, CA: Stanford University Press.
Simmonds-Duke, E. M.
  1987   "Was the Peasant Uprising a Revolution? The Meanings of a Struggle over the Past." *East European Politics and Societies* 1(2):187–224.

Sinyavsky, Andrei
1990 *Soviet Civilization: A Cultural History.* Joanne Turnbull and Nikolai Formozov, trans. New York: Little, Brown.
Siu, Helen F.
1989a *Agents and Victims in South China: Accomplices in Rural Revolution.* New Haven, CT: Yale University Press.
1989b "Recycling Rituals: Politics and Popular Culture in Contemporary Rural China." In *Unofficial China: Popular Culture and Thought in the People's Republic,* P. Link, R. Madsen, and P. Pickowicz, eds., pp. 121–37. Boulder, CO: Westview Press.
1990 "Introduction: Social Responsibility and Self-Expression." In *Furrows: Peasants, Intellectuals, and the State: Stories and Histories from Modern China,* H. Siu, ed., pp. 1–28. Stanford, CA: Stanford University Press.
Siu, Helen, and Zelda Stern, eds.
1983 *Mao's Harvest: Voices from China's New Generation.* New York: Oxford University Press.
Staniszkis, Jadwiga
1991 *The Dynamics of the Breakthrough in Eastern Europe.* Chester Kisiel, trans. Berkeley: University of California Press.
Starr, John Bryan
1973 *Ideology and Culture: An Introduction to the Dialectic of Contemporary Chinese Politics.* New York: Harper and Row.
Strauss, Leo
1952 *Persecution and the Art of Writing.* Chicago: University of Chicago Press.
Suny, Ronald G.
1980 "Georgia and Soviet Nationality Policy." In *The Soviet Union since Stalin,* S. F. Cohen, A. Rabinowitch, and R. Sharlet, eds. Bloomington: Indiana University Press.
1989 *The Making of the Georgian Nation.* London: I.B. Tauris.
Sutton, Donald S.
1990 "Ritual Drama and Moral Order: Interpreting the Gods' Festival Troupes of Southern Taiwan." *Journal of Asian Studies* 49:535–54.
Szelenyi, Ivan
1982 "The Intelligentsia in the Class Structure of State-Socialist Societies." In *Marxist Inquiries: Studies of Labor, Class, and States,* M. Burawoy and T. Skocpol, eds. Chicago: University of Chicago Press.
Szporluk, Roman
1988 *Communism and Nationalism: Karl Marx versus Friedrich List.* Oxford: Oxford University Press.
Tadić, Ljubomir
1988 "Kominterna i Nacionalno Pitanje Jugoslavije (The Comintern and the national question in Yugoslavia)." *Knji evne Novine* 760, September 15, 1988:1,5.
Taussig, Michael
1987 *Shamanism, Colonialism and the Wild Man: A Study in Terror and Healing.* Chicago: University of Chicago Press.
Teiser, Stephen F.
1986 "Ghosts and Ancestors in Medieval Chinese Religion: The Yü-lan-p'en Festival as Mortuary Ritual." *History of Religions* 26:47–67.
1988a *The Ghost Festival in Medieval China.* Princeton, NJ: Princeton University Press.
1988b "'Having Once Died and Returned to Life': Representations of Hell in Medieval China." *Harvard Journal of Asiatic Studies* 48:433–64.
Thurston, Anne
1987 *Enemies of the People: The Ordeal of the Intellectuals in China's Great Cultural Revolution.* Cambridge, MA: Harvard University Press.
1990 "Urban Violence during the Cultural Revolution: Who Is to Blame?" In *Violence in China: Essays in Culture and Counterculture,* J. Lipman and S. Harrell, eds., pp. 149–74. Albany: State University of New York Press.
Tolstoy, Nikolai
1986 *The Minister and the Massacres.* London: Century Hutchinson.

Tomorkhuleg, T.
1990   "VIII Zhavzandamba Khutugt Yamar Khun Baiv? (What kind of man was the eighth Javzandamba Khutagt?)." *Utga Zokhiol Urlag*, June.

Tudjman, Franjo
1990   "Bespuća Povijesne Zbilnosti (The wasteland of historical reality)." Zagreb: Nakladni Zavod Matice Hrvatske.

Turton, Andrew
1986   "Patrolling the Middle-Ground: Methodological Perspectives on 'Everyday Peasant Resistance'." *Journal of Peasant Societies* 13(2):36–48.

Uyanga, Sh.
1991   "Yesdugeer Bogd Khezee Todrox Ve? (When will the ninth Bogd be reincarnated?)." *Ardyn Erkh*, July 23.

Vansina, Jan
1985   *Oral Tradition as History*. Madison: University of Wisconsin Press.

Verdery, Katherine
1991a   *National Ideology under Socialism: Identity and Cultural Politics in Ceaucescu's Romania.* Berkeley: University of California Press.
1991b   "Theorizing Socialism: A Prologue to the 'Transition'." *American Ethnologist* 18(3):419–39.

Vladimirtsov, B. Ya.
1927   "Etnologo-lingvisticheskiye issledovaniya v Urge, Urginskom i Kenteyskom Rayonakh (Ethnological-linguistic researches in Urga and the Urga and Kentei districts)." In *Severnaya Mongolia* II. Leningrad: Izdatel'stvo Akademii Nauk SSSR.

Wagner, Rudolf
1987   "The Chinese Writer in His Own Mirror: Writer, State, and Society—the Literary Evidence." In *China's Intellectuals and the State*, M. Goldman with T. Cheek and C. L. Hamrin, eds., pp. 183–232. Cambridge, MA: Council on East Asian Studies/Harvard University.
1990   *The Contemporary Chinese Historical Drama*. Berkeley: University of California Press.
1992   "Reading the Chairman Mao Memorial Hall in Peking: The Tribulations of the Implied Pilgrim." In *Pilgrims and Sacred Sites in China*, S. Naquin and C. Yü, eds. Berkeley: University of California Press.

Wakeman, Frederic
1985   "Revolutionary Rites: The Remains of Chiang Kai-shek and Mao Tse-tung." *Representations* 10:146–93.
1988   "Mao's Remains." In *Death Ritual in Late Imperial and Modern China*, J. L. Watson and E. S. Rawski, eds., pp. 254–87. Berkeley: University of California Press.

Walder, Andrew
1986   *Communist Neo-Traditionalism: Work and Authority in Chinese Society*. Berkeley: University of California Press.

Wang Meng
1991   Preface to exhibition catalogue of photographs by Jiang Zhenqing. Dalian, Oct. 24–Sept. 1.

Wang Xiaoyi
1988   "Woguo fengjian shehui de jingzi: Mulianxi sixiang neirong chutan (A mirror on our country's feudal society: Preliminary discussion on the thought and content of Mulian opera)." *Xiqu yanjiu* (Opera Research) 28:118–33.

Ward, Barbara E.
1979   "Not Merely Players: Drama, Art and Ritual in Traditional China." *Man* 14:18–39.

Wasserstrom, Jeffrey
1990   "Student Protests and the Chinese Tradition, 1919–1989." In *The Chinese People's Movement: Perspectives on Spring 1989*, T. Saich, ed. Armonk, NY: M. E. Sharpe.

Watson, James L.
1982   "Of Flesh and Bones: The Management of Death Pollution in Cantonese Society." In *Death and the Regeneration of Life*, M. Bloch and J. Parry, eds., pp. 155–86. Cambridge: Cambridge University Press.
1985   "Standardizing the Gods: The Promotion of T'ien Hou ('Empress of Heaven') along the South China Coast, 960–1960." In *Popular Culture in Late Imperial China*, D. Johnson, A. J. Nathan, and E. Rawski, eds., pp. 292–324. Berkeley: University of California Press.

n.d.   "The Protection of Priviledge: Self Defense Corps and the Satellite Village System in South China, 1850–1980."

Watson, James L., and Evelyn Rawski, eds.
1988   *Death Ritual in Late Imperial and Modern China.* Berkeley: University of California Press.

Weller, Robert P.
1985   "Bandits, Beggars, and Ghosts: The Failure of State Control over Religious Interpretation in Taiwan." *American Ethnologist* 12:46–61.
1987   "The Politics of Ritual Disguise: Repression and Response in Taiwanese Popular Religion." *Modern China* 13:17–39.
1994   *Interpreting Resistance and Resisting Interpretation.* New York: Macmillan.

White, Hayden
1982   "Historicism, History, and the Imagination." In *The Tropics of Discourse,* by Hayden White. Baltimore, MD: Johns Hopkins University Press.

Whyte, Martin
1988   "Death in the People's Republic of China." In *Death Ritual in Late Imperial and Modern China,* J. L. Watson and E. S. Rawski, eds., pp. 289–316. Berkeley: University of California Press.

Will, George
1991   "When Congress Wrote the News." *New York Times Book Review,* June 30.

Williams, Raymond
1979   *Modern Tragedy.* Rev. ed. London: Verso.

Wittfogel, Karl A.
1957   *Oriental Despotism: A Comparative Study of Total Power.* New York: Vintage.

Wolf, Arthur P.
1974   "Gods, Ghosts, and Ancestors." In *Religion and Ritual in Chinese Society,* A. P. Wolf, ed., pp. 131–82. Stanford, CA: Stanford University Press.

Woodward, Susan
1989   "Reforming a Socialist State: Ideology and Public Finance in Yugoslavia." *World Politics* 41:267–305.

Wu Peiyi
1984   "Varieties of Chinese Self." In *Designs of Selfhood,* V. Kavolis, ed., pp. 107–31. Associated University Presses.

Xiong Foxi
1936   *Xiju dazhonghua zhi shiyan* (Experiments in the popularization of opera). (Place of publication unknown): Zhengzhong shuju.

Xue Ruolin
1988   "Han'gai duoyuan sixiang, rongbao duozhong yishu: Lun Mulianxi jianji haineiwai de yanjiu qingkuang (Containing thought from many sources, holding many types of art: On Mulian opera and the state of research at home and abroad)." *Xiqu yanjiu* (Opera Research) 28:104–17.

Yang, Martin C.
1968   *A Chinese Village: Taitou, Shantung Province.* New York: Columbia University Press.

Yang, Mayfair Mei-hui
1988   "The Modernity of Power in the Chinese Socialist Order." *Cultural Anthropology* 3(4):408–27.

Yang Zhensheng
1955   "Huiyi wesi" (Recollections of May Fourth). *Renmin wenxue* 55:100–113.

Yeh Sheng-tao
1978   *Schoolmaster Ni Huan-chih.* Beijing: Foreign Languages Press.

Yi Mu and Mark Thompson
1989   *Crisis at Tiananmen: Reform and Reality in Modern China.* San Francisco: China Books.

Young, James
1992   "The Counter-Monument: Memory against Itself in Germany Today." *Critical Inquiry* 18:267–296.

Yu Mok Chiu and J. Frank Harrison, eds.
 1990   *Voices from Tiananmen Square: Beijing Spring and the Democracy Movement*. Montreal: Black
        Rose Books.
Yue Daiyun and Carolyn Wakeman
 1985   *To the Storm: The Odyssey of a Revolutionary Chinese Woman*. Berkeley: University of Cali-
        fornia Press.
Zagorin, Perez
 1990   *Ways of Lying: Dissimulation, Persecution, and Conformity in Early Modern Europe*. Cam-
        bridge: Harvard University Press.
Žanko, Želimir, and Nikola Šolić
 1990   *Jazovka*. Zagreb: Vjesnik.
Zarrow, Peter
 1990   *Anarchism and Chinese Political Culture*. New York: Columbia University Press.
Zhou Yang
 1955   "Fayang Wusi wenxue de douzheng chuatong (Develop the militant tradition of May
        Fourth literature)." *Renmin wenxue* 55:45–63.
Zito, A. R.
 1987   "City Gods, Filiality, and Hegemony in Late Imperial China." *Modern China* 13:333–71.
Zweig, David
 1989a *Agrarian Radicalism in China, 1968–1981*. Cambridge, MA: Harvard University Press.
 1989b "Struggling over Land in China: Peasant Resistance after Collectivization, 1966–1986."
        In *Everyday Forms of Resistance*, F. Colburn, ed. Armonk, NY: M. E. Sharpe.

Index

SCHOOL OF AMERICAN RESEARCH ADVANCED SEMINAR SERIES

SCHOOL OF AMERICAN RESEARCH ADVANCED SEMINAR SERIES

Participants in the advanced seminar "Secret Histories:
The Politics of Memory under Socialism." School of American
Research, Santa Fe, 1991.

Seated, left to right:	*Standing, left to right:*
Vera Schwarcz	Ellen R. Judd
Paul G. Pickowicz	Gail Kligman
Rubie S. Watson	Andrew Lass
Robert M. Hayden	Stephen F. Jones
Caroline Humphrey	Richard Madsen

www.ingramcontent.com/pod-product-compliance
Lightning Source LLC
Chambersburg PA
CBHW020531270326
41927CB00006B/534